Exploding the Castle

A volume in
Psychological Perspectives on Contemporary Educational Issues
Jonathan Plucker, *Series Editor*

Exploding the Castle

Rethinking How Video Games and Game Mechanics Can Shape the Future of Education

edited by

Michael F. Young
University of Connecticut

Stephen T. Slota
University of Connecticut

INFORMATION AGE PUBLISHING, INC.
Charlotte, NC • www.infoagepub.com

Library of Congress Cataloging-in-Publication Data

A CIP record for this book is available from the Library of Congress
http://www.loc.gov

ISBN: 978-1-68123-935-4 (Paperback)
          978-1-68123-936-1 (Hardcover)
          978-1-68123-937-8 (ebook)

Printed in the United States of America

CONTENTS

TEN

TWIST

KETSU

CONCLUSION

FOREWORD

Certain technologies have had magical effects. They have utterly changed the world. Writing turned language—a creature of sound rapidly decaying in time—into a creature of visual images fixed in space. Writing made meaning permanent, inspectable, public, and able to travel great distances. It gave rise to logic, libraries, science, and the state. The telegraph and its heirs collapsed time and space. The world shrank and humans became one big discourse community interacting in real time. The washing machine freed half the human race (women) in the developed world to work and thereby created modern economies. New technologies to clean water will free the same half in the developing world to go to school and work, instead of traveling long distances each day to hydrate. Computers have changed the very nature of work, and—combined with the Internet—they are well on the way to creating a nearly jobless future.

Any powerful technology can do good, evil, or nothing depending on how, when, and where it is used. Books have led to great things, indeed. Nonetheless, millions and millions of lives have been lost because someone read a book (e.g., the Bible, the Koran, or *The Turner Diaries*) and thought it was telling them to kill other people. And, of course, many people think God wrote a book; they just don't agree which one. Literacy is truly powerful.

The jury is still out on video games. They are too new and are changing too fast and furiously for us to know much yet about how powerful they will be. For now, there are very few people who think a video game told them to go on a murderous crusade, and no one thinks God designed a video game (leaving aside the small number of people, like me, who think Will Wright is God).

But video games have the *potential* to be as important (for good *and* bad) as writing, the telegraph, washing machines, and water nanofilters. Human beings are built in such a way—it is part of our human nature as it has evolved—to learn best only under certain (and rather narrow) conditions. These conditions are socially interactive and collaborative immersion in well-designed and well-mentored embodied experiences of problem solving where the cost of failure is greatly lowered. This is how language acquisition works and how socialization and enculturation work whether in a family, culture, or profession.

For centuries, we humans have been constrained in the creation of such learning experiences by the limitations of—and grave dangers in—the real world and by the limitations of our human senses and our middling (not to say piddling) size (we are way too big to see and do some things, like play with electrons, and way too little to see and do others, like jump from solar system to solar system). But video games have the potential to transform these limitations.

Video games can allow us to create brand new worlds and embody our bodies and minds in them via surrogate bodies (avatars). They can immerse us in experiences no human has ever had before in history. And, in the words of an ad for the first *Portal* game, they can change the way we humans "approach, manipulate, and surmise the possibilities in a given environment" (STEAM, 2007, n.p.). The world today is a royal jumble of interacting, nearly out-of-control complex systems set awry by utter human stupidity. We had better surmise some new possibilities—and soon.

So, let us explode the castle and shape the future, by all means. A lot is at stake in this excellent collection aiming to test and expand the limits of video games and learning.

—**James Paul Gee**
Arizona State University

REFERENCES

STEAM. (2007). *Portal* [video clip]. Retrieved from http://store.steampowered.com/app/400/

PREFACE

When we first started investigating game-based teaching and learning in 2009—known at the time as "gamification" or "serious gaming"—we figured it would be fun but nevertheless more of the same old thing. After all, we'd studied multimedia software, web quests, and programmable robots before, and nothing about video games (as a technology) struck us as terribly unique or complex. But, in the span of about six months, the relatively straightforward research trajectory we originally planned to follow turned into something quite different.

We knew then (and have argued passionately since) that quality games research starts with understanding *how* and *why* players play games. Unfortunately for educators and scientists, gameplay changes from day to day, quest to quest, and even from one battle to the next. When individual goals for play change, the nature of the gaming experience changes; likewise, when the gaming experience changes, the potential for various academic benefits changes. Individuals playing *World of Warcraft* as a Gnome Warrior may choose to max out their engineering skill in part due to a parallel interest in real world chemistry and physics. But when those same individuals engage in player-versus-player battle, they will modify their behavior to fulfill new goals that rely on collaborative problem solving and self-regulation (i.e., 21st-century digital work and learning skills) rather than chemistry- or physics-based thinking. Such in-the-moment, on-the-fly adaptations are logical and reasonable (Why waste time and energy on skills that aren't pertinent to the immediate situation?) but make it incredibly difficult to reduce variables like engagement, motivation, and achievement across time and individuals, as traditional t-tests in educational research require. That made us wonder: Do players recognize when their goals shift during play? If they do, do they recognize when, why, and how it occurs? What happens when player goals misalign with designer goals? And, perhaps most importantly, will the answers to these questions ever enable us to answer broad questions such as whether games are "good" or "bad" for education?

Initial attempts at examining these big "how" and "why" questions led us to realize that traditional educational research strategies would only ever lead to mixed and uninterpretable results as different players played their games for different reasons across time. That meant our idyllic "castle upon a hill"—the one containing our game-based learning princess (i.e., our understanding of games as an instructional resource)—was probably much further off in the distance (and in greater disrepair) than we thought.

That's why, in October 2015, we invited a number of leading games scholars to collaborate on an edited volume as a means of "resetting" our collective approach to games research. Doing so meant replacing traditional studies with situated analyses aimed at answering newly revised, more granular questions like, "What does the wise integration of games into classrooms actually look like in practice?" and "How can we evaluate the value-added nature of various game mechanics and components if they can't be standardized and administered to students like prescription medication?"

This book is the fruit of our effort.

As you'll see, we have taken a holistic approach to educational gaming. Some of our contributing authors focused on video games, while others focused on text-based games and other forms of play. Some focused on assessment, and others focused on teaching practice or how theory can inform design. Naturally, this gives us quite a bit of complex content to unpack, but we've tried to make it as accessible as possible for any educator, administrator, researcher, designer, or gamer with a general interest in game-based instruction.

Additionally, given our penchant for using princess/castle/plumber-themed analogies, we've decided to organize our thoughts using the classic Chinese, Japanese, and Korean story structure *kishōtenketsu* (起承転結), a Nintendo favorite when it comes to designing stages, mechanics, and player goals for the *Super Mario* series. In *kishōtenketsu*, the overarching narrative is broken into four parts:

1. Introduction (*ki*): Introduces the story's setting and main characters.
2. Development (*shō*): Follows from the introduction, develops the story, and leads to a twist.
3. Turn/Twist (*ten*): Brings the story in a new direction that includes the climax (*yama* ヤマ).

4. Conclusion (*ketsu*): Ties together story threads to provide a cohesive ending (*ochi* 落ち).

Our *ki* opens with an anchor chapter that explains why we so intensely believe games are unique learning ecologies with potentially powerful instructional affordances. This sets up our major "characters," games and their affordances, for Roger Travis to elaborate on in Chapter 2. Through his contribution, we discover that game-based teaching and learning are as old as the art of storytelling and why Socrates (yes, *that* Socrates) should be considered the very first "gamer." In Chapter 3, Trent Hergenrader expands on Travis' storytelling-as-play by exploring how the overlapping features of games and other media can be used to guide creative writing instruction and practice, especially with respect to narrative world-building.

Next, opening our *shō*, Amanda Bell and Melissa Gresalfi address the need for classroom and technology supports capable of helping teachers successfully incorporate video games as part of their standard instructional practice. Jackie Barnes and Melissa Gresalfi take this a step further in Chapter 5 by exploring case study evidence to help us understand whether children playing games in school view and play them like the games they play at home or if they view and play them like other school activities (e.g., worksheets, tests). Their work raises important questions about whether and how we should use games to tackle assessment, which serves as the focal point for Peter Wardrip and Sam Abramovich's Chapter 6 on badging systems. Chapter 7, penned by Sasha Barab and Anna Arici, broadens the assessment scope to include data-rich activities that take place outside of play (i.e., the meta-game), like visiting cheat/hint sites, discussing game play online/in-person, and extending game narratives by writing fan fiction.

Of course, to understand games' educational potential, researchers must also understand that play is only one piece of the gaming experience. That's why our *ten* begins with Ian O'Byrne and Nenad Radakovic's Chapter 8, which utilizes a series of future studies to orient us toward our end goal, the construction of a "castle" where games research is situated in a rich, dynamic learning ecology. Meeting that goal, according to our Chapter 9 authors Valerie Shute, Seyedahmad Rahimi, and Chen Sun, hinges on our understanding of testing in game-based learning environments. Like O'Byrne and Radakovic, they explore a possible game-infused future but emphasize the benefits and implementation strategies associated with "stealth assessments," activities or tasks embedded into games as a means of tracking longitudinal student growth and achievement. In Chapter 10, Jennifer Dalsen, Craig Anderson, Kurt Squire, and Constance Steinkuehler bring us deeper by discussing the "data exhaust" that flows out to teachers and researchers via game and learning analytics, from a player's first key press, chat post, and menu decision to their last.

Finally, we reach the *ketsu*, where we synthesize our findings into recommendations aimed at helping teachers, designers, and learning scientists improve their game-based instruction and research. This includes our Chapter 11 contributors—Jeffrey Holmes, Kelly Tran, and Elisabeth Gee—sharing a study of distributed teaching and learning systems to optimize game-based instruction, and our volume editors—Stephen Slota and Michael Young—deconstructing a series of educational technology projects to pinpoint why and how we should replace the game-based learning "castle" as it currently exists with one grounded in situated cognition.

It's our hope that this book will convince you of the instructional potential inherent in the treatment of games as learning ecologies. We know, as with any good boss fight, one attempt may not be enough, but that's why we're glad to have an audience as vested in game-based education as we are. With your help, this work can and will continue. The more teachers, researchers, and game players who join the cause, the closer we'll come to understanding how and why students learn through play. And, given enough time and attention informed by high-quality research, we're confident that the games community will be able to create greatly improved game-based instructional tools for 21st century education.

Thank you so much for joining us on this adventure.

—**Stephen T. Slota**
Michael F. Young

KI

INTRODUCTION

CHAPTER 1

CASTLE UPON A HILL

Michael F. Young and Stephen T. Slota
University of Connecticut

Hearing the words "game" and "school" together, you might think of activities like tag or kickball being played on the playground during recess. Or maybe you'd think of thumbs rapidly clicking on a control pad as children move avatars through imaginary Mario or Madden Sports worlds, rewarding themselves for finishing comparatively dull schoolwork, homework, or testing. Some might balk in disapproval at the violent behavior, bullying, racist overtones, sexist exploitation of women, and addiction often associated with video game play, while others—including teachers, business owners, and politicians—may be envious of the sustained engagement games can induce in audiences who often have little time for (or interest in) a given subject. For more than a decade, learning scientists have taken the latter perspective, framing games as a pathway to content engagement rather than a simple, recreational pastime. They have presented video games as a strategic and potentially transformative tool in the struggle to adapt to myriad political, economic, and social constraints that influence and create objectives for schooling, corporate training, and other kinds of formal and informal learning. But is belief in the potential of games as learning tools well-founded? Is it misplaced? Or is the issue of game-based

Exploding the Castle, pages 3–17
Copyright © 2017 by Information Age Publishing
All rights of reproduction in any form reserved.

instruction simply too complex and nuanced to discuss in terms of an up-or-down judgment?

Over the coming chapters, we—experts in education and game design—will contend that games can and should be viewed as a positive influence on the future of public and private, formal and informal education, particularly with purely online learning in mind—but only insofar as they fill a particular instructional/curricular need. That is, while video and board games have the potential to be a great resource for educators, they should not be taken as the sole, ideal means for delivering curricula in the schools or corporate and military training facilities of tomorrow. *They are one tool in the toolkit, not likely a substitute for teachers and classrooms entirely.* The playful learning inherent in many forms of games results from understanding game mechanics as a particular instructional delivery mechanism, good for establishing a learning ecology for particular kinds of content and types of thinking. The context in which games are played can completely influence the experience, so when high-stakes outcomes like grades are made contingent on play, content is less likely to be explored and certainly less likely to be seen as "fun." Making games "work" in business, the sciences, museums, and massive online open courses (MOOCs) relies on a full understanding of how people interact and learn in game environments, generally, and how particular learners with particular experience sets are led to adopt and fulfill particular, designed game objectives aligned with prespecified student learning outcomes. This is quite different from what frequently occurs in practice: randomly overlaying game mechanics onto curricular content and waiting for efficient, engaging learning to emerge by virtue of being gamified (despite the fact that students are quite adept at identifying [and ignoring] "school" games as knock-offs of "real" games designed for entertainment).

Lacking a digital crystal ball, we cannot precisely predict the future of education or the exact instructional role games will come to play going forward, but there are several trends beginning to take hold that suggest possible paths toward innovation and transformation within the American education system in support of playful learning. Such trends include pedagogical shifts with "just-in-time," personalized student-centered learning and primarily online delivery services for freely-available, rigorous content from university and business sources; increased academic enrollment of adults as a function of an aging population (retooling for changing job demands) and the need for workers to change careers frequently, redefine themselves, and become lifelong learners; the growth of innovative assessments such as learner-adaptive testing, big data learner analytics, and artificial intelligence inferencing engines that can customize learning to the performance level of the student; and high-bandwidth mobile devices that enable learners to interact with clarity through technology (e.g., augmented reality) across the globe. Taken together, these developments provide a framework for how video games and associated mechanics could be wisely integrated to support novel, effective learning ecologies.

Of course, this does not in and of itself answer the question, "How might easy access to free, game-infused instructional materials from universities and global businesses change the field of education?" Circa 2017, academic researchers and other leaders remain undecided on exactly what a wise integration of games into instruction should look like. Various stakeholders seek to improve education for political, economic, or other ends, and it is unclear if any single solution—even a game-based one—can comprehensively address individual, academic, governmental, and industry instructional needs. Yet many state the issue of games in learning in terms of such a global outcome. Higher education has made the landscape of information online widely available as top-tier research institutions have begun openly sharing their instructional materials in the context of MOOCs and similar approaches, but their efforts are just one piece of the larger game-based learning puzzle. At least superficially, it would be straightforward to develop content beyond traditional one-way, passive reading/viewing through the use of collaborative, social, and constructive experiences coupled with traditional, fact-based instruction—for instance, ubiquitously accessible, online and "on-time" 24/7 courses that combine accessibility to digital/multimedia information, virtual experiences, and synchronous/asynchronous interactions for those willing and able to participate in open courses. But after this simple adaptation of classic classroom learning, the vision for how games might be part of a truly different educational system is quite unclear.

While we don't believe games hold the potential to address all of what is broken in Western education (see McGonigal, 2011), one thing we *do* believe is that they will play an increasingly prominent role in the future of formal K–12 and higher education environments as well as informal learning in zoos, museums, and the like. This means members of existing game design and education communities (say, the collaborating authors of this book) will have to choose between being passive observers or active contributors to the complex and often political process of weaving together pedagogy, technology, and culture. We'll have to agree that games—or, more specifically, game mechanics and the engagement in joyful learning that they engender—are not only critical for shaping online and classroom instruction but also in line with the evolution of schooling as a whole. We'll likewise need to endorse a hard push beyond questions like "Are video games 'good' or 'bad' for education?" and "Are games 'better' for all students than traditional face-to-face, lecture-style teaching?" to questions about how game experiences vary with individual learner goals as an interaction with the parameters of an educational environment. Simply put, we'll need to form a cohesive, compelling argument in support of the notion that *games create learning ecologies in and of themselves, and to understand them as ecologies, we need to view learning as situated.* In turn, we need to apply cognitive science to understand game-based playful learning as it emerges in rich dynamic interactions within applied and formal settings (as well as how it interacts with location, curricular goals, and human and digital learning supports).

This chapter is designed to anchor our collective thinking with respect to the value-added nature of games as learning ecologies and the dynamic complexities involved in player experience, narrative cocreation, and player–game interactions. As you might expect, we are not interested in defining or detailing parameters of gamification, debates about game violence, evaluating individual game quality, and other topics that have become standard fare in extant games literature and the blogosphere. Instead, we seek to emphasize issues of instructional scalability, the induction of players to adopt curricular-related game goals, affordances of game-based instructional environments for support student-based learning, the relationship between play and transfer to applied contexts, and the value of games as part of an ecological psychology worldview. As long-time contributors in a field that has made a habit of playing it safe—pun intended—we seek to bring the dialogue in a more granular and meaningful direction.

LET US PLAY

Play is a form of wish fulfillment and serves a purpose in the evolution of society and culture that educators cannot ignore. That is why, before we share our vision for the future of games and education, we'd like to establish how (apart from *video* games) other forms of games and play are and always have been essential to the way in which children learn. As an example, a pillar of educational psychology is Lev Vygotsky's social constructivist theory, which described play as crucial for a child's sociocultural development (Vygotsky, 1933/1976). For Vygotsky, imaginative play provided a way for children to enact behaviors that they could not fulfill in real life—for example, a small child imagining herself as a horseback rider by picking up a stick and "riding" it long before growing big and strong enough to ride an actual horse. He furthered this point by explaining how roleplaying activities enabled children to develop a vocabulary by giving voice to different characters and encouraging them to imitate others' more advanced language utterances. In so doing, they were able to learn by internalizing the world and reenacting events helpful for socializing them to the surrounding environment (e.g., a child playing "family" and saying to herself, "Now, let's wash our hands and eat supper"). According to Vygotsky, such "inner speech" emulated adult action and enabled the child to reflect on, experiment with, and understand activities in ways not possible when directly dealing with the exigencies of real life.

Naturally, this perspective raised an important question about the relationship between playful learning and "fun." "Fun," an emotional reaction, has often been applied in a dualistic fashion where the individual assigning a given activity has determined how it should be perceived (i.e., work or play) rather than the individual experiencing it. Consider the pressure and stress of professional sports as a form of play, or the outcome of a traditional classroom teacher who—as a class assignment—requires all of their students to play 15 hours of *Marvel Heroes 20XX* lest they fail Creative Writing 101. In these cases, play very likely will not be experienced emotionally as fun whatsoever even though game rules, strategies, and the notion of "winners" and "losers" still apply. Conversely, mundane tasks like mowing the lawn or folding laundry can become personal challenge sessions where participants time themselves on how quickly they can complete parts of each task and reward themselves for setting new personal bests. In 1990, Mihaly Csikszentmihalyi described this "work can be fun, and play can be work" concept using the term "flow," a sense of cognitive engagement in which one loses track of time and narrows their focus to a single goal. When "flow" occurs, the individual experiences a sense of pleasure and accomplishment akin to "fun" in spite of the goal-fulfillment process appearing nonplayful to an external observer.

In the interest of scholarly dialogue, we suggest adopting working definitions for "play" and "fun" that clearly distinguish between the two as concepts:

> *Play:* A behavior that is not always fun but involves thinking (i.e., cognition), strategy, rules, and often imagination and creativity in the context of a game setting and mechanics (e.g., scores, timed responses, competition).

> *Fun:* An emotional response that is orthogonal to play. Work tasks can be experienced as fun, and play can be experienced as un-fun (e.g., losing, playing a game for professional gain or high-stakes competition).

A NOTE ON GAMES & SIMULATIONS

In many ways, disambiguating "games" and "simulations" has proven to be even more challenging than operationally defining "play" and "fun." The phrases "educational game," "role-playing," "social simulation," and "simulation game" were first conflated with "simulation" during the 1970s (Blaga, 1979), and scholars have had trouble meaningfully differentiating and categorizing them in the time since. Games are frequently catalogued as a subset of simulations, while simulations are equally often catalogued as a subset of games. Associated definitions are regularly re-written to satisfy the conceptual needs of the individual studies in which they apply (Gehlbach et al., 2008; Leigh & Spindler, 2004; Marsh, 1981), inadvertently creating problems for replication, meta-analytics, cataloguing, and more (see Young et al., 2012). Marc Prensky wrote in 2007 that the distinction between games and simulations is that "simulations are about things (or systems) and how they behave, and games are about a fun user experience" (2007, para. 1). Others have proposed that designers and researchers need to distinguish between games and simulations on a case-by-case basis rather than applying umbrella terminology, highlighting differences in story amount and quality, types of situations, decision-making required, rules involved, linear versus nonlinear progression, feedback measures, and completion goals (see Petroski, 2012). Unfortunately, the former distinction is not true across all simulations and games, and the latter relies on distinctions for which there are often more exceptions than cases that fit the rules.

To optimally categorize and describe the tools featured in this text, we recommend taking a middle path: adopting definitions for "game" and "simulation" that treat them as interconnected and occasionally overlapping tools rather than the same thing, direct subsets of one another, or synonyms for the increasingly common word "gamification."

> *Game:* A tool with design goals (e.g., boss fights, winning) that require interaction with an environment—virtual or real—and can include simulated elements of reality (e.g., gravity, momentum) but is not limited by parameters of the real world. Games are governed by rulesets (both designed and emergent), take full advantage of imagination and creativity, often include scoring criteria and/or measurable win/loss outcomes (e.g., competitive among multiple players, collaborative with all players working to beat the game, an individual competing against the game or herself), and are explicitly directed toward playfulness.

> *Simulation:* A goal-driven tool that requires interaction with an environment—virtual or real—and often shares some mechanics with games (e.g., points, missions, timers) but is explicitly designed to veridically emulate some real-world interaction, process, situation, or phenomenon (e.g., flight simulator, medical simulator). While simulations are also governed by designed and emergent rulesets, play is attenuated in order to represent the target interaction, process, situation, or phenomenon as accurately as possible. Naturally, the real-world aspects of simulations add much to their educational affordances, but they should be discussed separately—not as part of this book.

GAMES AS LEARNING ECOLOGIES

In order to fully explain what is meant by "games as learning ecologies," we must first describe what a learning ecology is and how it relates to gameplay in general. For this we draw on the ecological psychology of James and Eleanor Gibson and on the cognitive psychology of situated learning and embodied cognition.

The phrase "learning ecology" encompasses the full set of actual and possible interactions between an agent, its goals, and its environment as defined within the school of *ecological psychology*. It has roots in the epistemology of rationalism (i.e., emphasizing knowing through reason over intuition, introspection, or the inherent nature of man), empiricism (i.e., emphasizing that learning about the world occurs through perception, not inborn understandings), and models of agent–environment interaction used in the hard sciences (e.g., biology, physics) that help to explain thinking and learning as adaptive processes rather than representational information processes like the internal workings of computers. Ecological psychologists presume that learners have a basic "comportment" to explore the world and learn by using their senses to guide action (e.g., Heidegger, 1927/1996), preferring an integrated agent–environment view of learners as "embodied and embedded" in everyday cognition (Merleau-Ponty, 1962). As a subset of more general psychological research, ecological psychology grew out of Gibson's (1983) seminal description of how vision results from direct perception-action rather than a reconstruction of meaning from lower-level cell function and the detection of energy properties requiring complex geometrical cerebral processing. This is often cited as the basis for the situated cognition worldview (e.g., Brown, Collins, & Duguid, 1989; CTGV, 1990, 1993; Greeno, 1994, 1998; Hodges, 2014; Young, 1993).

Drawing on Eleanor Gibson's description of perceptual learning (Adolph & Kretch, 2015; Gibson & Pick, 2000), the ecological approach to learning has as its basic tenet that learning is a refinement process represented by an improvement of *attention* and *intention* via experience with the world. This stands in contrast to information processing theory, which posits an accumulation of knowledge defined by representational memory storage and retrieval processes. Generally speaking, ecological psychologists believe that learning is a continual refinement of perception that is mostly unrelated to memory and enables individuals to "see" things that were always environmentally present but went undetected prior to experience with the world. Improved perception-action can thus be summarized as the goal-driven education of attention (as mentioned above). This model is completed by an ontology of goals that also emerge from an agent's interaction with the world, drawing fundamentally on our general comportment to explore the world.

Complex organisms like humans are defined as having a hierarchy of goals and intentions that unfold across various space-times and can be either simultaneously addressed or conflicting. At any given moment, a particular goal serves as the focus of an individual's interaction with the world and sets the boundary constraints on what can be done to progress toward goal fulfillment. Importantly, this also explains the individual motivations that underlie behavior. For example, as a player hacks and slashes through a game like *Diablo III*, they may be in pursuit of more powerful armor and weapons in addition to helping other players level-up their character avatars, providing strategic advice for boss fights, and contributing their knowledge to the game's external community (e.g., posting information in a shared online space like the official *Diablo III* forums, Reddit, etc.). Together, the player's individual goals lead to a particular behavior (i.e., playing), and it becomes clear how they can pursue multiple goals at the same time.

Yet, there are often competing goals embedded in an individual's goal hierarchy. Returning to our *Diablo III* player, there might also be a desire to make progress in a different video game, weed the garden, or finish an overdue writing assignment. The way competing goals are narrowed to the particular moment when an intention establishes the boundary constraints of action is called *ontological descent*, the individual's movement toward an occasion that defines a particular situation or behavior. Of course, even when a situation is established and an interaction with the environment is underway, other goals can intervene and create a different situation that constrains behavior. For instance, as our player sits to complete a dungeon, the phone could ring or they might develop thirst, and a new goal (e.g., acquiring a glass of water) would take over to define what is seen and what actions are taken in the world. Such events are referred to as *dynamics of intentions* (i.e., how individuals shift from one goal or set of goals to another).

Fluctuations in intentionality lead to substantial variations in the way we—as particular individuals—experience and behave in the world, meaning that our goals ultimately determine what we "see" (a concept described by James Gibson and others in terms of *affordances*). Affordances are the possibilities for action in the environment as defined by our perceptual detection systems (e.g., sight, smell, taste, hearing, proprioception) and mediated by existing and emerging goals like those of the *Diablo III* player described above. With respect to gaming, specifically, they include all possibilities for interaction with the game world as designed (i.e., developer-intended rulesets) as well as any possibilities for interaction that arise from creative play and interaction with other players (i.e., emergent rulesets). At any particular time and in any particular place, there may be a nearly infinite number of affordances available, but only a small portion—rooted in the context of a player's in-the-moment intentions—will be detected on that occasion.

Delving further into this idea requires familiarity with how affordances are codefined by an agent's *effectivities*, or its ability to act on the environment (Shaw, Turvey, & Mace, 1982). If, for instance, we were to position a small closet doorway beside a healthy human adult capable of walking through the frame, the doorway could be described as having the affordance "passable." Yet, if the same human adult were to use a wheel chair or had to carry a large box, the doorway would no longer have its passable affordance. The same would be true if an elephant or giraffe attempted to walk through a human-sized frame; neither would fit, so the door would not have the passable affordance it held for the healthy human adult. This implies that the doorway's passable affordance does not exist abstractly as part of the world for all time and for all agents, but instead emerges *in situ* given a particular individual with a particular goal, occurring only when there is an immediate need and possibility for action. Put another way, the affordance emerges in the moment when an individual agent with particular effectivities acts toward the fulfillment of some goal.

Understandably, this may seem to fall outside the scope of our broader thesis regarding games as learning ecologies and be written off as (a) a matter of philosophy that bears minimal impact on the real world (much less the gaming world), (b) an exercise in semantics, and/or (c) nothing particularly new or exciting in the realm of learning science. But the notion of player–game–context interaction carries important implications for the way we categorize play in general and study the consequences of gameplay specifically. There are many game designers and researchers who *believe* that they address player–game–context interaction in their work, but their products do little to exemplify the terms and concepts described thus far and even undermine the mechanics that make games instructionally valuable to begin with. In fact, many have inadvertently done more to obscure the value-added benefits of games than take full advantage of them (e.g., engagement vs. fun, productive failure vs. trial-and-error, embodied cognition vs. simple kinesthetic movement, learning vs. test achievement). In a field seeking to grow and improve rather than shrink into inconsequentiality, this is not something to be taken lightly.

On the whole, we have not adequately attended to the way individuals form dialectics with their respective in- and out-of-game environments. We have adhered to unsubstantiated assumptions about how and why individuals take particular game and metagame actions. Peer-reviewed literature, for instance, has seldom described metagame activities like trolling as part of an emergent ruleset (e.g., *World of Warcraft*'s affordance for players to merge individual intentions, effectivities, and existing game mechanics [i.e., rideable mounts and a water-walking spell] as a means of interrupting others' in-game fishing activities). Likewise, few (if any) pieces have evaluated learning among participants who willfully work in *opposition* to a desired learning outcome (e.g., *SimCity* users who sink their citizens in a nearby river instead of building a bustling metropolis). While neither of these situations may align with the achievement of *desired* learning outcomes (at least not those relevant in a classroom setting), they can and should not be dismissed as counterindicative of critical thinking and problem solving. To the contrary, they must be understood as evidence of higher-order thinking that has for too long gone overlooked.

We would suggest that achievement tunnel vision is the primary reason games researchers have discovered game "goodness" and "badness" to be roughly equivocal in K–12 and higher education (see Clark, Tanner-Smith, & Killingsworth, 2016; Wouters, van Nimwegen, van Oostendrop, & van der Spek, 2013; Young et al., 2012). After all, only students holding goals related to academic outcomes can be expected to improve on measures of traditional scholastic learning in the first place, and the same student playing on different days with different goals is likely to interact with a given game entirely differently from one session to the next. In the proverbial words of Heraclitus, you can never step in the same river twice, so it should come as little surprise that we have met with an uninterpretable zeroing effect where only some students improve their school performance through some games on some occasions as part of some studies.

The challenges we face as a result of our collectively limited and predominantly nonecological approach demonstrate how general questions about the net benefits of game-based instruction almost certainly mask individual situated cognitive consequences of classroom game use. In our opinion, learning scientists, teachers, and game designers would do well to focus on the game elements, mechanics, and affordances that further a range of educational and player goals including—but not limited to—traditional academic achievement (e.g., trolling, creative play, participation in metagame experiences). Doing so would allow for the tracking and analysis of highly individualized ways in which play and learning emerge in game contexts as well as reinforce our understanding of player-game-environment dynamics as "situated"—that is, a rich interaction between player goals, game affordances, and the broader social context in which play occurs. We further propose that this is the only way that the field of game-based instruction will experience major shifts in design and research, by taking on the Mario-like task of exploding the game-based learning castle of the early- and mid-2000s to build another grounded in ecological psychology and situated cognition.

Changing course will not be simple or easy. In our meta-review (Young et al., 2012), we recommended that researchers and designers more deeply consider the way individual differences in player skill (as well as their goals adopted in-the-moment) affect play and any resulting learning. Now, more than five years later, we are asking that you help us spread this sentiment by reflecting upon and incorporating the warrants for a situated view into your own research, publications, and presentations. Without such a collaborative effort, it will become increasingly difficult to keep educational games work relevant and productive as we look ahead to the future.

We offer the following pillars of research and design in hopes that they will serve as a rallying point for anyone seeking to join our cause:

> *Player–Game Interaction:* The experience of gameplay that leads to student learning outcomes (SLOs) is codetermined by the player's goals and intentions for play, and the affordances of a game serve as parameters for engagement as established by the game designers. Gameplay experiences are not always the experiences intended by the designers or those using the game instructionally since players can use game elements in unexpected and/or unintended ways (e.g., modding, hacking, trolling), some of which may have instructional value.

> *Game Ecosystem:* Games researchers must consider all interactions that emerge from gameplay, not simply those that occur within the boundary constraints of the game as conceived by the game's designers. These include "metagame" interactions (e.g., cheat, hint, player community forums) where games are discussed and strategies/play are analyzed outside the game. Peripheral contexts may hold equal or more value than games themselves as they draw on player reflection, analysis, and collaboration.

WHERE TO BEGIN?

Before we flip the world of game-based learning on its head, we suggest considering how the games and game mechanics utilized in your everyday work best fit as tools to reform and improve the way we "do" education. As noted throughout this chapter, not all games can or will have the same affordances for instruction and learning, but they can all play some part in standing against the current, dominant model for industrial age schooling (i.e., efficiency and productivity analogous to assembly line manufacturing). As in the early 1900s, students are tracked by age and grade level so the same curriculum can be efficiently presented to large classes. Metrics related to Carnegie units and seat time are still implemented to enable productivity and quantify achievement. The spiral curriculum, developed so students would have a predictable schedule, continues routinizing our school days. The one-room schoolhouse and Dewey's (1938) belief in student-centered pedagogy have long been rejected in mainstream public education.

Take a few moments to think about the following trends and whether they may impact your vision for the classroom of tomorrow.

Trend 1: Widely Available, Free Online Content

The notion of free, online content began with universities—many of them top-tier research institutions—providing instructional materials in the context of MOOCs. One of the emergent benefits of this trend has been learner control, allowing individuals of nearly any age to access content of their choice. As changes in job requirements and workforce makeup have necessitated a perennial update of employee skills and knowledge, the development of diverse, cross-age-group learning communities has reshaped the way professional development and other learning opportunities can unfold.

We believe that game narrative is one way to further expand this area, bringing disparate groups together as part of a shared environment. This is similar to watching a feature-length film that suddenly stops mid-story: while most of the audience has little in common upon entering the theater, at the moment the film is paused, they share a common experience history with the story and are equally prepared to anticipate what is coming next and provide advice to the characters. This may also lead to the emergence of common intentions (e.g., seeing how the story plays out), which, if used in conjunction with other mechanics, could be a powerful means of leveraging the adoption of particular learner goals.

Trend 2: Mobile, "Just-in-Time" Personalized Learning

Mobile technology has increasingly enabled students to learn at their own pace anywhere and at any time. It has also made learning more student-centered and allowed individuals to carve their own paths through the curricular landscape. If content is universally available at little or no cost (e.g., Bring-Your-Own-Device programs), students are free to select desired content and only that content—a figurative buffet of learning. Of course, this comes with many pitfalls, including the likely loss of commitment to general education as learners direct their attention to only chosen interests or career skills and leave behind the exploration of new areas or the development of interdisciplinary concepts (e.g., intercultural competence). Yet efforts to make learning personal through mobile tools might well be supplemented with advice and support—human or digital—that can ensure broader perspectives are gained while each unique path toward career preparation is navigated based on students' individual choices (i.e., adaptive, cross-discipline mobile games).

Trend 3: Competency-Based Curricula and Grading

Another trend that can potentially support just-in-time, personalized learning is competency-based grading. Many K–12 institutions have begun moving away from traditional, zero-to-100 grading schemes to avoid averaging scores into vague letter grades (i.e., A through F). The adoption of state and national standards has enabled teachers to enumerate the actual skills that students should be able to demonstrate if they have mastered curricular content, and, in so doing, have led to (a) more meaningful individual and project-based assessments, and (b) the creation of report cards that list contextually meaningful learning objectives. Electronic or paper portfolios of student work can document student skills in ways that are much more transferable from school to school and provide a much richer basis on which to make educational decisions (e.g., job promotion, college admissions).

We contend that standards-based assessment has much in common with many game mechanics, including the acquisition of gear that shows levels of achievement, badges for completing specified tasks, and even status on metagame websites where records of user contributions can be maintained and rated (for usefulness) by other players. This simple observation suggests to us there is potential for educational researchers to understand how game design has implemented such assessments and apply those mechanics to the mastery of the more traditional curriculum.

ONWARD AND UPWARD

While the general trends highlighted above may substantially impact when and where students learn, games—or, more specifically, game mechanics and the engagement in joyful learning that they engender—have the potential to change the *way* we teach in the future, both online and in the classroom. Using games to influence instruction as a whole depends on how we understand both games and contemporary trends in education to support player (and learner) engagement. This leads us to ask a different question about games and learning than the simplistic "do games 'work' in schools?"—specifically, discussing games as not simply as an instructional tool but a holistic framework (which, as we will find, necessarily starts with deconstructing the "games" used in ancient education).

With that, we wish you a warm welcome to the world of games as learning ecologies. Happy reading, and happy gaming.

IT'S DANGEROUS TO GO ALONE! TAKE THIS

To more easily track and understand the authors' shared reasoning, we recommend a quick review of the following questions before beginning each new chapter:

- Can particular game narratives induce player goal adoption centered on designed learning outcomes and standardized core curriculum content?
- How can and should games be designed to optimize community interaction, meaning making, and measurable, real-world impact, rather than abstract fantasy entertainment?
- How can educational games be made scalable from the individual level up through the course, program, and system levels?
- What innovations in research methods are required to understand games and learning as situated?
- What games or game mechanics have deep value for researchers and designers but have largely gone overlooked?
- How can the game-based learning community better work to support a situated cognition, ecopsychological approach to research and design?

REFERENCES

Adolph, K. E., & Kretch, K. S. (2015). *Gibson's theory of perceptual learning.* Retrieved from https://www.google.com/url?sa=t&rct=j&q=&esrc=s&source=web&cd= 1&cad=rja&uact=8&ved=0CB4QFjAAahUKEwiz_Oy78oDIAhXLcD4KHVX_ CXw&url=https%3A%2F%2Fpsych.nyu.edu%2Fadolph%2Fpublications%2F AdolphKretch-inpress-GibsonTheory.pdf&usg=AFQjCNHIVVb_aO34yDyPRs PJwqokdlorVg&sig2=RmphLzPqG48eUklkP0SigQ

Blaga, J. J. (1979). Simulations: An evaluation. *The High School Journal, 63*(1). 30–35.

Brown, J. S., Collins, A., & Duguid, P. (1989). Situated cognition and the culture of learning. *Educational Researcher, 18*(1), 32–42.

Clark, D. B., Tanner-Smith, E. E., & Killingsworth, S. S. (2016). Digital games, design, and learning: A systematic review and meta-analysis. *Review of Educational Research, 86*(1), 79–122. doi: 10.3102/0034654315582065

Cognition and Technology Group at Vanderbilt (CTGV). (1990). Anchored instruction and its relationship to situated cognition. *Educational Research, 19*(6), 2–10.

Cognition and Technology Group at Vanderbilt (CTGV). (1993, March). Anchored instruction and situated cognition revisited. *Educational Technology,* 52–70.

Csikszentmihalyi, M. (1990). *Flow: The psychology of optimal experience.* New York, NY: Harper & Row.

Dewey, J. F. (1938). *Experience and education*. New York, NY: Kappa Delta Pi.

Gehlbach, H., Brown, S. W., Ioannou, A., Boyer, M. A., Hudson, N., & Niv-Solomon, A. (2008). Increasing interest in social studies: Social perspective taking and self-efficacy in stimulating simulations. *Contemporary Education Psychology, 33*(4), 894–914.

Gibson, J. J. (1983). *The ecological approach to visual perception*. Boston, MA: Houghton Mifflin.

Gibson, E. J., & Pick, A. D. (2000). *An ecological approach to perceptual learning and development*. New York, NY: Oxford University Press.

Greeno, J. G. (1994). Gibson's affordances. *Psychological Review, 101*, 336–342.

Greeno, J. G. (1998). The situativity of knowing, learning, and research. *American Psychologist, 53*(1), 5–26.

Heidegger, M. (1996). *Being and time* (J. Stambaugh, trans.). Albany: State University of New York Press. (Original work published in German in 1927)

Hodges, B. H. (2014). Righting language: a view from ecological psychology. *Language Sciences, 41*, 93–103.

Leigh, E. & Spindler, L. (2004). Simulations and games as chaordic learning contexts. *Sim Gaming, 35*(1), 53–69.

Marsh, C. J. (1981). Simulation games and the social studies teacher. *Theory Into Practice, 20*(3), 187–193

McGonigal, J. (2011). *Reality is broken: Why games make us better and how they can change the world*. New York, NY: Penguin Press.

Prensky, M. (2007). Sims vs. games: The difference defined. *Edutopia*. Retrieved from https://www.edutopia.org/sims-vs-games

Merleau-Ponty, M. (1962). *Phenomenology of perception* (C. Smith, Trans.). New York, NY: Humanities Press.

Petroski, A. (2012, February). Games vs. simulations: Why simulations may be a better approach. *TD Magazine*. Retrieved from https://www.td.org/Publications/Magazines/TD/TD-Archive/2012/02/Games-Vs-Simulations-When-Simulations-May-Be-a-Better-Approach

Shaw, R. E., Turvey, M. T., & Mace, W. M. (1982). Ecological psychology. The consequence of a commitment to realism. In W. Weimer & D. Palermo (Eds.), *Cognition and the symbolic processes* (Vol. 2, pp. 159–226). Hillsdale, NJ: Erlbaum.

Vygotsky, L. (1976). Play and its role in the mental development of the child. In J. S. Bruner, A. Jolly, & K. Sylva (Eds.), *Play: Its role in development and evolution*. New York, NY: Basic Books. (Original work published in 1933).

Wouters, P., van Nimwegen, C., van Oostendorp, H., & van der Spek, E. D. (2013). A meta-analysis of the cognitive and motivational effects of serious games. *Journal of Educational Psychology, 105*(2), 249–265.

Young, M. F. (1993). Instructional design for situated learning. *Educational Technology Research and Development, 41*(1), 43–58.

Young, M., Slota, S. T., Cutter, A., Jalette, G., Mullin, G., Lai, B., . . . & Yukhymenko, M. (2012). Our princess is in another castle: A review of trends in serious gaming for education. *Review of Educational Research, 82*(1), 61–89.

CHAPTER 2

WHAT HOMERIC EPIC CAN TEACH US ABOUT EDUCATIONAL AFFORDANCES OF INTERACTIVE NARRATIVE

Roger Travis
University of Connecticut

We know very little about the education of Socrates, Plato's mentor and thus the catalyst, if not the founder, of Western philosophy. Though Plato, in his dialogues, reports him as discussing the subject of education over and over, all that we can gather about how he and the other elite men of Athens—those who created the cultural context that continues to make most of the Western world who we are—acquired the skills they needed to function as Athenian citizens comes from oblique, almost off-hand statements that reference what both Socrates and his interlocutors already know.

Based on those hints and hints dropped by other writers, though, we can say for certain that the interactive storytelling of the homeric epics—the *Iliad* and the *Odyssey*—played an absolutely decisive role in the educations of Socrates, Plato, Thucydides, Aeschylus, Sophocles, and Euripides, to name only the writers whose works I will draw on here. When the moment came

Exploding the Castle, pages 19–37

for Socrates (and/or Plato, through Socrates) to make incendiary statements about the inadequate education of the Athenians and to lay out the new system of interactive storytelling he hoped might replace it—the system we call Platonic philosophy—the relation of the educational technology they endorse to the epics that shaped their own educations tells us much more about how we should design our own situated learning environments than is immediately apparent to a reader who lacks a thorough knowledge of (a) ancient Athenian culture and (b) video games.

To make the potential benefit of this chapter clear (before diving into quoted passages from ancient literature), I'm going to begin by speculating about what Socrates' education might have been like. Because I want to start you out with an idea of where I'm headed with this strange-sounding argument about how the *Iliad* and the *Odyssey* are some of our earliest game-based learning environments, I'm going to make certain parallels clear between ancient and modern. You'll probably find them jarring, and you may want to see my evidence and argumentation right away; I promise that I'll back up each of the parallels as the chapter goes on.

As we move forward, you may notice that I don't capitalize "homeric." That's because, though the topic remains controversial, I (like many of my fellow classicists) don't believe in a man named "Homer" but rather in a tradition of homeric bards who developed the *Iliad* and the *Odyssey*, along with several other epics now mostly lost, over the course of hundreds of years. To put it another way, the *Iliad* and the *Odyssey*, written down as we now have them, are fossils of a once-living epic tradition in which bards performed new versions of their stories night after night, just as a gamer, night after night, performs a new version of her favorite game (see Lord, Mitchell, & Nagy, 2000, for the basic theory and Travis, 2012, for an application of it to digital games). This is why Socrates, night after night, almost certainly reimagined his own role in the epic of his own life, even without an XBox or a Playstation or a dungeon-master.

SOCRATES THE GAMER

Picture a group of boys, ages 10 to 14, seated on wooden benches in the shade of a portico in the courtyard of the house of one of their families. A slave—a prisoner of war, perhaps, from one of Athens' campaigns in the islands—is telling them about today's lesson.

"It's time for you young men to learn your letters," he says, holding up a wax tablet on which he has engraved with his stylus the word MHNIN (*mēnin*: "wrath"). "Who can tell me what this says?"

Grumbling ensues among most of the boys. Surely writing is for the slaves who keep the accounts, not for real Athenians like them?

Socrates doesn't grumble. He has been working out what the inscriptions on the Acropolis and in the porticoes say since he was five years old, pestering his *paidagōgos*—pedagogue, the slave who leads boys to their lessons—to tell him what the letters sound like. "That's *mēnin*," he says excitedly.

Some of the other boys stop their protests. Another of the more enthusiastic ones can't restrain himself, and bursts out, "*Mēnin aeide, thea, Pēlēiadeō Akhilēos!*"

"Exactly," says the *paidagōgos*, looking pleased. "Today we're all going to practice writing the very first words of the doer's work."

Maker. Doer. Composer. Poiētēs: poet means someone who does, and makes, Socrates realizes not for the first time.

Oh, how he loves the poet: Homer, the wandering bard with his stories of adventure and his two great heroes—Achilles, greatest of warriors, who refused to lose his fame but sat out of battle and lost his friend Patroclus, and Odysseus, who told so many tricksy tales to get home to his wife, then killed so many men so cleverly to complete the homecoming. One day, as Plato tells us, Socrates will decide that as stirring as these stories are, they are not fit for young people. We can have no doubt, though, that this repudiation arose directly from how readily the boy took to the stories he heard recited over and over from the moment he could understand human speech.

With the boys sitting next to him, about to learn how to write, he has played countless games of "Achilles and Ajax," "Odysseus and Diomedes," and "Odysseus and the Cyclops." He has sat next to them at the All-Athens festival and listened to the reciters tell the tale of how Odysseus shaped his stories to win his passage home, and countless treasure, from his hosts on a magical island.

Above all, he heard the story of the choice of Achilles: how he stayed at Troy even though he knew he would die. In the final moments of his trial for trying to change the way Athens educated her youth, he would tell the jury that he had the example of Achilles' self-sacrifice before his eyes as he decided that he would embrace the death-penalty, if they bestowed it upon him.

Plato would have him say in the *Republic* that the philosopher who has ascended from the cave would feel as dead as Achilles feels in the *Odyssey* when Odysseus meets him in the underworld: that he would rather learn what philosophers learn than get all the honors in the school of the prisoners of the cave—though they slay him just as the Athenians slew Socrates.

Socrates did not wield a controller as he played the interactive narratives of the *Iliad* and the *Odyssey*. He wielded a stick, perhaps, and he wielded his imagination. These epics were born prior to the Greek alphabet in oral song traditions that featured a good deal more obvious interactivity between the bard and his epic tradition. In the classical Athens of Socrates' youth, however—a world without digital games but in which humans had the very same need to play—epic remained a living occasion. The performances of the reciters, or *rhapsodes* (as an adult Socrates, suspicious now of the poet's power, in one of Plato's earliest dialogues, *Ion*, shows us), had the effect of bringing the time of legend vividly alive.

Socrates was a gamer. My research suggests that he and his fellow Athenians played the stories of Achilles and Odysseus every time they heard them because we always play adventure stories, whether we hear them or read them or watch them and whether we have explicit, if fake, control over some portion of the story or not. Remember that every choice you can make in a digital game is programmed into that game's software, and remember that every choice you can make even in a tabletop role-playing game must fall within the rules. If it works better for you, though, simply imagine Socrates and his friends playing Achilles or playing Odysseus. At the end of his life, those games became even more interactive as Socrates chose to become a new Achilles.

As mentioned above, Plato writes Socrates as delivering an incredible story about all this: the famous allegory of the cave. We'll return to the story in detail at the end of this chapter, but for the moment it's enough to mention that Socrates introduces it as being a story about "education and the lack of education," establishing that what the prisoners chained to their benches *do* when they watch the shadow-puppet play is to *interact* with it. They win prizes for predicting which shadow will come next and in what order the shadows will come. I'm not making that up: They're all gamers, playing the worst game ever: *School.*

Socrates and Plato tell us that the interactive narratives of the *Iliad* and the *Odyssey* represent an educational technology so powerful that they can make people chained to a bench in a cave feel good about it, and we can leverage the very same affordances in the service of much better education. Plato's solution is, in fact, his dialogues themselves—a new game and a new way to play.

He and Socrates weren't the only Athenians who grew up in and found fault with this educational system. Throughout the rest of this chapter, I'll take you on a quick tour of some of the others. In each case, we'll find that the writer has, in resisting and/or transforming the lessons of the homeric epics, pointed to their educational affordances—affordances we can use today in our instructional design. I'll then return to Socrates, Plato, and the cave to explain a classicist's vision for the future of interactive narrative and highlight where we can find the affordances of homeric tradition at work (once we know what to look for).

THUCYDIDES: HISTORY IS NOT A GAME (THE OPENNESS LESSON)

There is no more telling indication of the crucial educational function of homeric epics like the *Iliad* and the *Odyssey* in ancient Athens—birthplace of so many ideals we still hold for citizenship 2500 years later—than Thucydides founding the first true example of history via a debunking of pseudo-evidence found in the *Iliad*:

> The greatness of cities should be estimated by their real power and not by appearances. And we may fairly suppose the Trojan expedition to have been greater than any which preceded it, although according to Homer, if we may once more appeal to his testimony, not equal to those of our own day. He was a poet, and may therefore be expected to exaggerate; yet, even upon his showing, the expedition was comparatively small. For it numbered, as he tells us, twelve hundred ships, those of the Boeotians carrying one hundred and twenty men each, those of Philoctetes fifty; and by these numbers he may be presumed to indicate the largest and the smallest ships; else why in the catalogue is nothing said about the size of any others? (Thucydides, Bk 1, Ch. 10, tr. Crawley, 1903)

Here at the start of his history, where the first true historian (we'll deal with Herodotus, who was doing something else, in just a moment) concerns himself to show that the war he has chronicled outstrips all previous conflicts, the primacy of the homeric epics shows itself. Though Thucydides understands that poets exaggerate, he has no choice but to use the evidence that constituted such a decisive part of his own education to clarify the hard facts of history for his audience. In trying to investigate the events of the deep past, to compare them, as historians must do, with those of more recent times, Thucydides engaged with the interactive storytelling of the *Iliad* just as he must have done when he first heard the "Catalogue of Ships" in Book 2, the marvelous passage that demonstrates the bards' skill in "remembering" (really, recomposing for the occasion) all the contingents who sailed to Troy. His view displayed a good deal of skepticism, but the catalogue lived on in his mind, always there to play with, as he reworked a young literary tradition into something brand new, that would, he hoped, last forever.

The primacy of homeric epic receives corroboration and shape from some of the most stirring historical words ever written, at the end of Thucydides' prologue:

> Any one who upon the grounds which I have given arrives at some such conclusion as my own about those ancient times, would not be far wrong. He must not be misled by the exaggerated fancies of the poets, or by the tales of chroniclers who seek to please the ear rather than to speak the truth. Their accounts cannot be tested by him; and most of the facts in the lapse of ages have passed into the region of romance. At such a distance of time he must make up his mind to be satisfied with conclusions resting upon the clearest evidence which can be had. . . . And very likely the strictly historical character of my narrative may be disappointing to the ear. But if he who desires

to have before his eyes a true picture of the events which have happened, and of the like events which may be expected to happen hereafter in the order of human things, shall pronounce what I have written to be useful, then I shall be satisfied. My history is an everlasting possession, not a prize composition which is heard and forgotten. (Thucydides, Bk. 1, Ch. 21–22, tr. Crawley, 1903)

The first historian rejects the interactive storytelling of homeric epic as "exaggerated fancy," but—as we saw above—he cannot avoid the way it has shaped him. He sees the recitations of the rhapsodes as evanescent "prize compositions"—just as Plato gives us the image of the prisoners in the cave competing to name the shadows as they pass and just as, say, the significance of an individual game session of *World of Warcraft* seems to vanish even if captured to video—but those ephemeral, interactive, living prize compositions form the educational backdrop without which true history, based on hard evidence, could never have been born.

What can we take away, then, from Thucydides' reaction against his education via the interactive storytelling of the *Iliad* and the *Odyssey*?

I see the most important lesson for designers and teachers grounded in the way Thucydides decides to play the game. Rulesets that foster learning will always be the ones that permit the kind of exploration in which the first historian engaged, and the *Iliad* and the *Odyssey* represent vast sandboxes of narrative material. As we'll see, that freedom allowed history, tragedy, and philosophy to develop out of them not as creations *de novo* but as iterations upon the rulesets of the bards.

As we consider the sorts of interactive storytelling we bring into our learning environments, we must pay careful attention to how much opportunity we're giving our students to "do a Thucydides."

HERODOTUS: INQUIRY AS PLAYING WITH HOMER (THE BREAKING-THE-GAME LESSON)

I've left Herodotus to second even though he performed his "Inquiry" (the actual meaning of *historia*—specifically not what Thucydides calls his work) before Thucydides wrote of the Peloponnesian War and in spite of the fact that Thucydides intended his work to counter Herodotus' own. Although the principal events Herodotus told of—his work clearly designed for oral performance—lie in the distant past, this Inquirer worked in Athens, having come as an emigrant from Ionia when Thucydides was a young adult. Both Thucydides' and Herodotus' approaches to homeric education, along with that of the tragedians and that of Plato, were available alongside one another during the classical period.

Herodotus began his Inquiry with a diss—a burn, even—of the homeric epic tradition:

> This is the display of the inquiry of Herodotus of Halicarnassus, so that things done by man not be forgotten in time, and that great and marvelous deeds, some displayed by the Hellenes, some by the barbarians, not lose their glory, including among others what was the cause of their waging war on each other. . . . [A]fter this (the Persians say), the Greeks were very much to blame; for they invaded Asia before the Persians attacked Europe. "We think," they say, "that it is unjust to carry women off. But to be anxious to avenge rape is foolish: wise men take no notice of such things. For plainly the women would never have been carried away, had they not wanted it themselves. We of Asia did not deign to notice the seizure of our women; but the Greeks, for the sake of a Lacedaemonian woman, recruited a great armada, came to Asia, and destroyed the power of Priam. Ever since then we have regarded Greeks as our enemies." (Herodotus, Bk. 1, Chs. 1–4, author translation)

Glory is the mainspring of the homeric tradition: the glory of the heroes of the Trojan War and the glory of the war itself—and of the account of the war, along with that account's author. We saw Thucydides arguing that his war—the Peloponnesian War—would be judged greatest, if one examined the evidence. Here, Herodotus begins his account of the Persian Wars with a claim put into the mouths of Persians that the war "Homer" narrated was the work of fools.

Herodotus doesn't accuse "Homer" of exaggerating the way Thucydides does, but rather makes clear that his mode of interactive storytelling is vastly superior: He will interact, he claims (though often this claim is demonstrably false), not just with the homeric epics but also with the accounts given by other cultures. Like Thucydides, he learned most of what he knows of the past from the interactive homeric narrative to which he must have been even more thoroughly exposed, coming from Halicarnassus in Ionia, the birthplace of the homeric tradition. While Thucydides elected to create a new game as an iteration of epic, though, Herodotus did something that might be compared to glitching in a video game: He used the basic ruleset of homeric epic, with its demand for glory, but travelled beyond its boundaries to a world where the rules no longer applied.

Herodotus' work delights and frustrates. Without it, Thucydides might well not have become frustrated enough to write his own account of his own war. Perhaps Herodotus began to tell stories because of his own frustration with the songs of the homeric bards. The desire to break a game for fun and profit (compare a subset of videos to be found on YouTube of gamers demonstrating their prowess at glitching) coexists with the desire to design better games.

From Herodotus, then, we might learn not to regard game-breaking behaviors as necessarily negative. Students confronted by a ruleset that doesn't fit their needs from their learning environment might well be able to find ways to break the rules helpfully, though maybe not always delightfully. Game designers, dungeon masters, and teachers tend to want everything to run on smooth rails. Herodotus tells us that as annoying as it can be to have a game's (or a course's) limitations pointed out, the deconstruction of those limitations can lead to progress for student and designer alike.

TRAGEDY: THE HEROES' NEW GAME (THE CHARACTER LESSON)

Theatre is interactive storytelling. I'm fairly certain I don't need to argue much for that proposition, but it may help to think of a script as a set of rules for performing a play. When we move to more improvisatory forms of drama, the point becomes even more obvious: At least for the performers on stage, what you have in a live drama—night after night—is closely akin to successive play-throughs of a digital game.

The debt of Athenian tragedy (what we usually call "Greek tragedy") to homeric epic can be easily overlooked. With one very complicated exception (Euripides' *Rhesus*), no surviving tragedy tells the same story as any part of the *Iliad* and the *Odyssey*. What this failure to overlap conceals, however, is that in skirting the edges of the homeric epics, the tragedians (i.e., Aeschylus, Sophocles, and Euripides) *interacted* with the epic tradition, creating what we might think of as new games and/or a new kind of epic learning environment.

Because, while the stories don't overlap, the *characters* do. Agamemnon and his family are the most striking examples, but the exception that proves the rule is the family of Oedipus of Thebes, whom many today don't realize was originally the subject of a different epic tradition—the *Thebaid*—which some ancients attributed to Homer. If we had the *Thebaid* (rather than some very fragmentary summaries of its plot), we would have a much clearer picture of the interactivity inherent to Athenian tragedy. But the way our three surviving tragedians treated the family of Agamemnon (remember, Helen of Sparta/Troy—cause of the Trojan War—is the sister of Clytemnestra, adulterous wife and murderer of Agamemnon) can give us the design lessons we're looking for.

The most famous tragedy to treat the horrific events of the House of Atreus (Agamemnon's father) is Aeschylus' *Agamemnon*, the first tragedy in the trilogy known as the *Oresteia* (after Agamenon's son and avenger Orestes). The most important thing to know about *Agamemnon* as a set of performance materials (that is, a ruleset for interactive narrative) is that Aeschylus turned the figure of the homeric hero who disastrously offends Achilles in the *Iliad* into a disastrous civic leader—the kind you might find in the Athens of Aeschylus.

That is, Aeschylus, older than Socrates but educated in the same way (i.e., through the interactivity of homeric epic) gave his fellow Athenians (all educated the same way) a new means of interacting with narrative. Above all, he gave them a way to see themselves and their mistakes in a figure who would have seemed quite distant to them as portrayed in the homeric performances of the rhapsodes.

Take, for example, Agamemnon's return from Troy:

> For a woman's sake, the beast from Argos,
> born from the belly of that wooden horse,
> in the night, as the Pleiades went down,
> jumped out with their shields and razed the city.   970
> Leaping over walls, the ravenous lion
> gorged itself on blood of royalty.
> So much for my long prelude to the gods.
> As for your concerns, I've heard your words,
> and I'll keep them in mind. I agree with you—
> we'll work together. By nature few men
> possess the inborn talent to admire
> a friend's good fortune without envy.
> Poisonous malice seeps into the heart,
> doubling the pain of the infected man,   980
> weighing him down with misfortunes of his own,
> while he groans to see another's wealth.
> I understand too well companionship
> no more substantial than pictures in a glass.
> (Tr. Ian Johnston, 2016)

Excessive aristocratic display is a problem for a great many societies, but Aeschylus wrote the *Agamemnon* at a time when such displays had become an incredibly serious issue for Athens (i.e., the aftermath of the Persian Wars). Agamemnon announced on his entrance that he would curb it, for the sake of civil order, as he put his city's government back together. The returning generals of Athens quite probably said the same.

However, when the queen, Agamemnon's wife Clytemnestra, had rich tapestries laid down for him to walk on as he entered the palace (thereby ruining them), the Athenians must have recognized a parallel even closer to their own lives:

My fame proclaims itself. It doesn't need
foot mats made out of such embroideries.
Not even to think of doing something bad
is god's greatest gift. When a man's life ends
in great prosperity, only then can we declare
that he's a happy man. Thus, if I act,
in every circumstance, as I ought to now,
there's nothing I need fear.   930
CLYTAEMNESTRA
Don't say that just to flout what I've arranged.
AGAMEMNON
You should know I'll not go back on what I've said.
CLYTAEMNESTRA
You must fear something, then, to act this way.
You've made some promise to the gods.
AGAMEMNON
I've said my final word. I fully understand,
as well as any man, just what I'm doing.
CLYTAEMNESTRA
What do you think Priam would have done,
if he'd had your success?
AGAMEMNON
That's clear—
he'd have walked across these tapestries.
CLYTAEMNESTRA
So then why be ashamed by what men say?
AGAMEMNON
But what people say can have great power.
CLYTAEMNESTRA
True, but the man whom people do not envy
is not worth their envy.
AGAMEMNON
It's not like a woman
to be so keen on competition.   940
CLYTAEMNESTRA
It's fitting that the happy conqueror
should let himself be overcome.
AGAMEMNON
And in this contest
that's the sort of victory you value?
CLYTAEMNESTRA
Why not agree? Be strong and yield to me,
of your own consent.

AGAMEMNON
Well, if it's what you want . . .
Quick, someone get these sandals off—
they've served my feet so well. As I now walk
on these red tapestries dyed in the sea,
may no distant god catch sight of me,
and, for envy, strike me down.

(Tr. Ian Johnston, 2016)

A marital argument, reinforced by human nature's desire to flaunt power and wealth, overcomes Agamemnon. When Clytemnestra kills him, the people don't come to his aid because he has gone back on his claim to humility—just as Clytemnestra intended.

Through this new kind of interactivity—interactivity of the theatre—Aeschylus gave the Athenians something quite different. Yet, that lesson only became possible as a consequence of Athenians' education in their older form of interactive narrative, homeric epic.

As the 5th century BCE wore on, Sophocles and then Euripides would turn to this same story, playing not just according to the rules of the homeric bards but also the newer rules laid down by Aeschylus. Sophocles' extraordinary *Electra* and Euripides' even more extraordinary—deranged, even—*Andromache, Hecuba, Electra, Trojan Woman, Iphigenia Among the Taurians, Helen, Orestes,* and *Iphigenia at Aulis,* all concern the house of Atreus in relation to the stories of the Trojan War sung by the bards and representing a part of Athenian education so decisive that the epics themselves might be called the learning environment.

In each of the tragedians' successive dramas—building on the work of those who had come before—they provided what might crudely be thought of as lessons for living in Athens. Most strikingly, perhaps, Euripides' *Electra* parodied Aeschylus' treatment of the same character in *Libation Bearers,* the second tragedy of the *Oresteia,* by suggesting that the qualities associated with character authenticity (and thus what made for impactful interactive storytelling) had progressed from Aeschylus just as Aeschylus himself had progressed from the homeric epics.

The design lesson emerging from study of tragedy in relation to the older interactive narrative of the *Iliad* and the *Odyssey* lies in the way Agamemnon, brought vividly to life by a live actor in a mask and a costume (though of course when we watch "authentically" staged tragedy today the mask and the language make the character much less vivid for us—we've moved on in our interactive storytelling, too), engaged the audience through their identification with him. Here, identification involves a great many more parts of a creative performance than character, but the role of strong, recognizable characters should never be overlooked given how they provide a special sort of identification, whether they're the formalized Iliadic Achilles, with whose unstoppable bravery Socrates clearly felt a kinship, or the more vivid tragic Agamemnon, who evokes our sympathies in his intractable dilemma.

PLATO: LEAVING THE CAVE (THE MIMESIS LESSON)

Growing up with the same education as the historian, the inquirer, and the tragedians—and probably knowing most of them personally—Socrates and his young friend Plato greatly valued the interactive storytelling of the *Iliad* and the *Odyssey*. At the same time, it seems clear that Socrates also, from a young age, could see deep flaws in the decisive role the works of the homeric bards played in making Athenians who they were.

It's not possible, much as scholars have tried over the centuries, to reconstruct any sort of biography of Socrates from the dialogues of Plato. Even the simplest and earliest of those dialogues bear the marks of Plato's fictionalization of his friend. This fictionalization inevitably seems strange to us who are accustomed to the facts of a person's biography—even a person without any sort of lasting fame—being verifiable and immutable. We must understand Plato, however, as creating in Socrates a new hero—a new Achilles—and also a new *kind* of hero.

In the end, Plato's reshaping of Socrates will be the true design-lesson of this chapter, but we must first analyze that reshaping process as carefully as possible.

To call this new Achilles an "epic" hero begs a question of the highest degree: What is *epic*? If we confine the word strictly—as the Greeks did with *epos*, their word for poetry in dactylic hexameter (the meter of the *Iliad* and the *Odyssey* and the literally countless other now-lost epics of the epic cycle)—then Plato's Socrates is *not* an epic hero.

But to call Socrates a "philosophic" or even an "educational" hero threatens to leave out what I would suggest is the most valuable takeaway from this chapter: that neither Socrates nor his new form of interactive storytelling (that's what Plato's dialogues are at their foundation, strange as it might seem if you're accustomed to being tortured with them in Western Civilization classes) would have come into being without Plato's driving will to make his martyred friend into the truly ethical hero that Achilles (still less the liar Odysseus) could never be.

In fact, the only way to capture the true valence of Plato's remaking of Socrates, I think, is to recover the real meaning of the word *hero*. For Socrates and Plato, heroes weren't role models (see Agamemnon and Oedipus!); they were human beings of the past worshipped somewhere as a cult divinity entombed in the earth. Some heroes, notably including Achilles and Odysseus, were never actually worshipped in hero-cult, but their roles in the *Iliad* and the *Odyssey* are predicated on belonging to the class of the cult hero, worshipped as a kind of communal ancestor.

Thus, when I argue that Plato created in Socrates a new hero and a new kind of hero, I'm invoking that technical, culturally contextualized sense of *hero*. Dead Socrates received a new kind of glory, and he would be the heroic foundation of a new kind of interactive, educational storytelling: philosophy, as brought to life in the dialogues of Plato, all but one of which feature Socrates either as the main character or as a presiding quasi-divinized character (*Laws,* almost certainly Plato's last dialogue).

When we examine the things Plato said through Socrates and other characters about the homeric epics (keeping the new interactive-narrative hero in mind), we see that from the very beginning, Plato was giving a design lesson in which the new hero spoke in complimentary—if revisionist—terms of the old (positioned paradoxically in the *Apology of Socrates*, the end of Socrates' life):

> Someone will say: And are you not ashamed, Socrates, of a course of life which is likely to bring you to an untimely end? To him I may fairly answer: There you are mistaken: a man who is good for anything ought not to calculate the chance of living or dying; he ought only to consider whether in doing anything he is doing right or wrong–acting the part of a good man or of a bad. Whereas, according to your view, the heroes who fell at Troy were not good for much, and the son of Thetis above all, who altogether despised danger in comparison with disgrace; and when his goddess mother said to him, in his eagerness to slay Hector, that if he avenged his companion Patroclus, and slew Hector, he would die himself—"Fate," as she said, "waits upon you next after Hector"; he, hearing this, utterly despised danger and death, and instead of fearing them, feared rather to live in dishonor, and not to avenge his friend. "Let me die next," he replies, "and be avenged of my enemy, rather than abide here by the beaked ships, a scorn and a burden of the earth." Had Achilles any thought of death and danger? For wherever a man's place is, whether the place which he has chosen or that in which he has been placed by a commander, there he ought to remain in the hour of danger; he should not think of death or of anything, but of disgrace. And this, O men of Athens, is a true saying. (Plato, *Apology of Socrates*, ch. 28, tr. Jowett, 1870)

The adjustment Plato made as he fictionalized Socrates' final speech is subtle but telling. The overarching story of the *Iliad* is Achilles' anger and the destruction it causes. This moment of bravery that Plato's Socrates highlighted comes after Achilles' wrath has caused the death of his friend. To call Plato's move whitewashing or obfuscation, though, doesn't do it justice, because he clearly did it not with the intent of having his Socrates insult the epic tradition but to go it one better—much better.

Socrates, in dialogue here with the city in which he grew up, taught to be a citizen through the interactive narrative of the *Iliad* and the *Odyssey*, invites them to identify with him through their own educations in that same narrative. As Plato writes him, he doesn't expect to live. He does expect to inaugurate a new way of looking at what young Athenians can learn—as well as what everybody can learn, from 399 BCE all the way through 2016 CE—from interactive storytelling.

When Plato returns to the story of Socrates' death, in allegorical form, explicitly discussing the difference between education and lack of education, it is to Achilles and Odysseus he returns, having his fictionalized Socrates endorse Achilles' sentiment, as recounted by Odysseus, that he would rather be alive than be honored among the dead:

> And now, I said, let me show in a figure how far our nature is educated or uneducated:—Behold! human beings living in a underground den, which has a mouth open towards the light and reaching all along the den; here they have been from their childhood, and have their legs and necks chained so that they cannot move, and can only see before them, being prevented by the chains from turning round their heads. Above and behind them a fire is blazing at a distance, and between the fire and the prisoners there is a raised way; and you will see, if you look, a low wall built along the way, like the screen which marionette players have in front of them, over which they show the puppets.
>
> . . .
>
> And if they were in the habit of conferring honours among themselves on those who were quickest to observe the passing shadows and to remark which of them went before, and which followed after, and which were together; and who were therefore best able to draw conclusions as to the future, do you think that he [a man who has been released and seen the outside world] would care for such honours and glories, or envy the possessors of them? Would he not say with Homer [in the Odyssey, Bk. 11],
>
> 'Better to be the poor servant of a poor master,' and to endure anything, rather than think as they do and live after their manner?
>
> 'Yes, he said, I think that he would rather suffer anything than entertain these false notions and live in this miserable manner.
>
> 'Imagine once more, I said, such an one coming suddenly out of the sun to be replaced in his old situation; would he not be certain to have his eyes full of darkness?
>
> 'To be sure, he said.
>
> 'And if there were a contest, and he had to compete in measuring the shadows with the prisoners who had never moved out of the den, while his sight

was still weak, and before his eyes had become steady (and the time which would be needed to acquire this new habit of sight might be very considerable), would he not be ridiculous? Men would say of him that up he went and down he came without his eyes; and that it was better not even to think of ascending; and if any one tried to loose another and lead him up to the light, let them only catch the offender, and they would put him to death.

'No question, he said. (Plato, Republic Bk. 7, 514a–517a; tr. Jowett, 1870, slightly modified)

Earlier, Plato's Socrates has had some harsh judgments to render about an educational technology that goes by the Greek name *mimēsis*. In the final book of *Republic* Plato will return, through his hero, to the matter and use it to issue a condemnation of the homeric epic tradition as a means of education. We need to be very careful about the meaning of *mimēsis*, which has traditionally been translated "imitation." That translation is especially inaccurate when we consider the matter from the perspective I take here—that of educational technology—because it leaves the imaginative aspect of the concept entirely out of it. *Mimēsis* actually means something much closer to "playing pretend" than it does to "imitation." When we grasp that difference, Socrates' pronouncements make a great deal more sense, and they have an essential, decisive connection to the allegory of the cave and above all to his invocation of the *Odyssey* in it.

First, the epic tradition, as performed by the rhapsodes—the way Socrates and Plato, as well as Herodotus, Thucydides, and the tragedians, would have known it—involved what Plato's Socrates calls *mimēsis* in Book 3 of *Republic*. The rhapsodes pretend to be the characters when they deliver the speeches of the heroes. Tragedy, says Socrates, involves even more *mimēsis*: that is, even more playing pretend. This, for Plato's Socrates, makes epic and tragedy the ultimate educational technologies, because playing pretend (as we know well from modern educational psychology) is a powerful way to learn a great many things. It also makes epic and tragedy very dangerous, because it's too easy for those participating in the performance—and in this Plato clearly includes the audience—to acquire the wrong skills, such as lying like Odysseus and giving way to their emotions like the characters of Euripides.

In the allegory of the cave, we see Plato, through his Socrates, take this idea of *mimēsis* to its logical, frightening conclusion: a world of interactive play in which the learning environment emphasizes the wrong skills and values but is nevertheless so involving (remember that the prisoners don't actually *need* the chains!) that no one wants to give it up, even when someone comes to tell them of the better world outside. In the process, he creates a paper-prototype of the very first video game and offers the first criticism of gamers refusing to leave the literal basement man-cave. More germanely for our purpose, he makes absolutely clear that his critique of homeric, interactive-narrative *mimēsis* is aimed very precisely not at removing *mimēsis* and interactive narrative from the ideal educational environment he envisions, but at transforming them into something new and better: Platonic dialogue.

Consider the way Plato sets up *Republic*. It's a first-person narration by Socrates to an unknown conversational partner (not just unnamed; this interlocutor never appears at all) of a dialogue that purports to have taken place the previous day. It begins, "I went down to the Piraeus yesterday," and proceeds to tell the massive tale of a conversation that starts off to be about old age, and then turns to the meaning of justice, and finally to the plan for the ideal city-state.

There is absolutely no possible reason for Plato to frame *Republic* this way *unless he wishes to make Socrates do* mimēsis, pretending to be not only the interlocutors of the dialogue *but also himself*. Consider that in a world in which silent reading was considered strange, the reader of *Republic* would himself have to pretend to be Socrates and his interlocutors.

Plato is not rejecting *mimēsis*: He's telling us how to do it right—at least as far as he's concerned. His interactive storytelling platform created Western philosophy, so perhaps we have a design-lesson or two to learn from him. These lessons may not teach us how to engage kids: I can say with certainty that Platonic dialogue, though I believe it's a good deal less boring than most people think, will never be able to do that and couldn't do it even in Plato's day, when he himself declared that he wanted it to be hard to undertake a philosophical education, in order to weed out the unworthy. On the other hand, given that the interactive narrative he created changed the intellectual world—reshaped some big part of it, even, in philosophy's own image—there might be something there that could help us attain prosocial goals with our learning environments.

The two most important lessons I find in Plato for the design and implementation of interactive storytelling as an educational technology are (a) the ubiquity of metacognitive scaffolding and (b) the persistence of theme over a single dialogue and among dialogues. I don't have space in this chapter to delve deeply into these lessons, but a sketch of their broad outlines will I think demonstrate at least their importance.

By *the ubiquity of metacognitive scaffolding* I really mean just what I pointed out above with regard to the narrative framing of *Republic*. Every one of Plato's greatest dialogues has a dramatic (don't forget that that must also by Plato's own analysis also mean a mimetic—that is, an interactive narrative) context that forces the thinking reader to "go meta" on the experience both of reading the dialogue and of doing philosophy. Just as a single prisoner in the cave is released from his chains and forced to take the hard way to the surface, the reader of a Platonic dialogue, involved interactively in the story of the particular conversation held by Socrates and his interlocutors through the mimetic process of reading (remember, all reading was reading aloud), is forced to think of his own participation in the story as part of what might be called the adventure of philosophy.

Plato erects this scaffolding in different ways in different dialogues (in addition to *Republic,* some of the more astounding examples are to be found in *Symposium, Timeaus–Critias, Parmenides,* and *Theaetetus*). I want to suggest that by studying the various ironies involved in this invitation to metacognition, or to put it another way the places where Plato demands that the player of his game search for another meaning, à la *BioShock* (see Travis, 2010), we can learn to build similar opportunities for reflection into our interactive narratives.

By *the persistence of theme* I mean the way Plato, from dialogue to dialogue, makes clear the importance of active learning, through interactive, playful participation in the ongoing story of a citizen's education. Each dialogue, and each book of a vast dialogue like *Republic,* has its own theme and examines its own problems with living as a wisdom-loving citizen in the imperfect world of the Greek city-states in the 4th century BCE. But in part through the ubiquity of the metacognitive elements that I sketched above, and in part through the ongoing story of Socrates' career as the self-appointed true teacher of the Athenians that unites all the dialogues, Plato's interactive learning environment as a whole gives the playful participant an ideal with which to identify.

This persistent theme of Platonic dialogue stands in direct contrast to the themes of the *Iliad* and the *Odyssey* that provide their audiences with an ambivalent warrior ideal: Achilles who sulks and loses his friend because of it; Odysseus who lies and slaughters his way home. The theme of Plato's interactive story is Socrates as the figure for the man of examined life, and although this story may not appeal to the broad adventure-seeking range of citizens who will always love stories like those of the homeric bards, nevertheless we as designers and implementers of learning environments can ourselves learn a great deal from Plato about how sophisticated and analytical such stories can be, when they go meta and present a persistent theme.

THE ODYSSEY: ADVENTURE FOR THE AGES (THE IMMERSION LESSON)

In the end, Plato's achievement in his new type of interactive narrative, which nevertheless necessarily looks back to the education he and Socrates got through the interactive narrative of the homeric epics, gives us very good reason to turn back to those epics to see whether, through the lens of Thucydides', Herodotus', the tragedians', and Plato's development of epic affordances, we can make out the outlines of those affordances more clearly.

One moment in the *Odyssey*, above all, seems to me to embody the potential of ancient interactive storytelling, even if it does so in a way that none of the enlightened Athenians we've consulted so far might approve. Odysseus here speaks to the bard of the magical land of the Phaeacians, who has been entertaining them with songs (epic songs, that is) of the Trojan War.

> Demodocus I praise you above all mortals.
> Either the Muse, daughter of Zeus taught you, or Apollo.
> For all too well, in order, you sing the trouble of the Achaeans,
> All the things they did and suffered and all the things the Achaeans
>   toiled at,
> as if you yourself were there, or heard from another.
> But come, change it up, and sing the making of the horse—
> the wooden one—the one Epeius made with Athena,
> which once heroic Odysseus brought as a trick to the city-center,
> having filled it with the men who sacked Troy.
> If you tell me this, giving due attention,
> immediately I'll proclaim to all people
> that the god willingly awarded you a divine song.
>   (Homer, *Odyssey*, Book 9, author translation)

To explain fully why this moment means so very much about the learning affordances of interactive narrative in the context both of the *Odyssey* and of the *Iliad*—indeed in the context of the entire epic cycle and even of the entire epic tradition from Gilgamesh to *Fallout 4*—I'd have to write at least one book. I hope to do that sometime soon.

But I think I can make one learning affordance entirely clear just by pointing out that after Demodocus sings the epic bit about the horse (whether or not you accept as true the very intriguing possibility that Odysseus is actually asking him to improvise it), Odysseus' reaction causes Alkinoos, the king of the Phaeacians, to demand that Demodocus stop singing and Odysseus give his own bardic performance of the epic of his adventures on his way from Troy to the land of the Phaeacians. The end product of that performance is a ride home and a huge haul of wealth with which to rebuild Odysseus' prosperity, currently and literally eaten up by the young men of Ithaca who seek Penelope's—Odysseus' wife's, that is—hand in remarriage.

The extraordinary ins and outs of the process that unfolds in Odysseus' narrative at the banquet of the Phaeacians, including Odysseus' praise of Demodocus and of the epic occasion, his manipulation of his story to include clearly fictional elements, his matching the story to the nature of his audience, and finally the satisfaction of Alkinoos' request that he tell (or improvise) the tale of meeting the souls of Agamemnon and Achilles in the underworld, all spring from this moment in which Odysseus makes a bargain about his lesson plan, and requests that Demodocus help him deliver a learning module about the greatness of Odysseus.

There are, as I said above, many, many design lessons to take away for our use of interactive narrative, but one is perhaps so obvious that it can stare us in the face for a long time before we notice it: Odysseus wants to teach his audience about who he is, and he designs a curriculum that does it so well—through interactive storytelling, no less—that the world continues learning about him today in one of the most enjoyable books we assign our children to read.

REFERENCES

Crawley, R. (Trans.). (1903). *A history of the Peloponnesian War, by Thucydides*. London, England: J. M. Dent.

Johnston, I. (Trans.). (2016). *Aeschylus: The Oresteia*. Retrieved from https://records.viu.ca/~johnstoi/aeschylus/oresteiatofc.htm

Jowett, B. Tr. (1870.) *The dialogues of Plato*. London: Oxford UP.

Lord, A. B., Mitchell, S. A., & Nagy, G. (2000). *The singer of tales*. Cambridge, MA: Harvard University Press.

Travis, R. (2010). BioShock in the cave: Ethical education in Plato and in video games. In K. Schrier & D. Gibson (Eds.), *Ethics in game design* (pp. 86–101). Hershey, PA: IGI Global.

Travis, R. (2012). Epic style: Recompositional performance in the BioWare Digital RPG. In G. Voorhees, J. Call, & K. Whitlock (Eds.), *Dungeons, dragons, and digital denizens: The digital role-playing game* (pp. 235–256). New York, NY: Continuum.

CHAPTER 3

STRUCTURES OF PLAY

Literacy, Games, and Creative Writing

W. Trent Hergenrader
Rochester Institute of Technology

At the conclusion of my first semester teaching college-level creative writing, I had an unmistakable feeling of despair. I entered graduate school with a stable of short story publications in some very well-regarded markets. My career plan, as with most creative writers seeking graduate degrees, was to support myself with a university teaching position while working to publish a steady stream of short stories and novels. I was far from being a recognized name as a fiction writer, but I felt that in the span of my short fiction writing career that I had learned the basics of entering the publishing industry: namely, how to find the right markets for my work; properly formatting and submitting a manuscript; and, most importantly, I'd learned the subtle tweaks and tightening of language that meant more often than not my work at least avoided instant and rejection and, at least some of the time, I came out on top amid intense competition. In short, I was confident I had something important to offer and that plenty of people would want to learn

Exploding the Castle, pages 39–63
Copyright © 2017 by Information Age Publishing
All rights of reproduction in any form reserved.

how to graduate from talented amateur to professionally published writer. I didn't give actual instruction much thought.

My program required that I spend one year teaching first-year composition while taking a course entitled Teaching College Composition before I could teach a section of Introduction to Creative Writing. I was astounded by those students' poor writing skills and their disengagement from the act of writing altogether. Likewise, I was smugly confident that once I started teaching creative writing, I would ride through each class on a wave of enthusiasm as I doled out golden tips on what constituted "good writing" and how with hard work, students may have the gratification of seeing their words in print. Much to my shock, my desire to impart my hard-won trove of knowledge was met with indifference by my first group of creative writing students. As it turned out, few of my creative writing students had any interest in pursuing publication whatsoever. The creative writing workshop method that had so improved my writing, where participants share and critique each other's work, produced limp, perfunctory exchanges in classroom. Student A didn't want to read Student B's sloppily crafted story, and Student B didn't want to read Student A's. Minutes crept by as students went through the motions of providing critique, only speaking when I crossed into their group's half of the room. It was a dull, tepid affair and I didn't know whom to blame more—the students for not caring about the finer points of writing, or me for forcing us all to suffer through each class session.

My dissatisfaction in teaching creative writing combined with my desire to be more marketable in a brutal job market led me to pick up an added specialization in professional writing. I hoped to offset my lack of teaching experience with the business and technical skills I'd developed in my administrative career prior to grad school, particularly my project experience working with software documentation. I was surprised how little students understood about the digital technologies they were using, and the research paper I did for my Teaching College Composition course examined how digital tools were reshaping writing disciplines. Composition and professional writing had a healthy catalog of theorizing what it meant to be a writer in the 21st century, there was virtually no research on digital creative writing. In fact, there was precious little creative writing research of *any* kind, much less focused specifically on digital approaches. Due to the lack of creative writing research on digital writing, an advisor pointed me to the field of game studies and the explorations of narrative in digital spaces. This in turn introduced me to the principles of game-based learning and, within a year of passing my preliminary doctoral exams, I had designed and taught my first creative writing course that blended collaborative writing, digital tools, and role-playing game mechanics.

Today, virtually all of my creative writing classes are either explicitly game-based or my lessons lean heavily on game-like structures and game mechanics. Now that I've turned my course objectives away from publishing concerns, I accomplish more and foster much deeper student engagement than I ever did with traditional workshop approaches. From time to time I have employed the workshop method, usually at the behest of students who have had them in other creative writing classes and feel like they're missing out if the course lacks that component. The results vary widely, and unfortunately there's not much an instructor can do to guarantee a good experience for all students. Workshops go well if the participants are eager about sharing manuscripts, but they are almost useless if the participants are unmotivated or simply don't do the work. This explains how the instructional method of "the creative writing workshop" that I learned so much from can function in a selective program—namely because everyone cares about writing—and yet be of minimal value at the undergraduate level, especially for introductory courses that students may be taking as a requirement or to fill a hole in their schedule, not because they love writing and want to see their name in print.

One of the major benefits of my game-based approaches is that it keeps everyone engaged in a collaborative project. This approach liberates the creative writing discipline from preoccupation with romantic notions of the secluded lone author toiling away in a garret (Brodkey, 1987) and redirects it to a more contemporary notion of the kinds of distributed and collaborative authorship made possible through networks and digital tools such as wikis, blogs, forums, GoogleDocs, video media, and more (Amato & Fleisher, 2002). The narratives that emerge are inherently unpredictable because they emerge through evocative, even sometimes contentious group dynamics (Cover, 2010). The unknowability of what comes next in an RPG helps rethink how we use the time and space afforded in the creative writing classroom, and it provides a model for making an important and overdue ideological shift in the creative writing classroom, namely switching from the historical focus on final *products*—the literary artifact intended for print publication—to the ongoing *processes* of writing (Harper, 2010).

One common bit of creative writing conventional wisdom is that we need to teach beginners how to "read like a writer" (Prose, 2006). By this, we mean that a novice should read widely and keep an eye on issues of craft by separating the experience of the story from the subtle techniques that make a piece of writing tick—the deft turn of phrase, the rich variety of verbs, actions, or utterances that reveal volumes about a character's personality. While this is generally sound advice for anyone serious about their writing, the complication comes in when beginning writers aren't sure how to start or even what to write about when it comes to producing their own work. When we ask students to read a published work of fiction and then use that as a model for their own writing, we're asking them to move from one product (the published story) to another product (their attempt at a story) without sufficient attention paid to what kind of work happens during this transition. In contrast, games foreground the *processes*—the rules and structures of games provide many different choices that must be considered—and the final product that results from the gameplay is the accumulation of those choices.

The transition from product-based to process-based thinking isn't an easy one. Creative writing in higher education is heavily invested in traditional notions of literacy and the romantic notions of what it means to "be a writer." Broadening our understanding of what literacy means the 21st century is a crucial step in opening up creative writing to a larger student population. Rather than obsessing about the reproduction of print literary culture, we can instead engage with questions about what it means to be a writer in the digital age, how literacy now includes multiple forms of media, and the ethical dimensions of creative production.

UNSTOPPABLE FORCES AND IMMOVABLE OBJECTS: MULTILITERACIES AND CREATIVE WRITING

Anyone who watches toddlers play on tablets or smartphones can see that the way they explore digital texts is very different than the way they handle printed books. Digital texts tend to be interactive and full of motion, objects to manipulate, and unique sounds. Kids who play with digital texts naturally wish to create digital texts too, and they can begin building them using programs like ScratchJr, Minecraft, and Roblox before they have mastered reading and writing. As they develop more skills, their digital projects become more sophisticated. By the time my son was six years old, he was creating simple animations with timed audio events in ScratchJr, and he built elaborate Minecraft worlds and literally left signposts to help guide visitors through the structures he'd created. This is different than scrawling with crayons on paper—though he does that too—because what he's creating involves images, and sounds, and motion, and they're environments that he can share with his friends and family to interact with. And this is as natural and normal for him as it is exotic and bizarre for his grandparents.

In an effort to describe this set of emergent communication practices, the New London Group (1995) coined the phrase "multiliteracies," folding a range of visual and auditory elements used for meaning making and sharing into what would traditionally be described as literacy. They urged educators to incorporate the notion of multiliteracies into their pedagogical practices in order to better equip students to critically engage with these rapidly evolving technologies. They write of the available designs—the various structures, rhetorical moves, and genre conventions of different forms of media that can be blended or remixed—that 21st-century writers choose from when creating a new text. If we can teach students to be cognizant, critical, and deliberate in their choice of composing tools today, they argue, the students will be better equipped to adapt to the changes yet to come and thus have greater agency in determining their own futures in both their personal and professional lives.

Of course, the need for multiliteracies extends to everyone, not just the very young. The explosion of Web 2.0 technologies in the early 2000s dissolved centuries-old gatekeeping practices that separated producers from consumers, by first vetting content and then distributing it through traditional media outlets. Seemingly overnight, anyone with access to a computer and the Internet could publish blog posts decorated with images and embedded video. Even before the pre-Internet boom, media theorists like Henry Jenkins (1992) had been investigating participatory culture, whereby people participate in both the consumption and production of popular media; Jenkins's best known work, *Convergence Culture: Where New and Old Media Collide* (2006), examines rapid growth and diversification of participatory culture facilitated by web technologies that foster cooperation, creative expression, and collaborative knowledge building, often between complete strangers from opposite sides of the planet who meet on Internet chat rooms and message boards to share ideas and opinions on popular media.

James Paul Gee's landmark *What Video Games Have to Teach Us About Learning and Literacy* (2007) draws on the notion of multiliteracies as well, arguing that "meaning, thinking, and learning are linked to multiple modalities (words, images, actions, sounds, etc.) and not just to words" (p. 106), and that good videogames not only work with these modalities but also build good learning principles into their very design. He urges teachers to think about designing educational experiences to replicate what good videogames do—namely scaffolding learning so beginners are always urged to complete tasks within the context of a specific problem to be solved and gradually increasing the complexity of the problem as the learner gains competence.

Rebecca Black drew on both Gee's and Jenkins's work in her (2008) book *Adolescents and Online Fanfiction* to examine the phenomenon of online fanfiction writing spaces and make the case that, like videogames, online writing spaces are sites of deep and impactful learning that elicit a level of participation and investment dedicated teachers wish to see from their students. She further argued that affinity spaces formed around popular media feature many benefits for learners that include motivation and self-direction, authentic uses of technology, interactive communication skills, creativity and innovation, and social support (Black, 2008). Jayne Lammers, Alicia Magnifico, and Jen Scott Curwood have extended this work, connecting fanfiction, games, and multiliteracies as topics that can be used to build affinity groups in writing classrooms (Curwood, 2013; Curwood, Magnifico, & Lammers, 2013; Lammers, Curwood, & Magnifico, 2012). In short, as our habits of producing and consuming texts change over time, our pedagogies need to adapt in order to remain relevant; as technological advances continue to speed up, our culture adopts (and then often abandons) new digital tools at an astonishing rate.

For the writing scholar, our understanding of how audiences interact with texts has changed dramatically. The fields of composition and professional writing have steadily revisited their pedagogical practices in an effort to keep pace, shifting to teaching broad composing strategies for a digital age rather than focusing on the mastery of specific tools or platforms that may or may not be here tomorrow. This is possible in part due to the fact that despite the rapidly changing technologies, the basic principles of the rhetorical situation—or the examination of the space in which an author seeks to convey a specific message to an audience within a given context—remains more or less intact. It also helps that, as media theorists Bolter and Grusin (1999) noted, emergent media do not eradicate existing media in a sharp break, but rather establish new relationships in which knowledge of new media informs understanding of old media and vice versa. A discrete subfield of composition has come to examine the rhetorical choices made available through digital technologies like multimodal composition, remixing, and appropriation of texts; professional writing has focused on business practices, where today's textbooks integrate lessons on email etiquette, the creation of professional web presences, and the need for collaboration on digital projects with international teams. Careful attention to well-crafted, specific use of language has always remained a central part of the disciplinary identity of these branches of writing studies, even if a "well-written" assignment now might mean a compelling YouTube video rather than an essay printed on paper.

The field of creative writing, however, has remained entrenched in the position that traditional print culture is not simply culturally superior to other forms of narrative media, but that print literature *is* culture. How else can we interpret NEA Dana Gioia's (2009) proclamation that "cultural decline is not inevitable," noting the downward trend in reading ability "that was clearly documented in the first generation of teenagers and young adults raised in a society full of videogames, cell phones, iPods, laptops, and other electronic devices" (p. 2)? We are left to assume that the "reading ability" Gioia mentions does not include multiliteracies operating in sophisticated ways across communication channels. If the medium is the message, then for Gioia and likeminded creative writers, the medium must be print on paper in order for the message to hold any cultural relevance.

This outdated understanding of 21st century literacy—where print remains supreme and other modes of media are viewed as the enemy—is quite common among college-level creative writing instructors around the country, but there are signs that it may be changing. A small but growing contingent of academics working in the field of creative writing studies are offering alternatives to traditional approaches in books like Creative Writing Studies (Harper & Kroll, 2008), *Rethinking Creative Writing in Higher Education* (Vanderslice, 2010), *Key Issues in Creative Writing* (Donnelly & Harper, 2012), *Creative Writing Pedagogies for the Twenty-First Century* (Peary & Hunley, 2015), *Creative Writing in the Digital Age* (Clark, Hergenrader, & Rein, 2015), and *Creative Writing Innovations* (Clark, Hergenrader, & Rein, 2017). While diverse in their approaches and recommendations, they all promote creative writing as a field to recognize that the "available designs" for our craft now extend beyond the printed word on the page and transcend rigid genres of fiction, poetry, and creative nonfiction. We can incorporate visual literacy, interactive media, audio, and more and combine it with our expertise in language. Healey's (2013) concept of "creative literacies" is particularly apropos in the discussion of new horizons for the field as taught in educational institutions. Healey defines creative literacy as skills that include

> the ability to use language (along with visual images and many other media) to produce complex affective states in an audience; the ability to think and communicate in associative, metaphorical, non-linear, non-hierarchical ways; the ability to craft evocative stories with fully realized characters, personas, voices; the ability to manipulate or destabilize received meanings and to produce new meanings. (p. 63)

Thus creative literacy is essentially creative writing's way of shedding light on the multiliteracies educators have been encouraged to attend to in their classrooms. Untethered from the reproduction of literary print culture, creative writing might instead serve as a locus for innovation and experimentation that falls in line with what we expect from 21st century classroom environments.

One pressing problem is the apparent lack of models for what kind of work our classrooms might be transitioning *to*. Despite their low circulation rates, literary magazines do exist and function as the (alleged) destination for student writing. If we are to let go of our obsession with product—the published short story, the poem—what exactly is the process or processes that will claim our attention? By what means might we accomplish, or begin to accomplish, this paradigm shift? In other words, if you buy *why* we need to change creative writing, the next logical question is *how do we do it?* To put it in the language of literacy studies, what are some of the available designs outside traditional creative writing we should consider when developing 21st-century courses and a forward-thinking curriculum? Some instructors have incorporated techniques from our neighboring disciplines in the visual arts, performing arts, and graphic design. Others interested in electronic literature have connected the formal structures of poetry to the formal structures of coding and computation.

I've enjoyed success using games. First off, the idea of using games in the classroom is still new to most of my students so there's a hook with that initial curiosity. More importantly, I've found it very easy to align structures we find in different games—whether that's rules, strategies, or opportunities for collaboration and cooperation—with learning outcomes commonly found in creative writing. Creative writing has a long tradition of using prompts and exercises to get students to focus on discrete aspects of craft. In the following sections, I'll discuss different types of games and how they can be used productively in the creative writing classroom, as well as the work I do with role-playing games that bridges creative writing with critical thinking.

PLAYING GAMES WITH WORDS AND LANGUAGE

For many students, their first experience studying the craft of creative writing occurs in college. While almost everyone will have written a story or poem before then, most will not have had specific instruction on individual aspects of craft. Equally importantly, today's students are more likely to have consumed narratives across many different media and not just print literature. While the multiliteracy approach encourages them to deploy their skills across different media, creative writing's focus is on the affordances of language in general, and the written word in specific. So while a student might choose to shoot a short a video in lieu of writing a short story, there is still need to attend to language. For example, if the video has dialogue between characters, we can focus on how their diction, syntax, and choice of words can reveal information about the character and establish the tone of the piece. While we might have input on camera angles, lighting, and other aspects relevant for that medium, our expertise lies in the rhythms of language. Students tend to take for granted the need for deft use of language; after all, when we watch a film or TV episode or read a book, evidence of rough drafts have been erased and we're presented with the final product. In order to get to a smoothly polished final product, students must be attuned to the nuances of language. While this might seem a daunting task, especially if students don't self-identify as strong readers, games provide a good entry point for the novice to begin thinking about the structures of language.

Playful approaches to language use is nothing new. Broadly conceived, language is a symbolic system governed by a common set of rules that facilitate communication. While most of our communication practices attempt to be straightforward—we don't want to be confused by street signs, nor do we wish letters to clients to require sophisticated analytical skill to understand their point—the symbols of language and their rule set allow for creative and artistic expressions, as well as playful interactions that include verbal utterances such as puns and double-entendres, as well printed word arrangements that are games or game-like: acrostics, anagrams, crosswords puzzles, word finds, and so on. Letters and words as puzzle pieces remain popular in the digital age, with mobile apps like Words with Friends and Ruzzle offering new takes on classic Scrabble-like mechanics. Typically, such games divorce language symbols from any kind of communicative purpose and instead rely on pattern recognition and surprising combinations to entertain the player.

The connection between language, creativity, and play has been central to various literary and artistic movements, perhaps most obviously by the Surrealists in the early part of the 20th century and the post-war group Oulipo, which stands for *Ouvroir de littérature potentielle* or "the workshop of potential literature." As outlined by André Breton (1969) in his manifesto, surrealism sought to liberate the mind from the shackles of reason and access more pure thought through chance, dreams, and madness. Dozens of techniques such as "automatic writing" and collaborative parlor games like exquisite corpse, where participants take turns collaboratively adding lines to a poem without being able to read previous lines, have been compiled into *A Book of Surrealist Games* (Brotchie & Gooding, 1995), which could double as a set of unconventional creative writing prompts, exercises, or activities. Rather than the psychological approach, Oulipo (Mathews, Brotchie, & Queneau, 1998; Motte, 1986) wished to dispense with Romantic muse-inspired notions of the creative and instead plumbed computation and mathematics for their inspiration. Representative works include Raymond Queneau's (1961) *A Hundred Thousand Billion Poems*, a set of ten sonnets printed on strips that can be combined in more different orders than anyone could read in a lifetime; his *Exercises in Style* (1981) which retells a mundane scene using 99 different stylistic techniques; and Georges Perec's (1994) *A Void*, a nearly 300-page novel that features no words that use the letter 'e,' the most common letter in both French and English. Christian Bok's *Eunoia* (2005) is a book where each chapter features words that use one vowel. For example, this excerpt from Chapter O:

from Chapter 0
(for Yoko Ono)

Loops on bold fonts now form lots of words for books. Books form cocoons of comfort—tombs to hold bookworms. Profs from Oxford show frosh who do post-docs how to gloss works of Wordsworth. Dons who work for proctors or provosts do not fob off school to work on crosswords, nor do dons go off to dorm rooms to loll on cots. Dons go crosstown to look for bookshops known to stock lots of top-notch goods: cookbooks, workbooks—room on room of how-to books for jocks (how to jog, how to box), books on pro sports: golf or polo. Old colophons on school-books from schoolrooms sport two sorts of logo: oblong whorls, rococo scrolls—both on worn morocco. (p. 59)

Playing such a word game results in some surprisingly clever phrases, but more importantly the exercise attunes the writer's ear to the resonance and rhythm of the language. Australian creative writing scholar Hazel Smith (2005) draws from both Surrealism and Oulipo in her book *The Writing Experiment: Strategies for Innovative Creative Writing*, one of the few creative writing guides that foregrounds experimental techniques and new media production over received literary forms. One exercise from her book that I participated in involved drawing random words written by other students on scraps of paper and tossed into a pile. I cycled through several combinations until the pairing "blood engine" stuck with me, and I wrote a short story using a blood engine as a startling, central metaphor. It's unlikely that image would have ever emerged from my own imagination.

Employing such language games helps reduce the sense that every piece of creative writing must be some monumental work of literary genius. Instead, creative writing exercises can serve as methods for producing the unexpected twists and unpredictable turns. The literary structures of poetry and prose can seem daunting, but games put these structures into systems of play that are allowed to be absurd or even silly. Through playful approaches, language becomes more accessible, malleable, and generative.

Storytelling Games

Few games marketed as "storytelling games" teach players about language or story in a way that creative writers instructors would support. Story-centric card games such as *Once Upon a Time* (Lambert, Rilstone, & Wallis, 1994) use narrative archetypes—the princess, the ogre—to facilitate cooperative or collaborative play, but the meandering narrative does not adhere to any coherent structure that resembles the basics of plot (e.g., rising action, climax, denouement), primarily because the game is more competitive than cooperative. The desire for players to get their cards out of their hand in order to win compromises the integrity of the story. Similarly, the much advertised *Elegy for a Dead World* (Lambe & Scott, 2014) purports to have its players tell stories by assuming the role of an astronaut exploring dreamlike worlds inspired by the poetic visions of Shelley, Byron, and Keats, responding to game prompts via written notes, and sharing their notes on a server for other players to read and annotate. However, *Elegy* is at best a multimedia writing prompt with gorgeous scenery and an eerie soundtrack and, at worst, a means of encouraging players to think about narrative in a paint-by-the-numbers approach where bits of language can be plugged into a structure and thus produce something artistic.

Other games approach storytelling from more productive angles, such as in collaborative storytelling roleplaying games (RPGs) where players assume the identity of a single character to interact with various peoples, places, and problems. They can take the form of digital environments such as Failbetter's *Fallen London* (2009) and the crowdfunded *Storium* (Hood, 2103) platform as well as analog/tabletop environments like *Fiasco* (Morningstar & Segedy, 2009) and *Dungeons & Dragons*. All of these RPG experiences include some type of game mechanics and governing ruleset intended to guide and inform storytelling. While these may sound like great foundational tools for classroom instruction, the common problem from a creative writing instructor's perspective is that none require, or even encourage, close attention to language. The game mechanics tend to be plot-based, driving the story forward and often creating a spontaneous and entertaining storytelling experience, but it does little to incentivize thoughtful language use, encourage deep consideration of complex and/or conflicting character motivations, or facilitate contemplation of any portion of the narrative that does not explicitly contribute to plot. Just as reading a short story or poem alone do not teach the reader how to "do" literary criticism, the simple act of playing storytelling games or RPGs do not inherently teach the player about language and narrative. However, playing RPGs *can* be helpful with respect to providing basic storytelling structures for occasions where students need to capture narrative events in language. More importantly, however, RPGs foster the development of classroom spaces where students are required to think both dialogically and dialectically (Paul, n.d.)—that is, understanding how characters experience life in their fictional world and how authors represent those characters' stories in language and media.

Role-Playing Games as Collaboratively Authored Experiences

I will begin with an explanation of a tabletop RPG for those who might not know what it looks like. Broadly speaking, RPGs require a group of players—usually no fewer than three and no more than six—sitting around a table (or virtually in a shared online space) where one person assumes the role of game master (GM) and the rest of the participants are all players.

Each player controls a character, who is the player's avatar in the game world known as the player-character (PC). Each PC has certain skills and abilities recorded on a character sheet. The GM establishes the setting, describes the scene, and plays the role of every nonplayer character (NPC); the GM is also responsible for invoking the rules whenever the PCs attempt to do a nontrivial task. The GM presents the PCs with certain situations or obstacles that they must overcome in order to achieve a larger goal.

Here's a hypothetical example from a fantasy RPG we'll call the Tower Heist. The GM may create a duke who hires the PCs, a group of four adventurers—a thief, a wizard, a warrior, and a bard—to retrieve a magic scroll stolen from him. In the course of the mission, the players discover a clue suggesting that the scroll can be found in the top room of a tall tower. The PCs arrive at the tower, and the GM describes the scene:

> It's a cold, damp night and the uppermost window of the stone tower is illuminated by flickering candlelight. There's one door to enter the tower, and a tall, thick man stands guard, leaning on his spear with one hand and clutching his soaked cloak around his throat with the other. Just outside the entrance is an alarm bell hanging from a hook about six feet off the ground. The tower is set back from the town's main street, which is deserted. What do you do?

The players around the table confer about possible strategies for gaining access to the tower. The player controlling the wizard suggests casting a sleep spell on the guard, but the players nix that idea as the guard might hear the incantation from the shadows and sound an alarm. The thief suggests she sneak over and scale the outside of the tower. The players like that idea, and the bard volunteers to distract the guard by pretending to be a lost traveler trying to find his way back to the town square. The wizard and warrior agree to keep guard from the shadows, providing cover while they execute the scheme.

When the players describe their plan, the GM helps determine the sequence of events and begins a series of ability checks. He requires the thief to roll two dice to determine whether she remains undetected on her approach to the tower. She rolls the dice, refers to her "stealth" skill on her character sheet, and reports those to the GM. She rolls very high, and the GM says she makes not even a whisper on her way to the tower. The bard tells the GM his PC emerges from the shadows with his hands held high and calls to the guard with an embarrassed laugh, "Excuse me kind sir, could you point me back to the town square? I seem to have gotten myself turned around in these twisting streets." The GM asks the bard to check against his charisma score, and the dice say he passes the test with ease; the guard exasperatedly explains the directions. The action turns back to the thief, who begins her ascent. The GM explains that she needs to make two checks: one to see if she succeeds climbing the tower (agility) and whether she does so quietly (stealth). He assigns a penalty to the agility roll citing the slick stones from the mist, and the thief fails her roll. The GM says she climbed up about five feet but then slid back to the ground. She rolls again for her stealth, and fails again! The GM smiles and says to the wizard and warrior: "You hear a clatter of rocks hitting the cobblestones from behind the tower, and the guard's head whips around. He lowers the spear at the bard and growls, 'Don't you move,' and steps toward the alarm bell. What do you do?"

Though most players use some sort of visual implements—maps, models of the environments, or miniatures—the majority of the experience is created *in language* through player interactions. In his book *The Fantasy Role-Playing Game: A New Performing Art,* Daniel Mackay defines a tabletop RPG as

> an episodic and participatory story-creation system that includes a set of quantified rules that assist a group of players and a gamemaster in determining how their fictional characters' spontaneous interactions are resolved. These performed interactions between the players' and the gamemaster's characters take place during individual sessions that, together, form episodes or adventures in the lives of the fictional characters. (Mackay, 2001, pp. 4–5)

The definition contains a number of important components that relates to its suitability for teaching narrative: First, it's *episodic* in that the larger story is intended to be broken into narrative chunks. Second, it's *participatory*: There is no way to sit on the sidelines as a player in a tabletop RPG. Even if players choose to be idle in a given scenario, their presence may be called upon at any time. Third, it's about telling an ever-evolving *story* that is shaped by player decisions. Fourth, it's governed by nonarbitrary *quantified rules* that determine the success or failures of certain actions. Fifth, it requires a *group of players* in order to provide a variety of narrative choices, and sixth, their choices are *spontaneous* as they react to the situation as it unfolds. Seventh, the *individual sessions* act like scenes in a larger story, and eighth, that story is about *the lives of the fictional characters.*

These elements form a system where the structural elements of the rules meet the freeform play of player decisions. To recap the definitional portions in relation to the Tower Heist example, it is but one episode in a larger story that deals with how the party met the duke who gave them the mission. All the players participate, though the warrior and the wizard characters elect to stay silent in the shadows—though perhaps not for long. The story happens from moment to moment, beginning with the thief sneaking from the shadows, and the major PC decisions need to be ratified by successful skill rolls, such as the stealth and charisma checks. While players often challenge a GM on when and what types of rolls are required, everyone consents that the dice will be the final judge of successes and failures, and not merely the will of the players or the GM alone. The group must decide on their course of action, which requires them to think about the nature and the skillsets of the other PCs. In this example, they worked together to form a stealthy plan, but agreeing isn't mandatory. The player controlling the warrior could say that he's the impatient type and charges out of the shadows to attack the guard. A moment like that, or the moment that the guard detects something is amiss, foregrounds the spontaneous nature of the narrative. The PCs switch from planning what to do to *reacting* to unforeseen events. And the GM may add pressure by not giving the players time to confer. For example, it makes sense for the players to take time in hatching a plan together with their PCs in the safety of the shadows, but the players need to think on their feet once the plan breaks down. For example, the GM might say, "The guard is reaching for the bell. Tell me right now what your PC does or he rings it."

It's also possible that the Tower Heist *episode* might take more than one *session* to resolve. For example, if the players have three hours to play on a Friday night, in the story world that may be enough time for the PCs may get past the guard, enter the tower, and successfully retrieve the scroll from a chest armed with a magic trap. However, the PCs hear voices below and realize that a group of guards are preparing to rush up the stairs at them. Playing through that scenario will take more time than the players have that night, so the group agrees to adjourn that session and pick up again in a week. Finally, players care about the characters they play and what happens to them. They carry both treasure and wounds from episode to episode, creating the life story of the character with each choice made.

Though players might not recognize it at first, RPG sessions model the *process* of developing a narrative. Using the tower heist example, consider:

- The players must understand their characters' strengths and weaknesses in order to contribute to the narrative in a meaningful way. For example, the warrior is not the best candidate to distract the guard, and the wizard is ill-equipped to climb the outside of the tower. The strategy made sense in light of the thief's stealth skills and the bard's acting ability.
- The best laid plans can go awry. The failed dice roll adds an unexpected wrinkle that the PCs hadn't anticipated, and the way each character responds to this unforeseen event will tell us something about their nature.
- Language and concrete details bring the narration to life. It's not just night, but a cold, damp night. The guard clutching his wet cloak seems miserable. These not only contribute functionally to the narrative—that the wet stone will be more challenging to climb, and

that the guard might be more cranky than usual—but also evokes a distinct mood to the scene.

- Each PC experiences the session from a different perspective. The thief must worry about being detected, the bard must keep his cool and put on a convincing act, and the wizard and warrior must stay alert and be ready to act.

In my courses where I use RPGs, I would ask the students to use their session as a prompt for a writing exercise, where they need to write a vignette from the first person perspective of their character. Before they begin, we review craft concepts—reminders to use strong images, to evoke all five senses, to deploy sharp verbs, and that the language should set a tone that reflects the character's attitude—as a way of revisiting the process of the narrative as they experienced it. They also have to carefully consider what parts of the story they wish to focus on in the space they're given in the assignment, and that they need to do more than just relay a blow-by-blow of the events. E. M. Forster (1927) famously described a story as a series of events and plot as a series of events plus causality—for example, "the king died and the queen died" is story, whereas "the king died and the queen died of grief" shows causality. Using the compressed form of the vignette, students learn how to establish enough of a scene to invite readers in, and how to end on a moment of tension to keep them wanting more. It can take several sessions for them to get the hang of it, but the episodic structure of the sessions helps them see how a scene might expand into a short story, and how a short story might grow into a novel.

In my experience, writing vignettes based on play sessions produces much richer fiction than simply having them read short stories and then write their own fiction. While those stories usually have a certain stiffness and formality about them, stories derived from RPG sessions feel looser and more steeped in the character. It also opens up avenues for more interesting critique sessions as well. For example, the Tower Heist session would produce four vignettes from four different perspectives. Students can compare the imagery and language—how did different writers evoke the sense of dark, damp, and cold?—as well as how they interpreted fuzzier details, such as the height of the tower, or whether the discussion of the plan only happened out of game between players, or whether it happened between the PCs in the game as well. Then there are the matters of tone and perspective. Did the warrior resent being told to hide in the shadows? What went through the thief's head as she lost her footing on the tower? In such an exercise, the Tower Heist session ceases to be a single story, but rather a prism of storytelling possibilities shared from a number of subjective viewpoints. When students gather to critique the fiction based on the session, they do so with the intimate knowledge of the events, which builds their confidence when they provide observations and suggest amendments or way to improve the writing.

The Tower Heist episode illustrates how some of the structures within RPGs work so that players may collaboratively build a narrative. However, the structures themselves can also be objects of critical study, as well as providing generative writing exercises. The next section looks at how the structures of world building and character building in RPGs can be used to require students to think critically about the act of fiction writing and our obligations in representing fictional worlds and fictional characters.

COLLABORATIVE WORLD BUILDING[1]

Whether the setting of an RPG is a fantasy world with orcs and dragons or a cyberpunk dystopia set in our near future, there needs to be an environment for the players to explore. Many RPGs, like *Dungeons & Dragons*, provide a general concept for a world and perhaps a few sample locations but leave the details of developing the space up to the players. I import this into my classes by a process I call "critical worldbuilding" (Hergenrader, 2014), which is a dialogic, recursive conversation between the instructor and students, and between students working in peer groups. Student writers must come to a mutual agreement about the rules of their world, which in turn raises productive questions about the relationship between the shared fictional world they're creating and our subjective impressions of the reality we currently inhabit. While some questions about the world might be politically neutral, others are explicitly political in nature. For example, an innocuous question might be, "Does magic exist in your world?"—whereas a more politically charged question would be, "Is magic equally available to men and women in your world?" The first question is one any novice writer would be expected to answer; however, the second requires a good deal more unpacking to answer well.

Critical worldbuilding happens in four steps: *completing a world building survey, writing a metanarrative, populating a catalog,* and *plotting entries on a map.*

World Building Survey

Regardless of the type of world students build in my classes, we begin with some "big questions" using a precourse survey. For example, I ask students questions similar to the following ones if we're building a postapocalyptic world:

- How the apocalypse happened (biological warfare, nuclear war, pandemic, etc.).
- When the apocalypse happened (ancient, Renaissance, Industrial Revolution, early 20th century, present, near future, far future).
- How long ago the apocalypse had happened (yesterday to 100 years ago).
- The geographic features present (coastline, desert, forest, mountains, etc.).
- The season (winter, spring, summer, or fall).

Such questions provide a general framework for the fictional world and also stimulate their thinking about how answers might combine in interesting ways. For example, a world where a disease wiped out most of the population one year earlier will be quite different than a world 100 years after a nuclear holocaust. Beginning writers often fail to think about geography and season when starting a new story, yet shelter and travel are dramatically impacted based on the weather, and frigid winters and hot summers present unique challenges for characters, especially those living in a world with limited infrastructure.

We review the answers and look for points of consensus, usually running a series of informal voice votes to gauge the direction of the world. With the big questions more or less settled, we begin digging into the other structures of the world, namely:

- *Governance:* Including the level of government involvement in daily life, the rule of law, and provision of services like healthcare, education, and transportation to the community.
- *Economics:* Including the economic wealth, how wealth is divided throughout society, and the strength of agriculture and trade in the community.
- *Social Equality:* Including the distribution of rights to citizens along the lines of gender, race, class, and sexual orientation.
- *Cultural Influences:* Including the degree to which military, religion, technology, and arts and culture matter to the society.

Different combinations create wildly different worlds. A world with a strong economy but high inequality could either be primed for a popular revolution against those in power, or it could be fragmented with gang factions fighting in the streets over scarce goods. Either option could provide a rich backdrop for storytelling.

I also ask students to answer the questions for our *actual* world. For example, I've asked students where they think our society is in terms of gender equity. While no one suggests we have a matriarchal society, some (usually young men) suggest we're somewhere between equality and slight patriarchy. Predictably, other students (usually young women) take exception to that and argue that there are many biases in society. As instructor, I moderate the conversation as necessary, keeping discourse civil while suggesting questions students perhaps hadn't thought of themselves, such as, "If a world were *slightly* patriarchal, what would it look like? What would be the features that indicate inequalities along gender?" These discussions then get mapped back onto the fictional world we're creating.

This proves to be an interesting writing challenge for students, especially when they opted for pat answers. For example, if a class decides that the post-apocalyptic world has reached perfect gender equality, the logical question is, "That's never existed across human history, so how did that happen in this world?" Such questioning across all categories prevents the speculative world from becoming mere escapist wish fulfillment and requires the authors to think hard about how social, political, and economic realities come to pass, and then express that in the form of a narrative. This is what Mayers (2005) calls "craft criticism," or situating the act of creative writing within specific institutional, political, social and economic contexts. The quantitative answers from the survey help pose these "tricky questions" and the qualitative narrative descriptions attempt to answer them.

During this process, appointed note takers record class decisions and post them to a course wiki where the world will be built. Wikis have the advantage of being editable by any authorized user and each page features change logs and discussion threads. This prevents users from deleting content anonymously and also allows them to carry on conversations after class. I reserve class time for students to work in small groups across these four broad categories, and I insist that groups consult with each other as they write. For example, the students working on the world's economic system must be in constant discussion with the group writing about governmental structures. As instructor, I remain actively involved to steer any content away from genre clichés or essentialist depictions of groups of people, and I also prompt students to create new categories as they see fit. For example, in the postapocalyptic world scenario, I encouraged them to begin adding professions and political factions once the economy and governmental structures had been better fleshed out.

In a matter of a few weeks, the students building the postapocalyptic world produced roughly 8,000 words or over 30 pages of collaboratively written metanarrative. While some students contributed more than others (which I tracked and assessed via the wiki page histories), no one could claim sole authorship for the work, since all parts of the world were inextricably linked to the others. Students uploaded images they found on the Internet, added their own artwork, and redesigned the site's header and footer. Once the metanarrative phase winds down, it's on to the next phase: populating the catalog.

POPULATING THE CATALOG
WITH ITEMS, LOCATIONS, AND CHARACTERS

The wiki becomes a catalog of not only the metanarrative that tells a story about the world, but also for the people, places, and things that exist *in* the world. Wikis allow you to create templates, so that all pages of a certain type have the same basic structure. In the course with the postapocalyptic theme, students determined what attributes were necessary for each of three entry types: items, locations, and characters. I took the requirements for each type of entry and created a page template to ensure entries were completed consistently. For example, every item required a weight, value, and rarity—expressed either numerically or descriptively—and a brief narrative that gave it some context for how it is used in the world. Once the class understands what type of information is required for the different types of catalog entries, the world built out very quickly. Assigning students even a modest number of entries results in a very dense world. If every student creates only 5 locations and characters, in a 25-student class, the catalog will have 125 unique locations and characters available to them for fiction writing, all in a matter of a few weeks.

Plotting Entries on a Map

The last step in the collaborative worldbuilding process is pinning the wiki entries to a map. Figure 3.1 shows a close up of more than a dozen map markers—some of which are locations and some are characters—in

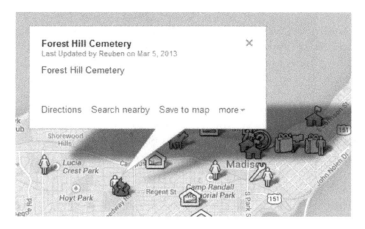

Figure 3.1   Map markers in post-apocalyptic downtown Madison in Google Maps.

postapocalyptic Madison. Note that the marker description contains a link to wiki entry so users can easily move between the map and wiki entries.

Students gain a better sense of spatial and temporal relationship between locations and characters through plotting locations on an actual place. For example, they generally have a concrete sense of how long it takes to walk from campus to the closest shopping district. Mapping over real-world locations also encourages them use monuments and other culturally significant spaces in their fiction in meaningful ways. It also encourages them to reimagine their own communities—and the social structures—through the lens of a fictionalized world.

Character Creation

With the completion of the critical worldbuilding portion of the course, the students should have a firm understanding of the multifaceted, complex world that will serve as an integral and active backdrop for their fiction. However, good stories need emotionally well-rounded characters too, lest the characters wind up feeling more like a "conglomeration of stats and types rather than the richly complex character that is the stuff of literature" (Martin, 2011), a problem that can plague bland or generic digital RPG characters.

Tabletop RPG players often create elaborate identities for their player-characters (PCs) and write stories about them that take place before, during, and after game sessions (Bowman, 2010; Cover, 2010). For my fiction writing courses, I have adopted the term "perspective characters" to describe the personalities the players assume when writing their fictions, and I refer to them using the same abbreviation (PC). Identifying the structures of character creation helps us talk about their motivations and decision making later on when we get to the RPG sessions and fiction writing.

First off, PCs should have at a minimum the same statistical categories as the wiki entries to ensure consistency across all characters in the catalog. Instructors will want to closely monitor the creation of PCs so students' characters have weaknesses as well as strengths and do not become larger-than-life superheroes. Aleatory techniques can also be used, such as dice rolls to determine numeric statistics, or students can balance any of their characters' above-average attributes with below-average ones.

Secondly, as an in-class activity, I ask a series of quantitative and qualitative questions inspired by creative writing textbooks (Bernays & Painter, 2010) and RPG character prompts (Bowie, 2013). This begins with their PC's "driver's license" and "tax return" information—height, weight, eye color, race, gender, occupation, level of education, economic class, current living situation, and so on. They then include more personal details such as tattoos, style of dress, or other distinguishing features. In summary fashion, I ask them how a stranger at a bus stop might describe the PC at a glance in one to three sentences.

Next we move to broader, evaluative questions. In three to four sentences, I ask them to describe their character's home life growing up and their attitude toward education; then I ask for three to four sentences on the character's social network, their attitudes toward the opposite sex, and their short- and long-term life goals.

Then we move into a series of quantitative aspects. I ask them to review a list of dispositions (angry, anxious, apathetic, ashamed, calm, contemptuous, curious, excited, joyful, melancholy) and choose the top two that best represent the character. I encourage them to offer any alternatives as well. Then I ask them to rank their characters' following attributes on a scale of 0 to 100:

- *Outlook*—from pessimistic (0) to optimistic (100)
- *Integrity*—from unscrupulous (0) to conscientious (100)
- *Impulsiveness*—from spontaneous (0) to controlled (100)
- *Boldness*—from cowardly (0) to daring (100)
- *Flexibility*—from stubborn (0) to adaptable (100)
- *Affinity*—from cold/aloof (0) to warm/hospitable (100)
- *Comportment*—from gruff/antisocial (0) to charming (100)
- *Interactivity*—from reserved/loner (0) to engaging/outgoing (100)
- *Disclosure*—from secretive (0) to candid (100)
- *Conformity*—from conservative/orthodox (0) to heterodox/shocking (100)

I then have them give five-word catch-phrase answers for their character's opinion on religion, general political views, sex and sexual relations, war and violence, drugs and alcohol, and the government.

The next section asks them to select their characters' two primary motivations and assign them values each between 1 and 99 so the sum of the two values equals 100: achievement, acquisition, balance, beneficence, chaos, competition, creation, destruction, discovery/adventure, domesticity, education, enslavement, hedonism, liberation, nobility/honor, order, play, power, recognition, rebellion, service, torment, tranquility, and understanding. They are also free to suggest other motivations not listed.

The final section is a series of 24 questions I ask in 24 minutes, or one minute per question. They range from "What is your PC's greatest fear?" to "What's your PC's idea of a perfect date?" to "What animal would your PC be and why?"

The PC customization process can be completed in one class session. The time limit forces spontaneous thinking similar to that required during an RPG session. To mix things up, I also choose certain attributes for students' PCs. For example, in my postapocalyptic class I had 70% of their PCs living in crushing poverty, which dramatically altered their relationship to the minority of wealthier characters.

Creative Play in the Critical Space

At the end of the process, the class will have a sprawling, collaboratively built world complete with a detailed history plotted onto a map, and each student will have a unique PC. In many classes, we proceed to RPG sessions followed by vignette writing and critique sessions. In other classes, I draw random items, locations, and characters from the wiki and assign them to students, where they need to use every wiki entry in a vignette or short story. They must think about the unique challenges different types of characters would face in the fictional world and then try to capture that experience in language. Again, it's a case of learning to map the structures present in the RPG catalog against traditional storytelling forms.

Whether it's experimental language games or full on RPG sessions, games provide useful scaffolding for teaching students fundamental aspects of language and storytelling. Using wikis or other websites to collect their writing means they can create hyperlinks to each other's work, where the classroom community's creative project is connected in ways not possible prior to the digital era. Games then provide an ideal, if unorthodox, model for reinventing the field of creative writing in the digital age.

NOTE

1. Portions of this section first appeared as "Dense Worlds, Deep Characters: Role-Playing Games, World Building, and Creative Writing" in the *Games+Learning+Society 10 Proceedings.* (Hergenrader, 2014) and in the forthcoming book Collaborative Worldbuilding for Writers and Gamers, due to be published by Bloomsbury Academic in 2018.

REFERENCES

Amato, J., & Fleisher, K. (2002, August 17). Reforming creative writing pedagogy: History as knowledge, knowledge as activism. Retrieved from http://www.altx.com/ebr/riposte/rip2/rip2ped/amato.htm#prelude

Bernays, A., & Painter, P. (2010). *What if?: Writing exercises for fiction writers.* Boston, MA: Longman.

Black, R. (2008). *Adolescents and online fan fiction.* New York, NY: Peter Lang.

Bolter, J. D., & Grusin, R. (1999). *Remediation understanding new media.* Cambridge, MA: MIT Press. Retrieved from http://search.ebscohost.com/login.aspx?direct=true&scope=site&db=nlebk&db=nlabk&AN=9351

Bowie, J. A. (n.d.). *Ash's guide to RPG personality and background.* Retrieved June 19, 2017 from http://www.ashami.com/rpg/

Bowman, S. L. (2010). *The functions of role-playing games how participants create community, solve problems and explore identity.* Jefferson, NC: McFarland & Co. Retrieved from http://public.eblib.com/choice/publicfullrecord.aspx?p=517013

Breton, A. (1969). *Manifestoes of surrealism.* Ann Arbor, MI: University of Michigan Press.

Bok, C. (2005). *Eunoia.* Toronto, ON: Coach House Books.

Brodkey, L. (1987). Modernism and the Scene(s) of Writing. *College English, 49*(4), 396–418. doi: 10.2307/377850

Brotchie, A., & Gooding, M. (1995). *A book of surrealist games: Including the little surrealist dictionary.* Boston, MA: Shambhala Redstone Editions.

Clark, M. D., Hergenrader, T., & Rein, J. (2015). *Creative writing in the digital age: Theory, practice, and pedagogy.* London, England: Bloomberg.

Clark, M. D., Hergenrader, T., & Rein, J. (2017). *Creative writing innovations: Breaking boundaries in the classroom.* New York, NY: Bloomsbury Academic.

Cover, J. G. (2010). *The creation of narrative in tabletop role-playing games.* Jefferson, NC: McFarland & Co. Publishers. Retrieved from http://public.eblib.com/choice/publicfullrecord.aspx?p=547921

Curwood, J. S. (2013). "The Hunger Games": Literature, literacy, and online affinity spaces. *Language Arts, 90*(6), 417–427.

Curwood, J. S., Magnifico, A. M., & Lammers, J. C. (2013). Writing in the wild: Writers' motivation in fan-based affinity spaces. *JAAL Journal of Adolescent & Adult Literacy, 56*(8), 677–685.

Donnelly, D., & Harper, G. (Eds.). (2012). *Key issues in creative writing.* Bristol, England: Multilingual Matters.

Failbetter Games. (2009). *Fallen London.* Retrieved from http://fallenlondon.storynexus.com/

Gee, J. P. (2007). *What video games have to teach us about learning and literacy* (Rev. and updated ed.). New York, NY: Palgrave Macmillan.

Gioia, D. (2009). *Preface. National Endowment for the Arts. Reading on the rise: A new chapter in American literacy.* Washington, DC: National Endowment for the Arts. Retrieved from http://purl.access.gpo.gov/GPO/LPS110100

Harper, G. (2010). *On creative writing.* Buffalo, NY: Multilingual Matters. Retrieved from http://site.ebrary.com/id/10393247

Harper, G., & Kroll, J. (2008). *Creative writing studies: Practice, research, and pedagogy.* Clevedon; Buffalo, NY: Multilingual Matters.

Healey, S. (2013). Beyond the literary: Why creative literacy matters. In D. Donnelly & G. Harper (Eds.), *Key issues in creative writing* (pp. 61–78). Buffalo, NY: Multilingual Matters.

Hergenrader, T. (2014). Dense worlds, deep characters: Role-playing games, world building, and creative writing. In A. Ochsner, J. Dietmeier, C. C. Williams, & C. Steinkuehler (Eds.), *GLS 10 Conference Proceedings* (pp. 118–124). Pittsburgh, PA: ETC press.

Hergenrader, T. (2017). *Collaborative worldbuilding for writers and gamers.* Manuscript in preparation.

Hood, S. (2103). *Storium.* Protagonist Labs. Retrieved from http://www.storium.com

Jenkins, H. (1992). *Textual poachers: Television fans & participatory culture.* New York, NY: Routledge.

Jenkins, H. (2006). *Convergence culture: Where old and new media collide.* New York, NY: New York University Press.

Lambe, I., & Scott, Z. (2014). *Elegy for a Dead World.* Dejobaan Games.

Lambert, R., Rilstone, A., & Wallis, J. (1994). *Once upon a time: The storytelling card game.* St. Paul, MN: Atlas Games.

Lammers, J., Curwood, J. S., & Magnifico, A. (2012). Toward an affinity space methodology: Considerations for literacy research. Retrieved from https://urresearch.rochester.edu/institutionalPublicationPublicView.action?institutionalItemId=27056

Mackay, D. (2001). *The fantasy role-playing game: A new performing art.* Jefferson, NC: McFarland.

Martin, P. (2011). The pastoral and the sublime in elder scrolls IV: Oblivion. *Game Studies, 11*(3). Retrieved from http://gamestudies.org/1103/articles/martin

Mathews, H., Brotchie, A., & Queneau, R. (1998). *Oulipo compendium.* London, England: Atlas Press.

Mayers, T. (2005). *(Re)Writing craft: Composition, creative writing, and the future of English studies.* Pittsburgh, PA: University of Pittsburgh Press.

Morningstar, J., & Segedy, S. (2009). *Fiasco.* Chapel Hill, NC: Bully Pulpit Games and Amusements.

Motte, W. F. (1986). *Oulipo: A primer of potential literature.* Lincoln, NE: University of Nebraska Press.

National Endowment for the Arts. (2009). *Reading on the rise a new chapter in American literacy.* Washington, DC: National Endowment for the Arts. Retrieved from http://purl.access.gpo.gov/GPO/LPS110100

New London Group, National Languages & Literacy Institute of Australia, & Centre for Workplace Communication and Culture. (1995). *A pedagogy of multiliteracies: designing social futures.* Haymarket, NSW: NLLIA Centre for Workplace Communication and Culture.

Paul, R. (n.d.). Dialogical and dialectical thinking. In *Richard Paul Anthology* (pp. 309–319). Retrieved from http://www.criticalthinking.org/pages/richard-paul-anthology/1139

Peary, A., & Hunley, T. C. (2015). *Creative writing pedagogies for the twenty-first century.* Carbondale, IL: Southern Illinois University Press

Perec, G. (1994). *A void.* London, England: Harvill.

Prose, F. (2006). *Reading like a writer: A guide for people who love books and for those who want to write them.* New York, NY: HarperCollins.

Queneau, R. (1961). *Cent mille milliards de poèmes.* Paris, FR: Gallimard.

Queneau, R. (1981). *Exercises in style.* New York, NY: New Directions.

Ritter, K., & Vanderslice, S. (2007). *Can it really be taught?: Resisting lore in creative writing pedagogy.* Portsmouth, NH: Boynton/Cook Heinemann.

Smith, H. (2005). *The writing experiment: Strategies for innovative creative writing.* Crows Nest, NSW: Allen & Unwin.

Vanderslice, S. (2010). *Rethinking creative writing in higher education: Programs and practices that work.* Wicken, Ely, Cambs, England: Professional and Higher Partnership. Retrieved from http://search.ebscohost.com/login.aspx?direct=true&scope=site&db=nlebk&db=nlabk&AN=462347

SHŌ

DEVELOPMENT

CHAPTER 4

THE ROLE OF DIGITAL GAMES IN A CLASSROOM ECOLOGY

Exploring Teaching With Video Games

Amanda Bell and Melissa Gresalfi
Vanderbilt University

Over two decades of research have established that computers, on their own, do little or nothing to change the nature of teaching and learning (Mouza, 2008; Penuel, 2006; Pierson, 2001; Windschitl & Sahl, 2002). However, there are exciting examples of what can happen when technologies are integrated into classrooms in ways that attend to the intersection between particular forms of technology, teachers' ideas about and knowledge of technology, and the particular content area that is being taught (Mishra & Koehler, 2006). Digital games in particular have demonstrated potential for supporting student learning across disciplines (Barab, Sadler, Heiselt, Hickey, & Zuiker, 2007; Pareto, Arvemo, Dahl, Haake, & Gulz, 2011; Squire, 2006). The diversity of game designs makes it challenging to pinpoint exactly why games support learning, but much has been said about the potential of games to motivate and capture student attention (Dickey, 2007; Garris, Ahlers, & Driskell, 2002; Lepper & Malone, 1987; Malone & Lepper,

Exploding the Castle, pages 67–92

1987), to situate disciplinary learning in realistic contexts (Barab, Petty-john, Gresalfi, Volk, & Solomou, 2012; Barab, Thomas, Dodge, Carteaux, & Tuzun, 2005; Clarke & Dede, 2009), and to offer consistent and substantive feedback about reasoning (Gresalfi & Barnes, 2016; Mayer & Johnson, 2010; Nelson, 2007; Rieber, 1996). Three recent meta-analyses compared learning from digital games to a nongame control for K–12 students and generally found that digital games led to higher cognitive outcomes (such as learning and retention) than traditional instruction (Clark, Tanner-Smith, & Killingsworth, 2015; Vogel, Vogel, Cannon-Bowers, Bowers, Muse, & Wright, 2006; Wouters, Van Nimwegen, Van Oostendorp, & Van Der Spek, 2013). These general findings support the enthusiasm around integrating game technologies into educational environments. However, all reviewers noted the small number of articles that they were able to include in their reviews based on the paucity of literature that compares games to other learning environments (Young et al., 2012).

Despite their potential, integrating digital games into schools is not simply a matter of making the tools available (Ertmer, Ottenbreit-Leftwich, Sadik, Sendurur, & Sendurur, 2012; Ertmer, Ottenbreit-Leftwich, & Tondeur, 2014; Takeuchi & Vaala, 2014). How and when games are used in relation to other instruction, the role that teachers take as they are playing the game, and how the game is integrated into the overall classroom ecology all play a role in whether and what students ultimately learn. Indeed, it could be argued that research that simply examines the "efficacy" of games misses out on what will ultimately be more generative—that is, the potential of games to transform (for good or for ill) the overall classroom learning ecology (Barron, 2004, 2006).

Currently very little is known about the integration of games into instruction, although we do know that teachers are using digital games. A recent survey of teachers (Fishman, Riconscente, Snider, Tsai, & Plass, 2014) found that 57% of survey respondents used games in their classrooms at least once a week, and over 80% say they are moderately comfortable using games in their classrooms. However, teachers also reported many barriers to implementing digital games, including the challenge of finding games that connect to the school's curriculum (47% of respondents) and being unsure about how to integrate games into instruction (33%). What integration looks like for these teachers, however, remains unclear.

This chapter seeks to contribute to our emergent understanding of what teaching using video games can look like, focusing on a specific example of a video game that was designed to incorporate teacher–student interactions, rather than to replace instruction. In this context, the teacher's role is central to implementing the game successfully. In this study, our goal was to understand diversity in implementation, and to explore whether and how teachers' practice around the game enhanced or decreased students' opportunities to learn. Here we are not talking about whether or not teachers implemented the game *with fidelity,* as is a common concern. Fidelity typically refers to the extent to which an innovation is used in ways that are consistent with the goals or plans of the designer. Instead, the decision to adopt this type of curricular innovation is, by Rogers and Murcott's (1995) definition, an "optional innovation-decision," in that teachers often have the autonomy to adopt and use innovations on an individual basis. Although an innovation offers potential benefits that the current practices do not, it by definition also involves newness and therefore a degree of uncertainty (Rogers & Murcott, 1995). Furthermore, what might appear beneficial to the designer might not be perceived as beneficial by the teacher. Clearly, adoption of a curriculum is not a one-to-one mapping or "rubber stamping" of the designed environment to the K–12 classroom. Instead, teachers must always adapt the curriculum for their local use, and this adaptation occurs as part of their goals, their students' needs, and the overall instructional context.

It is with this understanding that we investigated the use of an immersive video game called *Boone's Meadow. Boone's Meadow* is an interactive problem-solving experience that involves engaging mathematical ideas related to ratio and proportion, important and difficult concepts for middle school students to understand. Using four cases selected from three different schools, we explore how teachers integrated the game into their instructional practice by focusing on teachers' interactions with students during gameplay and the types of mathematical engagement afforded by those interactions. There are myriad questions to be posed about the role of the teacher in using and supporting games. As an initial starting point, we focused on teachers' interactions with students that specifically related to supporting their mathematical problem solving during gameplay. We think about problem solving as a movement between understanding the constraints of the problem, thinking mathematically about how to solve the problem, and understanding the outcomes of choices (depicted in the narrative of the game). Specifically, we investigated teachers' roles in supporting problem solving during gameplay by addressing the following research questions:

1. How do teachers support students' mathematical thinking?
2. Who has the mathematical agency to solve problems?
3. How do teachers interact with students around the narrative of the game?

We addressed these questions by analyzing four case study teachers using *Boone's Meadow.* The findings illustrate how teachers with similar resources can implement a game very differently, which points to needed improvements to the supports teachers receive when using games for learning.

THEORETICAL FRAMEWORK

Much of the video game research that has been published to date examines the effect of the game on student learning. This lens fails to account for how the introduction of a game into a classroom necessarily interacts with other elements of the classroom system, including the teacher. For that reason, in our research on how to design games to support student learning, we focus not only on the students' use of the game and students' learning, but also how other elements of the classroom system connect to the use of the game or are transformed or changed by the introduction of the game (Davis & Sumara, 1997; Osberg & Biesta, 2008). We conceptualize the classroom activity as only one aspect of the learning environment, based on significant prior work that has demonstrated that elements of the classroom system work together and influence one another in order to support (or thwart) student learning (Gresalfi, 2009; Hand, 2010; Wortham, 2004).

In this chapter, we consider two elements of the classroom system in relation to how the game was used and ultimately what students learned through playing it. The first has to do with what students already know and understand about the mathematical content targeted in the game. It is well known that individual students' prior knowledge about a particular topic strongly influences their problem-solving behavior (Bielaczyc, Pirolli, & Brown, 1995; Jonassen, 1997; Lee & Chen, 2009). Relatedly, we also know that when students are struggling with a problem, teachers are often tempted to step in to scaffold their thinking, thus reducing the cognitive load of the task (Henningsen & Stein, 1997; Stein, Smith, Henningsen, & Silver, 2000). Taken together, it is reasonable to assume that, when working on complex mathematical problem-solving tasks, the individual students' prior knowledge is likely to influence both how students act on the opportunities in the game and how their teachers support students' interactions with the problems in the game. Relatedly, the second element we consider includes teachers' interactions with students around problem solving and the narrative of the game. Together, these elements of the classroom profoundly influence to what extent a game can support learning.

BOONE'S MEADOW

Boone's Meadow is an immersive game that involves exploring a virtual world through the first-person lens of an avatar. Students play the central protagonist who has applied for a job as "wildlife rescue assistant." The core problem that students work to solve involves figuring out how to rescue and save an injured eagle, a task that is based on part of the *Adventures of Jasper Woodbury* series (Cognition and Technology Group at Vanderbilt, 1997). As in the Jasper series, students must decide which information they need to use to solve a complex, multistep problem, which has the potential to link to other curricula (we have seen teachers incorporate literacy standards, social issues, and some basic science concepts).

In the *Boone's Meadow* digital game, an eagle is located in a remote field, and the only way to get to her in time is by flying an ultralight (a small plane). Players must choose between three different ultralights to use based on fuel efficiency, speed, and payload (how much weight it can carry). Players must also plan the route to take to pick up the eagle and safely return her to the veterinary clinic in time, choosing whether or not to stop for gas along the way. Figure 4.1 shows a picture of the map of the game world with the veterinary clinic, the gas station, and Boone's Meadow as the three main points. If players decide to stop for gas once or twice at Hilda's Gas Station, they can choose to fill up the gas tank all the way or only partially. Cost is also a minor factor in the game, as the veterinary clinic hopes to save money to open a new animal shelter. Players have two attempts to save the eagle, and they can use the second try to find a more optimal solution (taking less time, using less gas, and spending less money) or test another route. The game includes several short writing prompts with questions about the choices students made in the game (route, plane, gas), whether or not they saved the eagle and why, and what convincing recommendation they would make to the veterinarian clinic as a final plan for saving the eagle. Teachers can respond to or return students' answers to the prompts using an online platform referred to as the Teacher Toolkit. Teachers can also use this platform to monitor students' progress in the game. The game is designed to take approximately three to four hour-long classroom sessions, including supportive instructional time.

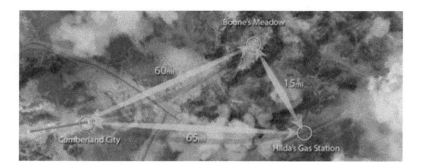

Figure 4.1   The map of the game world in *Boone's Meadow*.

Saving the eagle requires making calculations that involve ratio and proportion. Multiplicative reasoning is a foundational idea of ratio and proportion (Lobato, Ellis, & Zbiek, 2010), so we designed the specific problems students needed to solve so that they could be reasoned about multiplicatively, without needing any formal instruction about algorithmic solutions.

METHODS

We employed a contrasting case methodology (Stake, 1995) and examined a small number of cases because of our interest in broadening our understanding of how games are used differently in relation to elements of the classroom ecology. We selected contrasting cases for their potential to illuminate important patterns that can be hidden when looking at a small number of similar cases, then selected four teachers who worked with students who had very different prior knowledge about multiplication. Two 7th-grade teachers, Ms. Lynn and Ms. Donald, taught students with very limited prior knowledge about multiplication, as indicated by the teachers and evidenced by the presence of "multiplication charts" on all students' desks that were used and referenced repeatedly throughout the implementation. In contrast, Mr. Doyle and Ms. Vann taught 6th-grade students with higher levels of prior knowledge about multiplication; the majority of students were able to generate benchmark multiplication facts without support. Calculators were available to students in all four classrooms, although we did not encourage their use.

Prior knowledge of students is just one of many factors that could have been selected for these contrasting cases. We were especially interested in prior knowledge because we observed that what students already understood about math influenced how teachers interacted with students during gameplay. We wanted to explore this in more detail, particularly as games are often used either as remediation or reward. Thus, understanding how teachers connect with the content of the game based on what students already know has implications for the ways games are integrated into instruction.

Setting and Participants

This analysis focuses on four teachers: Ms. Lynn, Ms. Donald, Mr. Doyle, and Ms. Vann (pseudonyms). To recruit teachers, we first contacted principals and asked if they had teachers who might be interested in participating in our study; they connected us with math teachers at their schools, and we followed up with a meeting to describe the goals and content of the game. Importantly, we made it very clear that participation in this study was completely voluntary, and we discouraged principals who felt that all teachers should be using the game. Thus, teachers who worked with us did so because of interest.

All four teachers had more than 5 years of teaching experience, but this was their first time implementing *Boone's Meadow*. Ms. Lynn, Ms. Donald, and Mr. Doyle participated in a professional development session held by the researchers the summer before they implemented the game which lasted a full day; Ms. Vann, who played the game in Year 2 of the study, met separately with researchers during planning time. The PD session and the face-to-face meeting generally covered the same content, although in the PD session, teachers also had time to play the game, while in the face-to-face session, teachers were expected to play the game separately on their own time.

In the PD session and face-to-face meeting, we talked about students' difficulties with ratio, what teachers wanted students to learn from the game, the problems students solve in the game, and how teachers might fit the game into their curricula. The teachers wanted their students to develop good procedural understandings of the traditional ratio algorithm and to be able to solve problems involving rates. The design team had no commitment to teaching or using the traditional ratio algorithm, and in our meeting and PD session we actively encouraged teachers to instead support students' reasoning about unit ratios and the ways they scale (Lobato et al., 2010). Likewise, there was quite a bit of discussion about the fact that the game did not include a single correct answer and that in fact there were multiple ways to be right (and save the eagle) and multiple ways to be wrong (and kill the eagle). Some teachers thought this was a great feature of the game that would keep students' interested (Lynn, Donald, Vann). Others worried that this might confuse students and cause them to give up (Doyle). In sum, although the teachers were excited to use the game and had high hopes for their students' use of it, it was clear that their vision of what high-quality use of the game would look like was not identical across teachers, nor was it perfectly aligned with our own vision.

We also gave all four teachers a set of teacher materials, which we designed. The teacher materials included pacing suggestions, including which "missions" in the game students should complete each day; questions to guide whole-class discussions before and after gameplay each day (involving ratio, components of the narrative, and the use of tools in the game); suggestions for thinking conceptually about ratio; and supplemental mathematics problems to discuss rates, ratio, and proportion with students. The game implementations lasted 3 to 4 days in each classroom. Ms. Lynn and Ms. Donald used the problems from the teacher guide quite frequently;

Ms. Vann used the pacing guide by informing her students how far they needed to get each day; there was no evidence that Mr. Doyle relied on the teacher materials in any significant way.

Ms. Lynn and Ms. Donald both taught 7th-grade mathematics at school A. They each taught three mathematics classes every day, and they had large class sizes: over 30 students in each class. In school A, 92% of students were eligible for free or reduced lunch, 30% were English language learners, and only 26% scored proficient on the state math test.

In contrast, Mr. Doyle taught four classes of 6th-grade mathematics at school B, where 32.7% of students identified as economically disadvantaged, only 2% were English language learners, and 64.4% scored proficient or above on the state math test. His class size averaged 25.

Ms. Vann taught two 6th-grade math classes at school C, where 64.7% of students received free or reduced lunch, 3.4% were English language learners, and 70% scored proficient or advanced on the state math test. Her class size also averaged 25. From these school data, we can expect to see that Ms. Vann's and Mr. Doyle's students had higher levels of prior mathematical knowledge before playing the game. In fact, Ms. Lynn's and Ms. Donald's 7th-grade students struggled with multiplicative reasoning, which is a foundational concept for understanding ratio and proportion. On the other hand, Ms. Vann's and Mr. Doyle's 6th-grade students had strong multiplicative reasoning skills and good procedural understandings of ratio before playing *Boone's Meadow*.

Data Collection

Each day during the game implementations, a camera was set up in the back of the room to capture the teacher's talk and actions. A researcher panned and zoomed the camera to follow the teacher's movements. The entire class period on game days was recorded, so even if students only played the game for 10 minutes, the entire 50- to 140-minute class period was recorded (length of classes varied because of modified schedules and time students spent traveling and settling in between classes). Students were also given pre- and posttests to check their understandings of ratio and proportion. While data were collected for all class periods taught by teachers, we chose to analyze the class for each teacher with the highest pre- to posttest change. Since research already tells us about the difficulties of using games in classrooms, we wanted to focus on the classes that demonstrated the most learning gains in order to talk about what worked successfully. We interviewed a subset of teachers informally after the game implementations both years, and we used their responses to triangulate our findings. We also collected data on students' interactions using separate cameras on student groups, written work students produced in game notebooks, and students' progress and responses to questions in the game. However, since our goal was to analyze the teachers' practices, we mostly focused on the videos from the teacher cameras in this analysis.

Analysis

As previously stated, our goal is to understand how teachers integrate and potentially transform the game in their classroom instruction by considering how teachers supported student problem solving and learning as they played the game. To address these questions, we analyzed the pre- and postassessments as an initial indicator of learning, and then looked in depth at the interactions that took place between the teachers and students. We used common coding schemes across all four classrooms because our questions were comparative.

Assessments

A team of four researchers developed a system for scoring the pre- and posttests. Most questions were scored on a scale of 0 to 2, 0 being totally incorrect or no answer, 1 being correct calculations or procedures or evidence of thinking but some sort of error in the answer (either a calculational error or missing labels so it was not clear what their numbers referred to), and 2 being completely accurate. Using the pre- and posttest scores, we calculated the average pre- to posttest change for each class. We used these results to determine focal classes to analyze further.

Videos

To answer our questions about how teachers implemented *Boone's Meadow* in their classrooms, we transcribed the talk from the teacher videos from each of the focal classes. With our research team, we watched the teacher videos several times along with the transcripts to identify major themes around how teachers supported students' mathematical problem solving during gameplay. This helped us begin to identify codes that we could analyze further with each research question to determine what the teachers did differently during gameplay.

For our first research question, we asked about how teachers support mathematical reasoning during gameplay. To answer this question, we analyzed the talk in the interactions between teachers and students during gameplay. The teachers' talk was coded by utterance defined as a turn of talk (a switch in speakers) or a change in the person the teacher was addressing (if Ms. Lynn said something to student A and then said something else to student B, that was counted as two separate utterances). We used student responses to make sense of what the teachers were saying in context, but we coded teacher utterances because we wanted to capture what the teachers in particular were doing. Drawing on Gresalfi and Barab's (2011) work, we distinguished between four different types of mathematical engagement: (a) procedural—following procedures correctly, (b) conceptual—conceptual understandings of procedures or ideas, (c) consequential—examining how the procedures used relate to the outcomes, and (d) critical—questioning why one procedure should be used over another. Four researchers coded all the transcripts, and instances of uncertainty were discussed until we reached agreement.

We were also curious about how much time teachers actually spent interacting with their students during gameplay. The research team reviewed the teacher videos for the focal classes again and noted the video timestamps each time the teacher sat at her desk, got up from her desk, spoke with a researcher, talked with a student or group of students, ended a conversation with a student, wandered around the room, and so on. From these timestamps, we calculated the total time each teacher spent on these activities during gameplay to compare how much time teachers spent interacting with students.

Our second research question asked about the agency to solve problems in the game. To answer this question, we coded the gameplay transcripts by utterance again for teacher agency or student agency. We defined agency by asking who has the ability to decide how to approach a mathematics problem, which procedures to use, and what to do (Gresalfi, Martin, & Hand, 2009). We counted an utterance as *teacher* agency if the teacher gave an answer or specified a procedure to follow, meaning the teacher had the agency to solve the problem. We coded an utterance as *student* agency if the teacher asked an open question that gave the student agency to decide how to approach the problem and which procedures to use. Four researchers coded all the transcripts again, and uncertainties were discussed until we all reached agreement.

For our third research question, we asked how teachers interacted with students around the narrative of the game since the narrative provided the main source of feedback for students' problem solving in the game. The major narrative outcome of the problems in *Boone's Meadow* is saving the eagle, so we looked for instances when teachers interacted with students around saving or killing the eagle. We marked entire interactional episodes that involved talk about the eagle outcomes. An episode started when a teacher or student reacted to saving or killing the eagle and ended when the teacher changed to a different topic or left to talk to another student. These episodes were marked by two researchers, and uncertainties were discussed for agreement.

FINDINGS

Here, we present findings about each case and contrast the teachers with the goal of beginning to identify petite generalizations (Stake, 1995) about the integration of video games into classroom practice. Table 4.1 shows the average pre- and posttest scores from each teacher's classes. The pretest scores reveal information about students' prior knowledge, which matches the reported state test scores from each school. Ms. Lynn's and Ms. Donald's students had the lowest average pretest scores. The students in school A generally struggled with concepts of ratio and proportion, in large part because they had little familiarity with multiplicative reasoning. As an example, all students in these 7th grade math classes had a laminated multiplication chart on their desks, which they referenced frequently when doing multidigit multiplication and division problems. In contrast, Mr. Doyle's and Ms. Vann's students scored above 53% on the pretests for this study. They already demonstrated good procedural understandings of ratio before playing the game and appeared to be comfortable reasoning multiplicatively. Ms. Vann's students scored highest on the pretest but did not show any learning gains on the posttest, which we discuss below. Ms. Lynn's, Ms. Donald's, and Mr. Doyle's students all showed significant learning gains on the posttest. In what follows, we explore how teachers interacted with their students around the mathematics in the game and how that might relate to students' prior knowledge.

Question 1: How do teachers support students' mathematical thinking during gameplay?

To investigate how teachers supported students' mathematical reasoning, we coded teachers' talk for the types of mathematical engagement it afforded. Table 4.2 includes the code counts for each teacher across the four types of mathematical engagement (procedural, conceptual, consequential, and critical). We found that over 80% of the talk for each teacher was coded as procedural. This means that when teachers interacted with

TABLE 4.1 Average Pre- and Post-Test Scores for the Four Teachers' Classes		
Teacher	**Average Pre Score**	**Average Post Score**
Ms. Lynn	36.0%	51.9%
Ms. Donald	36.2%	42.6%
Mr. Doyle	53.2%	57.0%
Ms. Vann	67.8%	67.3%

TABLE 4.2 Number of Teacher Utterances Coded for Affording Types of Mathematical Engagement During Gameplay in Focal Classes

Teacher	Procedural	Conceptual	Consequential	Critical	Total
Ms. Lynn	68 (93.2%)	1	4	0	73
Ms. Donald	57 (82.6%)	9	3	0	69
Mr. Doyle	105 (100.0%)	0	0	0	105
Ms. Vann	17 (85.0%)	1	2	0	20

students around the mathematics in the game, teachers mostly created opportunities for students to engage procedurally with the mathematics, and teachers provided very few opportunities for students to engage more deeply. In particular, Mr. Doyle had the most math talk out of the four teachers, but all of his talk was procedural. The following interaction between Mr. Doyle and one of his students exemplifies how much of his talk afforded procedural engagement[1]:

1. **Mr. Doyle:** Rate is miles per hour. Distance is what?
2.   **Student:** 60.
3.   **Doyle:** Divided by
4.   **S:** *XXXX*
5.   **Doyle:** Rate. 60 miles. 60. Distance divided by rate, so, so it's gonna be 60 miles, and 90 miles an hour.
6.   **S:** So divided by 90.
7.   **Doyle:** Yeah. 90. 90. So distance, 60 divided by rate.

In lines 1–7 above, Mr. Doyle helped a student calculate the time it took a plane traveling at a speed of 90 mph to go 60 miles. He immediately proceduralized the problem by giving the student the definition of rate as "miles per hour" in this problem, and then in line 3 told the student to divide. In line 5, Mr. Doyle gave the student the procedure to follow: "distance divided by rate," and he even filled in the numbers ("60 miles, and 90 miles an hour"). He did not ask the student to think conceptually or critically about the problem. For instance, he could have asked why you divide to find the answer or if there is another way to solve the problem. Instead, Mr. Doyle's talk afforded procedural engagement in the mathematics. This was inconsistent with the way these problems were modeled in the teacher materials and the ways the game presented ratio. Instead, this framing of ratio was consistent with previous practice in Mr. Doyle's classroom, as further evidenced by Mr. Doyle frequently stating, "Remember how we did that kind of problem?"

Ms. Vann had very little math talk with her students (only 20 utterances across all four days of gameplay in her focal class). Since her students scored high on the pretests and already had strong procedural understandings of ratio, perhaps she thought her students could solve the game's ratio and rate problems on their own. However, like Mr. Doyle, when she did talk with students about the math, almost all of her talk afforded opportunities to engage procedurally.

It is interesting to note that Ms. Lynn and Ms. Donald, whose students had the lowest levels of prior knowledge, had the most utterances affording conceptual and consequential engagement. For example, when talking about one of the planes whose average maximum speed was 60 miles per hour, the following exchange occurred:

1. **Ms. Donald:** No, listen to what I'm asking. I'm asking you to find out how many miles you would go in one minute.
2. **Student 1:** So, do we divide it.
3. **Donald:** Would that make sense?
4. **Student 2:** One.
5. **Donald:** Why is it one?
6. **S2:** Because one is one minute.
7. **Donald:** Because one minute would be one mile, right?
8. **S1:** Yeah.

In the exchange, Ms. Donald worked with her students to think about how many miles an ultralight would travel in one minute based on its speed in miles per hour. Instead of telling the student which procedure to follow, Student1 suggested using division in line 2 and then Ms. Donald questioned why that might make sense in line 3. This was coded as conceptual engagement because Ms. Donald created an opportunity for the student to think about why you might divide to find the answer, rather than just following the procedure. She also followed up with the student's correct answer of one mile in one minute by asking "why is it one?" in line 5. In a few other exchanges like this, Ms. Donald went beyond reviewing procedures and helped her students think deeper about why the answers or procedures made sense.

Along with mathematical engagement, we also captured how much time teachers spent interacting with students during gameplay in Table 4.3. Not surprisingly, Ms. Vann, who had the fewest utterances coded as mathematical talk, also spent the least amount of time talking with her students during the game. Instead of interacting with students, Ms. Vann spent the majority of her time sitting at her desk, monitoring students' progress with the online Teacher Toolkit or working on other things. Ms. Vann mostly let her students

TABLE 4.3 Percent of Gameplay Time Teachers Spent Doing Different Activities

Teacher	Percent of Gameplay Time Talking With Students	Percent of Gameplay Time Sitting at Desk
Ms. Lynn	69.04%	6.93%
Ms. Donald	81.42%	5.37%
Mr. Doyle	88.99%	3.5%
Ms. Vann	7.33%	81.70%

play the game without help or management, an indication of Ms. Vann's confidence in her students' abilities to solve the problems in the game.

In summary, we observed some variation among the teachers in terms of the amount of time they spent talking with students and the kinds of questions that they asked. Perhaps surprisingly, interactions did not seem to be predictable based on students' prior mathematical reasoning. Across all four cases, almost all teacher talk emphasized procedural reasoning, despite the fact that the game and teacher materials emphasized justification and developing unique strategies to solve the problems. The interactions that we observed were consistent with teachers' practices before using the game, and thus it appeared that teachers' incorporated the game into their existing classroom routines. This is entirely consistent with previous research about technology integration and attempts to change teaching practices more broadly.

Question 2: Who has agency to solve problems in the game?

Figure 4.2 displays the results of our codes for teacher and student agency of teachers' talk, showing significant variations between the teachers. As we showed above, Ms. Vann spent little time interacting with her students about the math in the game, so she also had very few utterances coded for agency. On the other hand, Mr. Doyle spent almost all of his time interacting with students. But Mr. Doyle's talk involved almost exclusively teacher agency, meaning he often told students the answers to problems when they asked questions or he told students which procedures to follow. In several instances, Mr. Doyle took control of students' computers and typed in the answers for them. For example, the following was an interaction that began with a student asking for help:

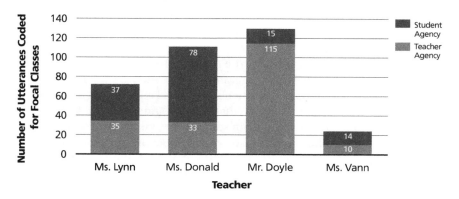

Figure 4.2 Number of teacher utterances coded for teacher or student agency during gameplay.

1. **Mr. Doyle:** Okay. Let's start filling this stuff. So your load is 78 pounds. You've got to use XX maximum fuel, 12 gallons. *[starts murmuring to himself]* 7 miles per gallon XXXXX. Confusing. Distance. *[Mr. Doyle orients the computer towards himself, begins clicking on the screen]* Fuel used is distance divided by miles per gallon.
2. **Student:** So 60.
3. **Doyle:** 60 divided by miles per gallon.
4. **S:** Seven.
5. **Doyle:** *[pointing to a calculator]* Calculator.
6. **S:** *[getting a calculator and beginning to type into it]* 60 divided by
7. **Doyle:** 7. Yeah, so this is a mixed number, so 8. Change to *[takes the calculator from student]* fraction decimal. 8 and 4/7 *[Types answer into the computer]* Time is equal.
8. **S:** Distance and rate.
9. **Doyle:** Distance divided by rate.

In this example, Mr. Doyle worked with a student on calculating the fuel used by one of the ultralights, using the procedure distance divided by miles per gallon (or fuel efficiency). In line 1, Mr. Doyle oriented the computer towards himself and typed in answers for him. Mr. Doyle also gave the student the procedures to follow, saying "fuel is distance divided by miles per gallon" and then specifying "60 divided by miles per gallon" in line 3. In these interactions, agency was distributed to the teacher, who made decisions and determined which procedure to use. Student agency in this interaction was limited to typing in numbers and observing the execution of the correct procedure.

Ms. Donald and Ms. Lynn had more balanced levels of student and teacher agency, meaning about half their utterances were coded as student agency and the other half as teacher agency. When students asked for help, both teachers responded by asking open questions that allowed students to think about their own solutions. In particular, Ms. Lynn scaffolded students' problem solving by first giving students the agency to solve the problems, then specifying some elements to pay attention to when students seemed confused, and finally helping students calculate precise answers using the procedures the students suggested. Ms. Lynn gave students agency, then took back some of the agency to scaffold their problem solving if students continued to struggle.

With respect to the distribution of agency, our cases looked quite different from each other, and this difference was somewhat surprising. Given the low number of teacher utterances in Ms. Vann's class, it is difficult to draw many conclusions about the distribution of agency (indeed, one could argue that Ms. Vann's class distributed almost all agency to the students and the game, given the low number of teacher utterances). When looking at the two lower performing classrooms, the amount of agency that was distributed to the students is surprising. In interviews with Ms. Lynn and Ms. Donald, they shared that they felt they needed to "reteach" the content that 7th-grade students should already have learned (multiplication, division), while simultaneously moving ahead with the 7th-grade standards (ratio, proportion). Thus, these moments when the teachers pushed students to declare how they might solve a problem might have been opportunities for teachers to gain insight into student understanding. In contrast, Mr. Doyle shared his opinion that "understanding" the content in the standards can be seen through accurate execution of procedures and thus did not feel it necessary to push beyond reminding students about "how to do" such problems. Thus, here again it seems clear that the larger context of the students' needs, combined with the teachers' vision of what it means to know and understand mathematics, framed the ways that the teachers interacted with students around the game, and particularly around the mathematics in the game.

Question 3: How do teachers interact with students around the narrative of the game?

Along with mathematical thinking and agency, the narrative outcomes of the game were an important source of feedback to students about their problem-solving efforts and, in the design of the game, were conceptualized as an important resource for mathematical thinking. We analyzed how teachers interacted with students around the narrative outcomes of the game—what happened to the eagle. To give a sense of scale, each student in the class had two opportunities to try to save the eagle, and thus, in each class, there were between 50 and 60 times when a student might have talked with the teacher about what happened to the eagle. Our observations of Ms. Lynn's and Ms. Donald's classes, who played the game first, suggested that teachers were not talking about the eagle outcomes as much as we had envisioned, and thus we sought to find a way to make the eagle outcomes more salient to teachers. To do this, we created eagle state stickers for sub-sequent implementations (beginning with Mr. Doyle, including Ms. Vann). These stickers showed either a live, injured, or dead eagle, and teachers were invited to distribute the stickers to their students based on their game outcome. Our goal in creating these stickers was to make in-game outcomes more salient to teachers, and, we hoped, to launch some conversations about why these outcomes took place. Students in all implementations have valued these stickers highly, displaying them prominently on their shirts, folders, and even faces, and as a consequence, students often tell teachers about their eagle outcomes. Thus, we would expect to see higher counts of discussion about eagle outcomes in Ms. Vann and Mr. Doyle's classrooms (with the eagle stickers) than in Ms. Donald and Ms. Lynn's classrooms (no eagle stickers). In fact, this was not quite the case; although Ms. Vann had many instances when she talked about eagle outcomes with her students, Mr. Doyle's discussion of eagle outcomes was quite low (see Figure 4.3).

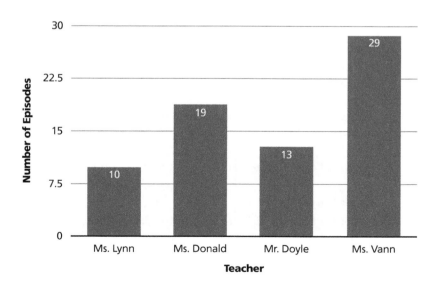

Figure 4.3 Number of interactional episodes around saving or killing the eagle.

Of course, merely talking about what happened to the eagle is not the same as leveraging the outcomes to prompt a discussion about mathematical problem solving (the ultimate goal for giving the feedback; c.f. Gresalfi & Barnes, 2016). Thus, we examined each episode when the eagle was discussed during game play and coded it for "narrative only," "problem solving," and "mathematics." An exchange was coded as "problem solving" when the teacher prompted the student to think about where the plan went awry (for example, running out of gas, choosing a route that took too long). A code of mathematics was reserved for times when the teacher and student talked about mathematical thinking or calculational errors that might have led to the eagle outcome. None of the teacher cases in this chapter discussed mathematical thinking in relation to the eagle outcomes.

Consistent with the findings about the distribution of agency in the classrooms, we found that Ms. Donald and Ms. Lynn were more likely to leverage the eagle outcomes as an opportunity to think about what went wrong than Mr. Doyle, whose response to eagle outcomes almost always involved acknowledgment of the outcome without any elaboration. Of the 13 times the eagle was discussed in Mr. Doyle's class, 9 of them involved no mathematical or problem solving elaboration. The other four times were coded as *problem solving,* such as in this exchange:

1.   **Doyle:** Did you make it? There you go. (*long pause*) You crashed and you killed the eagle.
2.   **S:** Ran out of gas.
3.   **Doyle:** Yeah you didn't plan your flight very well. When you're done, you need to go to the reflection piece. Answer those questions.

In contrast, Ms. Lynn and Ms. Donald were more likely to use the eagle outcome as an opportunity to discuss problem solving, although they did not delve into the mathematics behind decision making. For example, Ms. Donald discussed problem solving in 8/19 exchanges, such as in the following:

1.   **S:** I, I didn't quite get to the Dr. Remi in time. I know why though.
2.   **Donald:** Why?
3.   **S:** I, I took the risk of going to the gas station both times. Coming back.
4.   **Donald:** Oh to really make, I see. So now, next time, what are you gonna do different?
5.   **S:** Have . . . gas.

Likewise, Ms. Lynn also was more likely to discuss problem solving when talking about the eagle (7/10 exchanges were coded as problem solving). For example, in an exchange with one student, she said:

> It's saying, oh, no. You killed the eagle. Oh no. Oh no. You ran out of gas from, you didn't have enough gas to go to Hilda's. Oh no. Oh no. Okay. So, it's your first try. So, close out. And then, go, you're gonna tell Dr. Remi what you did. Okay. Tell Dr. Remi you killed the eagle, and then, try again using your mathematical calculations. You've gotta make sure you have enough gas!

Finally, as previously mentioned, Ms. Vann spent very little time talking about the math problems with her students and almost all of her time on the computer monitoring students' progress and responding to their written reports in the game. However, Ms. Vann had 29 episodes reacting to students saving or killing the eagle, the most out of all four teachers in this study. In these episodes, Ms. Vann cheered students who saved the eagle or teasingly booed students who killed the eagle, but she did not ask them to think carefully about how their choices led to those outcomes and how they could refine their plans to save the eagle. Ms. Vann focused her attention on the narrative outcomes, but she did not relate the outcomes to the mathematics in the game. For example:

1. **Student 1:** We killed the eagle!
2. **Ms. Vann:** Bad eagle killers! Aaaaaarggg. Dead Eagle alert!
3. **Student 2:** We saved the eagle!
4. **Vann:** Eagle salvation over there! *[rings bell]*

In summary, teachers' use of the narrative consequences of the game fit into the classroom system in predictable ways. Teachers who tended to turn agency over to students were more likely to use the feedback as an opportunity for students to think about what they had done wrong, or what they could do differently. Teachers who were more focused on accuracy used the feedback as an indicator of success or failure, but did not take the feedback further to open a discussion about problem solving or mathematical reasoning.

DISCUSSION

While we cannot generalize widely from only the four cases in this study, these close level analyses of interactions between the teachers and their students offer insight into teaching with video games and how to better support teachers to successfully integrate games into instruction. First, our four case study teachers demonstrate what an important role teachers play in the learning that occurs when students are playing games; teachers are a central part of the overall learning ecology that develops around the game. Perhaps this is most obvious when considering the case of Ms. Vann, who spent the majority of gameplay time sitting at her desk, not interacting with students. Additionally, almost all of Ms. Vann's talk with students involved reacting to the narrative outcomes of the game instead of talking about the math. Ms. Vann's students were the only ones out of the four case teachers' classes who did not show learning gains on the posttest, despite having room to grow; her students only scored 67.3% on the posttest. It is important to note that Ms. Vann wasn't a disinterested or unapproachable teacher; she prepared slides that framed the goals of game play and even created additional homework asking students to reflect about what they had learned from playing the game. However, while playing the game, Ms. Vann did not push her students to engage conceptually, consequentially, or critically with the mathematics. Therefore, we suggest that students learn more and have more opportunities to engage with the mathematics content of digital games if teachers interact with students and talk about the math during gameplay.

Second, we found that during teacher–student interactions about the math content, it is possible for teachers to appropriate student agency rather than allowing students to try their own solutions. This is consistent with literature about using tasks in classrooms, which suggests that when students have questions or are confused, teachers often narrow the problem, thus lessening the rigor of the task as designed (Stein et al., 2000). Instead of offering answers or procedures right away, teachers can scaffold students' problem solving with open questions that give students agency to develop solutions and procedures first. Ms. Lynn's work with her students exemplified this idea. When a student asked for help, she first asked him/her a question that allowed the student to suggest a strategy or procedure to use. If the student still struggled to come up with a solution, Ms. Lynn suggested what to do next or what the student might need to think about to solve the problem. We conjecture that this type of scaffolding helped her students understand different solution strategies; perhaps because of this, her students had the highest learning gains of all four teachers' classes on the posttest. On the other hand, in Mr. Doyle's class, most of the agency was distributed to the teacher, meaning Mr. Doyle offered a strategy or answer right away, thus diminishing some of the cognitive demand of the task. While the students in Mr. Doyle's class did have pre-post gain, we believe that the emphasis on teacher agency limited students' opportunities to think critically about the mathematics problems. We conjecture that students learn more if they are given agency to develop their own solutions to problems in digital games. This is a question worth further exploration.

Findings from this study also point to important design changes for *Boone's Meadow* and suggestions for others working with digital games. For instance, even if students perform well on tests and appear to have good procedural understandings of ratio and proportion, students can still learn from engaging conceptually, consequentially, and critically with the mathematics in the game. Therefore, we need to work more with teachers to help them recognize opportunities for students to engage deeply in the game's content and respond to narrative feedback from the game. Teachers do not always notice those opportunities or know how to support students to go beyond procedural engagement. We need more research on how teachers can recognize and scaffold potential moments of deeper mathematical engagement. In addition, we need to examine how *Boone's Meadow* and other educational games afford engagement in the content so that teachers can use games to improve students' understandings beyond just practicing procedures.

More specifically related to *Boone's Meadow*, we also need to work with teachers to make sure they understand how to use our teacher materials. We provided all four of our case study teachers with a packet of teacher materials, but we found that the teachers did not all find these materials useful. For future iterations of our designs, we need to work alongside teachers to make sure our materials are clear and easy for teachers to use to guide discussions and gameplay time. We also need to tailor the teacher materials to help teachers differentiate and support students based on the extent of their prior knowledge relevant to the game. Ms. Vann's and Mr. Doyle's students had much more relevant prior knowledge than Ms. Lynn's and Ms. Donald's students, so the teachers interacted with students and structured gameplay very differently. Our teacher materials were not originally designed to support these different groups of students, so we need to work with teachers to improve the materials for future use. After working with Ms. Lynn's and Ms. Donald's students who had low levels of multiplicative reasoning, we made specific changes to the *Boone's Meadow* game to support problem solving for similar students with low levels of prior knowledge. We are in the process of analyzing and writing about those changes to the game. Overall, we are working towards improving *Boone's Meadow*, the Teacher Toolkit, and teacher materials to make the problems in the game more accessible to students with different levels of prior knowledge and help all students build conceptual understandings of ratio and proportion.

IN CLOSING

One of the most salient conclusions to be drawn from this study is that teachers use games in amazingly diverse ways, and that diversity cannot be explained by some teachers implementing the game with more fidelity than others. Instead, our observations support the idea that classrooms are complex interactive spaces and that elements interact with and influence the behavior of other elements. As such, introducing a new element, such as a video game, undoubtedly changed the behavior of each classroom system, but in ways that were consistent with the other existing elements of the system. Thus, what students already knew about math appeared to interact with the ways that teachers talked about math with their students in the game. Likewise, teachers' ideas about what it means to know and do mathematics interacted with the game and influenced how open problems were treated. The four teachers in this study used mathematical thinking, agency, and narrative in different ways, which appeared to influence what their students learned from playing the game. These results demonstrate that we cannot simply make good games and give them to teachers with the expectation that students will learn.

If we take as given that a classroom ecology has many factors that interact to affect student learning, then if we want teachers to be able to integrate games successfully into their classrooms and improve students' understandings of the content, we have to understand teachers' practices around gameplay. Teachers need more resources and training to help develop their practice so that they can successfully integrate games into the classroom ecology. In this study, we led a professional development session for the teachers using the game and we provided a packet of teacher materials outlining gameplay sessions and discussion questions. However, the materials were not enough to help teachers identify opportunities for deeper mathematical engagement and support the learning of all students. An important area for future research includes questions about what kinds of supports or training teachers need in order to realize the potential of digital games for learning.

This chapter demonstrates the potential of problem-solving games like *Boone's Meadow* for supporting student learning, especially when teachers spend most of the gameplay time interacting with students. But it also points to the need for more detailed research on how teachers can support learning through deeper engagement in the content and points to the need to investigate in more depth whether and how the games that we design shift the learning ecology of the classroom.

ACKNOWLEDGMENTS

This material is based upon work supported by the National Science Foundation under Grant No. 1252380. The authors are very grateful for the work of Katherine Chapman, Panchompoo Wisittanawat, and Isaac Nichols in helping with data collection and analysis, and for the teachers and students who participated in this study.

NOTE

1. Transcript conventions: S indicates talk from a student, X represents talk that is inaudible, ... indicates a pause, and gestures/actions are written in brackets *[in italics]*.

REFERENCES

Barab, S. A., Pettyjohn, P., Gresalfi, M. S., Volk, C., & Solomou, M. (2012). Game-based curriculum and transformational play: Designing to meaningfully position person, content, and context. *Computers and Education, 50*, 518–533.

Barab, S. A., Sadler, T. D., Heiselt, C., Hickey, D., & Zuiker, S. (2007). Relating narrative, inquiry, and inscriptions: Supporting consequential play. *Journal of Science Education and Technology, 16*(1), 59–82.

Barab, S. A., Thomas, M., Dodge, T., Carteaux, R., & Tuzun, H. (2005). Making learning fun: Quest Atlantis, a game without guns. *Educational Technology Research and Development, 53*(1), 86–107.

Barron, B. (2004, June). *Learning ecologies for technological fluency: Gender and experience differences.* Paper presented at the Sixth International Conference of the Learning Sciences, Santa Monica, CA.

Barron, B. (2006). Interest and self-sustained learning as catalysts of development: A learning ecology perspective. *Human Development, 49*(4), 193.

Bielaczyc, K., Pirolli, P. L., & Brown, A. L. (1995). Training in self-explanation and self-regulation strategies: Investigating the effects of knowledge acquisition activities on problem solving. *Cognition and Instruction, 13*(2), 221–252.

Clark, D. B., Tanner-Smith, E. E., & Killingsworth, S. S. (2015). Digital games, design, and learning a systematic review and meta-analysis. *Review of educational research, 86*(1), 79–122.

Clarke, J., & Dede, C. (2009). Design for scalability: A case study of the River City curriculum. *Journal of Science Education and Technology, 18*(4), 353–365.

Cognition and Technology Group at Vanderbilt. (1997). *The Jasper Project: Lessons in curriculum, instruction, assessment, and professional development.* Mahwah, NJ: Erlbaum.

Davis, B., & Sumara, D. (1997). Cognition, complexity, and teacher education. *Harvard Educational Review, 67*(1), 105–126.

Dickey, M. D. (2007). Game design and learning: A conjectural analysis of how massively multiple online role-playing games (MMORPGs) foster intrinsic motivation. *Educational Technology Research and Development, 55*(3), 253–273.

Ertmer, P. A., Ottenbreit-Leftwich, A. T., Sadik, O., Sendurur, E., & Sendurur, P. (2012). Teacher beliefs and technology integration practices: A critical relationship. *Computers & Education, 59*(2), 423-435.

Ertmer, P. A., Ottenbreit-Leftwich, A. T., & Tondeur, J. (2014). Teachers' beliefs and uses of technology to support 21st-century teaching and learning. In H. Fives & M. G. Gill (Eds.), *International handbook of research on teacher beliefs* (pp. 403–418). New York, NY: Routledge.

Fishman, B., Riconscente, M., Snider, R., Tasi, T., & Plass, J. (2014). *Empowering educators: Supporting student progress in the classroom with digital games.* Ann Arbor, MI: University of Michigan School of Information. Retrieved from gamesandlearning.umich.edu/agames

Garris, R., Ahlers, R., & Driskell, J. E. (2002). Games, motivation, and learning: A research and practice model. *Simulation & Gaming, 33*, 441–467.

Gresalfi, M. S. (2009). Taking up opportunities to learn: Constructing dispositions in mathematics classrooms. *Journal of the Learning Sciences, 18*, 327–369.

Gresalfi, M. S., & Barab, S. A. (2011). Learning for a reason: Supporting forms of engagement by designing tasks and orchestrating environments. *Theory Into Practice, 50*, 300–310.

Gresalfi, M. S., & Barnes, J. (2016). Designing feedback in an immersive videogame: Supporting student mathematical engagement. *Educational Technology Research and Development, 64*(1), 65–86.

Gresalfi, M., Martin, T., Hand, V., & Greeno, J. (2009). Constructing competence: An analysis of student participation in the activity systems of mathematics classrooms. *Educational Studies in Mathematics, 70*(1), 49–70.

Hand, V. M. (2010). The co-construction of opposition in a low-track mathematics classroom. *American Educational Research Journal, 47*(1), 97–132.

Henningsen, M., & Stein, M. K. (1997). Mathematical tasks and student cognition: Classroom-based factors that support and inhibit high-level mathematical thinking and reasoning. *Journal for Research in Mathematics Education, 28*(5), 524–549.

Jonassen, D. H. (1997). Instructional design models for well-structured and ill-structured problem-solving learning outcomes. *Educational Technology Research and Development, 45*(1), 65–94.

Lee, C.-Y., & Chen, M.-P. (2009). A computer game as a context for non-routine mathematical problem solving: The effects of type of question prompt and level of prior knowledge. *Computers & Education, 52*(3), 530–542.

Lepper, M. R., & Malone, T. W. (1987). Intrinsic motivation and instructional effectiveness in computer-based education. In R. E. Snow & M. J. Farr (Eds.), *Aptitude, learning, and instruction: III. Conative and affective process analyses* (pp. 255–286). Hillsdale, NJ: Erlbaum.

Lobato, J., Ellis, A., & Zbiek, R. (2010). *Developing essential understanding of ratios, proportions, and proportional reasoning for teaching mathematics: Grades 6–8.* Reston, VA: National Council of Teachers of Mathematics.

Malone, T. W., & Lepper, M. R. (1987). Making learning fun: A taxonomy of intrinsic motivations for learning. In R. E. Snow & M. J. Farr (Eds.), *Aptitude, learning, and instruction: III. Conate and affective process analyses* (pp. 223–253). Hillsdale, NJ: Erlbaum.

Mayer, R. E., & Johnson, C. I. (2010). Adding instructional features that promote learning in a game-like environment. *Journal of Educational Computing Research, 42*(3), 241–265.

Mishra, P., & Koehler, M. J. (2006). Technological pedagogical content knowledge: A framework for teacher knowledge. *Teachers College Record, 108*(6), 1017–1054.

Mouza, C. (2008). Learning with laptops: Implementation and outcomes in an urban, under-privileged school. *Journal of Research on Technology in Education, 40*(4), 447–472.

Nelson, B. C. (2007). Exploring the use of individualized, reflective guidance in an educational multi-user virtual environment. *Journal of Science Education and Technology, 16*(1), 83–97.

Osberg, D., & Biesta, G. (2008). The emergent curriculum: Navigating a complex course between unguided learning and planned enculturation. *Journal of Curriculum Studies, 40*(3), 313–328.

Pareto, L., Arvemo, T., Dahl, Y., Haake, M., & Gulz, A. (2011). A teachable-agent arithmetic game's effects on mathematics understanding, attitude and self-efficacy. In *Artificial intelligence in education* (pp. 247–255). Springer Berlin/Heidelberg.

Penuel, W. R. (2006). Implementation and effects of one-to-one computing initiatives: A research synthesis. *Journal of Research on Technology in Education, 38*(3), 329–348.

Pierson, M. E. (2001). Technology integration practice as a function of pedagogical expertise. *Journal of Research on Computing in Education, 33*(4), 413.

Rieber, L. P. (1996). Animation as feedback in a computer-based simulation: Representation matters. *Educational Technology Research and Development, 44,* 5–22.

Rogers, E., & Murcott, S. (1995). Attributes of innovations and their rate of adoption. *Diffusion of Innovation, 4,* 204–251.

Squire, K. (2006). From content to context: Video games as designed experiences. *Educational Researcher, 35*(8), 19–29.

Stake, R. E. (1995). *The art of case study research.* Thousand Oaks, CA: SAGE.

Stein, M. K., Smith, M. S., Henningsen, M. A., & Silver, E. A. (2000). *Implementing standards-based mathematics instruction: A casebook for professional development.* New York, NY: Teacher College Press.

Takeuchi, L. M., & Vaala, S. (2014). *Level up learning: A national survey on teaching with digital games.* New York, NY: Joan Ganz Cooney Center.

Vogel, J. J., Vogel, D. S., Cannon-Bowers, J., Bowers, C. A., Muse, K., & Wright, M. (2006). Computer gaming and interactive simulations for learning: A meta-analysis. *Journal of Educational Computing Research, 34,* 229–243.

Windschitl, M., & Sahl, K. (2002). Tracing teachers' use of technology in a laptop computer school: The interplay of teacher beliefs, social dynamics, and institutional culture. *American Educational Research Journal, 39*(1), 165–205.

Wortham, S. (2004). From good student to outcast: The emergence of a classroom identity. *Ethos, 32*(2), 164–187.

Wouters, P., Van Nimwegen, C., Van Oostendorp, H., & Van Der Spek, E. D. (2013). A meta-analysis of the cognitive and motivational effects of serious games. *Journal of Educational Psychology, 105*(2), 249.

Young, M. F., Slota, S., Cutter, A. B., Jalette, G., Mullin, G., Lai, B., . . . Yukhymenko, M. (2012). Our princess is in another castle a review of trends in serious gaming for education. *Review of Educational Research, 82*(1), 61–89.

CHAPTER 5

MORE THAN AN AVATAR

Unmasking the Player's Impact on an Educational Game

Jackie Barnes
Northeastern University

Melissa Gresalfi
Vanderbilt University

Educational games are special sites of interaction because they contain both educational and game-like elements. They bridge the two seemingly disparate worlds of *school* and *games* as they incorporate playful elements into a design specifically intended for disciplinary learning. Similar to commercial games, most educational games take place within a virtual space that provides immediate feedback on game actions. Both the contrasts and the similarities between these two types of games are important, as they influence the ways that players *perceive* the game. A student who feels disillusioned in school may see an educational game as a boring classroom activity; a player who identifies as a gamer may see an educational game as a challenge to beat. Alternatively, a gamer might see an educational game as

Exploding the Castle, pages 93–115

fundamentally *educational* and may not consider what they're playing a *real* game (Squire, 2005). In other words, whether a student sees an educational game as game-like or as school-like is consequential—these are different ecologies and signal different kinds of affordances to anyone interacting within them. Thus, an educational game cannot be placed within a classroom with the assumption that students will think of it and interact with it as they would with any other game, and studies of games must take this larger ecology into account.

Much of the existing research on educational games reports on affordances of the games themselves—games afford immediate feedback on actions and understanding (Gresalfi & Barnes, 2015) and may also position children as experts, giving them voice that they cannot have in the real world (Barab, Gresalfi, Dodge, & Ingram-Goble, 2010; Gee, 2003; Squire, 2003) and are often more effective than nongame learning environments (Clark, Tanner-Smith, & Killingsworth, 2015). However, while it has been established that educational games have worthwhile affordances, fewer studies examine the players of educational games in their own right. Those that do focus on large categories rather than ecological elements like player perception. Therefore, while research on educational games to date has focused on their effectiveness for groups of learners, namely gender, age, and game experience, we propose that it is vital to look beyond these categories.

We suggest that players' experiences in the world fundamentally influence the game experience (Harteveld, 2011). Therefore, it is necessary to understand how the players themselves might impact the educational game design. In order to do this, we present two players who are similar according to the categories usually studied in games (i.e., gender, age, game experience, prior knowledge). The two players, Cameron and Lamia, are girls who are the same age, rate themselves as heavy gamers, and have similar prior knowledge (as measured by our pretest). Yet we show how their experiences diverge, in part, based on how they perceived the game as academic or playful. The goal of this chapter is to consider how players' perceptions of a game and their previous attunement to games and school influence the game that is ultimately played.

BACKGROUND

While the literature on game design and outcomes is growing substantially, there is limited work investigating players, the diversity of player experience, and, specifically, how players perceive educational or serious games. Nacke et al. (2009) echo this characterization, describing the difference between playability research focusing on the design of a game and player experience research focusing on the players and their perceptions and experience before and during game play. Historically, much of the research on game players has focused on gender differences in whether and how boys and girls tend to interact with games and other new technologies. Today, the vast majority of youth play some kind of video games, with 99% of boys and 94% of girls playing some kind of video game (Lenhart et al., 2008). In fact, the target sample of this study, 7th graders, represents a unique developmental stage marked by various types of social play through online gaming (Gross, 2004; Steeves & Kerr, 2005), where players experiment with avatar choices or through in-game interactions. However, boys and girls appear to perceive the purpose of their play differently; boys might be interested in beating the game while girls generally aim for exploration of the game tools and simulating multiple options (Squire, Barnett, Grant, & Higgenbotham, 2004). This finding is not uncommon; using interactive technologies such as games, girls often look for opportunities for social interaction and collaboration rather than competition (Cone, 2001; Passig & Levin, 2000; Volman & van Eck, 2001). In general, girls tend to take advantage of communication affordances of the technology such as discussion boards, email, or messaging, while boys often prefer to act upon affordances that provide control over the screen or game or creating content new material (Caleb, 2000). More recent research suggests these general trends have not changed; Appel (2012) found that board games, simulations, and Facebook games were much more popular among girls than among boys, whereas the preferences were reversed for first-person-shooters, action, and fantasy games. Overall, girls used the computer less for entertainment purposes and programming and more for emailing and schoolwork at home. Lucas and Sherry (2004) note that boys seek out video games as their method of social interaction, while girls usually do not.

Anxiety about playing video games seems to differ between the genders, with girls showing more anxiety about game play than boys (Appel, 2012), although this may be related to gaming frequency rather than gender. Relatedly, Appel (2012) has found very large differences between boys and girls in the computer knowledge scores, suggesting that girls might have more anxiety about computers because they are less likely to see technology and games as something they can control. Further, separate from game play, middle-school-aged girls are particularly at risk for confidence problems related to their learning—perceiving and reporting that they are doing worse than they really are (Chen & Pajares, 2010).

Another focus of research has been on whether and how gaming experience impacts play and learning. For example, Christou (2013) found that game experience impacted perceptions of usability—more frequent gamers saw games as more accessible, and appealing. This is supported by findings that suggest navigation and other game play dynamics are tougher for those who are not used to playing games (Tawfik, He, & Vo, 2009). In this way, players' personal histories must be considered as part of "the public and private contexts of digital play" (Mäyrä, 2007, p. 814), including game experience or social relationships among coplayers. For example, Orvis, Horn, and Belanich (2008) found that players with more video game experience performed better on a novel game than those with less experience, regardless of the level of difficulty of the game. The authors suggested that playing games activates familiar video-game-relevant schemas during game play. Experienced gamers also choose more difficult personal goals for game play and report higher self-efficacy for game play. Those with less experience may be overwhelmed or experience cognitive overload, while struggling with usability aspects such as navigation and directions (Tawfik et al., 2009). Further, Appel (2012) found that more time playing games contributed to a decrease in computer anxiety. Player anxiety may contribute to being overwhelmed by the options on the screen, such as understanding controls for navigation or game action. The study suggests that anxiety about game play influences what players notice in games.

However, although gamers have less anxiety about navigating new games, they tend to have different worries about their game play. Bringula, Lugtu, and Aviles (2015) observed that gamers were inclined to be more anxious about being defeated in a game as gaming became more frequent and length of years spent playing games increased. They also felt stressed when they were competing with a better player, especially as they reached higher levels in a game. Many gamers need to play games frequently in order to build up their game characters. To do this, gamers spend a lot of time and effort to achieve their gaming status and achieve accomplishments, and one mistake within a game may lead to a loss of earned resources.

The game used in this study is about Newtonian mechanics. Because of this, prior experience with physics might be relevant to how players interact with the content of the game. Novice and expert physicists see physical scenarios differently and take sharply different approaches to explaining them. Novice understanding often relies upon what physical phenomena one has seen in the world—one's own experiences. For example, when asked to explain why some bells have higher or lower pitch than others, novices might explain that thicker bells have lower pitches, indicating their attunement to the fact that bigger things have lower pitch (such is often the case with human voices). Those who have more physics expertise may relate the thickness of the bell to frequency of vibration (diSessa, 1993). Given this, players of a physics game who are novices to physics might rely upon their own experience in a world with friction and air resistance—they may assume that any object will slow down over time. However, those who have some exposure to Newton's laws might understand that objects moving in some places, like space, have little to no friction and may rely more upon the formula's inherent in Newton's laws than their own experience.

In addition to personal and social histories, the physical context in which a game is played matters. One might imagine that placing a game within a classroom context might necessarily communicate to players that what they are doing is educational. However, simply framing a task as educational or a game can be consequential. Lieberoth (2015) observed that framing an educational activity as a "game" and use of game artifacts increased interest and engagement, whether or not the activity actually had game mechanics. Similarly, Vandercruysse, Vandewaetere, Cornillie, and Clarebout (2013) conducted a study calling a task a "game" for some participants and an "instructional activity" to others. They found that many participants saw what they were doing as educational despite the activity being described as a game. They also found that those who were in the game group reported higher interest, enjoyment, and perceived competence after playing.

While perceptions related to video games are not well investigated, other media have been investigated in relation to perceptions of the environment purpose and the impact that has on learning. Salomon (1984) investigated this question in relation to educational television. Learners' perceived mental effort to learn material was lower if, for them, television was perceived as something watched for fun rather than for instruction. In this case, and in interactive media overall, it appears that how learners perceive the educational context and its purpose affects whether the technology actually impacts learning (Shuell & Farber, 2001). One explanation for this might be that students who perceive a task as very game-like or as a leisure activity might dedicate less mental effort to the task, which may result in little learning. By contrast, students who perceive the environment as school-like may dedicate more effort and learn more (Vandercruysse et al., 2013). In other words, how students perceive the medium and context of instruction affects its impact (Lowyck, Elen, & Clarebout, 2004; Entwistle & Tait, 1995). For example, an instructional game is likely to be affected by students' perceptions about games in general. However, stated previously, these learner perceptions related to games have remained largely examined.

Taken together, it seems likely that differences in players' histories, experiences, and contexts shape their game play. However, the literature to date has not explored whether or why this might be true. For this reason, we have selected two contrasting cases that are similar in terms of the categories that have been studied previously: two girls, with gaming experience, and low pretest scores. These categories should seemingly predict outcomes, or at least, would lead us to assume similar outcomes. But instead, we observed significant differences in the ways that the students played the game, and, ultimately, what they learned.

Our analysis of these cases focuses on the two players' perceptions of the game in relation to how they interact with it and the outcomes that occur as a result of those interactions. There is not an agreed-upon way to formulate or define perceptions of players. For the purposes of this study, we think of the ecological concept of perception (Gibson, 1986), meaning what the player see game affordances *as*, whether game or school. Seeing games as ecologies, we must look at game play as an interaction in order to understand player perceptions. The ecological framework that we use to frame our work and findings is articulated below. While the categorical characteristics of players were discussed here (i.e., age, game experience), our discussion that follows posits that an *ecological* consideration game play should shift the paradigm from considering categorical differences to differences in perception and interaction with a game design.

GAMEPLAY AS AN INTERACTION

The cases we present here have categorical similarities. The analysis focuses on how, despite these similarities, the players' perceptions and interactions differ. This discussion is driven by a shift in paradigm, or ontology, from categorical to ecological. Traditional studies of learning and game play often come from the tradition of cognitive science, with a focus on player characteristics as separate from game play interactions. These studies often consider the impact of categorical membership or individual characteristics on game play and learning (Bahr & Rieth, 1989; Ke, 2008; van Eck & Dempsey, 2002). Ecological frameworks of game play broaden the unit of analysis and focus on the interactions among the player, the context of the game play, and the designed elements of the game (Barab et al., 2010; Gresalfi, 2015; Gresalfi & Barnes, 2015; Squire & Jan, 2007). We analyze our cases using this latter perspective, using a framework of perception and affordances (Gibson, 1986). The premise of this framework is that every action taken by a player occurs in an ecology with myriad affordances that a player might perceive and choose to act upon. In a video game context, affordances would count as any opportunity for action (or reaction) during the game experience, such as the occurrence of a choice, a clickable object, or an event that can be responded to. Importantly, affordances also include *potential* actions taken within the context around the game. Educational games are played in a classroom space with its own rules and social interactions that existed before the game was used. Players within these spaces may perceive and act upon any number of things in the space around them.

In a video game, players often take actions differently over time as they get better at the game. Practice with the game can change the player's attunement—that is, contribute to the capabilities of a player to discriminate affordances of the game experience. For example, a person playing a game about physics might be attuned to the vocabulary used in the game from a previous science class. A different player, with no previous exposure to physics terms or concepts, might see the same features of the game but not perceive them as options that might, for example, add force or velocity, or allow him to navigate his ship. A third player who is a self-professed "gamer" may be attuned to the familiar game-like aspects of the screen in relation to games that they have played before. This might aid in her learning initial game mechanics, but she might be unfamiliar with the word and symbols related to understanding the concepts of Newtonian mechanics.

A focus on interaction highlights the importance of investigating both the affordances of a designed space and the histories of the players. The extant literature on games focuses primarily on the former, with limited conceptualization of the player. The work that has focused on players has primarily considered particular categories, such as gender, age, or game experience. Some findings related to these categories are presented here before discussing how two cases who represent many of the same categories can nevertheless diverge in game perceptions, game play, and learning.

SURGE FUZZY CHRONICLES

The game used in this study was *SURGE Fuzzy Chronicles* (Clark, 2011). *SURGE* supports users to experiment with Newtonian mechanics by placing forces on a spaceship to navigate through a trajectory of speed and mass gates, which have specific requirements for passage. Shown in Figure 5.1, players specify magnitude and direction of forces to place on their ship to make it through green speed gates and purple mass gates safely (i.e., at the correct speed or mass). If they attempt to travel through one of these gates at the wrong speed or mass, the ship will explode and they will need to start over. In later levels, players can also pick up or throw "fuzzies" to change the ship's mass and speed.

Players navigate through their "star map" (Figure 5.2) made up of levels differentiated by color. *Red* levels introduce game dynamics and support understanding of the relationship between force and velocity. *Blue* level trajectories increase in complexity and introduce the relationships between mass, force, and velocity, with the addition of "fuzzies," creatures weighing 1 kg that sometimes need to be picked up along the way. *Green* levels allow players to throw fuzzies, leveraging the principles of equal and opposite forces pushing back on their ship in a desired direction. For example, players can throw a fuzzy upward with 20N of force to propel their ship downward with the same magnitude of force. Yellow, purple, and orange levels follow as bonus levels that combine previous skills into increasingly complex trajectories.

SURGE supports specific types of interactions. Players can manipulate where, along the trajectory, to apply various actions: applications of force,

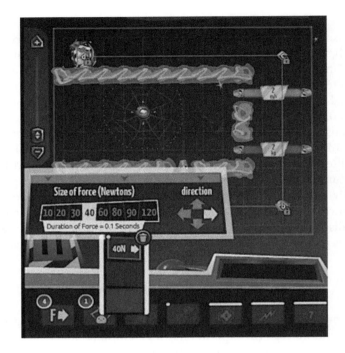

Figure 5.1   Choosing force magnitude and direction in "Blue Boss 1."

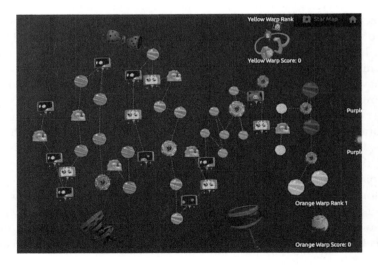

Figure 5.2   Players' "star map" in SURGE with red, blue, green, and additional levels.

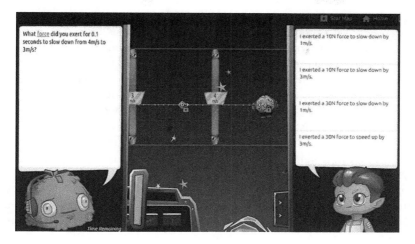

Figure 5.3 Example question at the end of the red warp missions.

fuzzy pickups, fuzzy throws, and switching of a lever to enact their plan. They can make any number of arrangements that do not result in their intended goal, and they can react to consequences of failure on the screen (i.e., the ship blowing up) either verbally or by iterating upon their plan until it works as intended. Further, there are countless affordances that can be perceived and acted upon, in addition to the affordances of the design itself, as part of the metagame. The different color levels scaffold different mechanics ideas. At the end of each set are "warp levels" that require a minimum score to be earned. At the end of warp levels, there are also multiple choice questions that pop out for players to respond to before proceeding (Figure 5.3). The questions ask about an action they took in that particular level, or what they might do in a similar hypothetical situation.

STUDY DETAILS

The cases discussed here came from a larger study of 97 7th-grade students across four STEM classes, taught by the same teacher. The game was played for five class periods, each of which lasted approximately 75 minutes. During the study, the regular classroom teacher largely handed over instruction to researchers. The activity was introduced by positioning students as playtesters who could give researchers feedback on the design of the game to improve it for future students, in part to set the intention with which the players would interact with the games as "experts in the use of their own media culture" (Marsh, 2011, p. 105). Students were encouraged to experiment with how to play the game on their own, with the intent of shifting expertise away from researchers regarding "how to play," and were encouraged to talk with their peers to share game strategies.

All participants took a pre- and posttest before and after the week of game play and a game engagement survey at the end of the week. Logged game data (e.g., time to complete a level, number of attempts) were also collected. The test questions aligned to the content players interacted with in the game, using more abstract scenarios and different objects (e.g., an alien or squirrel instead of a spaceship). The engagement survey asked players to rate their experience relative to four statements, with a rating from 1 (strongly agree) to 5 (strongly disagree). The statements were "I liked playing this game," "This game was difficult for me to play," "I worked hard to understand how to play the game and complete missions," and "I would like to play this game, or games like it, again in the future." They also responded to "How many times a week do you typically play video games?" with choices ranging from "I do not play," "Less than 1 hour," "1–2 hours," "3–4 hours," "5–7 hours," "8–10 hours," or "More than 10 hours."

To collect more substantial data for particular students with the aim of understanding nuance within study findings, 20 students were chosen as case studies based on having their consent form turned in at the beginning of the study, an equal distribution of gender, and a balance across classes. Case studies included 10 boys and 10 girls with 4–6 students drawn from each class that was observed. For these cases, screen capture videos were initiated each day of game play at the beginning of each class period. These videos captured the game screen, cursor movement and clicks, and audio using the laptop's internal microphone. They also captured the audio of the interviews and discussions we had with the case study students throughout their play.

FINDINGS

This chapter presents two of these 20 cases (i.e., Cameron and Lamia) to contrast their experiences. Cameron and Lamia are both 7th-grade girls, in separate classes (we have no evidence they know each other or interacted during the study), with similar pretest scores, who identified themselves as heavy gamers. They each reported playing over 10 hours of games per week and talked about their game play during the course of the study. Given these similarities regarding age, gender, prior knowledge, and game experience, it might be expected that these girls' experiences with the same game would also be very similar. However, that was not the case. Despite their identical categorical group memberships in these categories, and the known trends discussed above related to these categories, Cameron and Lamia diverged quite substantially in their game experiences.

While the two girls had the same pretest score (29%, slightly below the overall average of 33%), their posttest scores (71% for Cameron, 43% for Lamia) and engagement ratings reflected the vast differences in their experience of *SURGE* (Table 5.1). Further, Cameron reached level 28, or Orange Boss Mission 1, further than any other player of that version of the game, while Lamia only reached level 14, which was slightly below the average. Cameron and Lamia, despite their superficial similarities, experienced the same game quite differently.

Table 5.1 shows differences that appeared particularly at the end of the game play experience, not the beginning: posttest scores, highest level reached, and game engagement ratings were very different between Lamia and Cameron. They both thought the game was difficult, but while Lamia was neutral on enjoyment and effort, she strongly disagreed that she would play again. Quite differently, Cameron very much enjoyed what she was doing, perceived herself as working hard, and strongly agreed that she would play again. Our analyses sought to determine what happened during the experience to cause these different feelings about and learning from game play. Because of their categorical similarities, we suggest the difference in experience might be due to game interactions or the players' perception of what they're doing.

For example, we can examine how Cameron and Lamia played and how they progressed through *SURGE*. The logged game data provide some information about number of attempts per level and the types of actions taken, as well as the speed of progression through levels, which may all be indicators of engagement and success. As described previously, we initiated screen capture videos of each case study at the beginning of each day. For Lamia, a recording was captured each of the 5 days, but we have recordings for Cameron starting on the third day of the study, the day she brought in her consent forms.

By the beginning of day 3, Cameron was starting Green Boss 2, which is the very last green level before the yellow "bonus" levels begin. At the same time, Lamia was on Blue Warp on day 3 and appeared to be stuck on this level from day 2 to day 4. Because Lamia only got to Green mission 1 before the study completed, and because Cameron's screen captures did not begin until she was on Green Boss 2, past where Lamia achieved total through the week, we didn't have any overlapping recordings of the two girls to compare level-specific actions. Table 5.2 indicates the general progression through levels for both Cameron and Lamia, as judged from their screen capture videos. In particular, it appears that Lamia got stuck on Blue Warp, as she was working on that level over the course of several days. Rather than look at how the girls played a specific level differently, we can look at other game analytics that may indicate something about their experience.

TABLE 5.1 Summary of Lamia and Cameron

	Hours/wk (M = 4.3)	Pre (M = 33)	Post (M = 56)	Highest Level (M = 16)	"I Liked Playing"	"This Game Was Difficult"	"I Worked Hard"	"I Would Play Again"
Lamia	>10	29%	43%	14	Neutral	Agree	Neutral	Strongly Disagree
Cameron	>10	29%	71%	28	Strongly Agree	Agree	Strongly Agree	Strongly Agree

TABLE 5.2 Level Progression Comparison of Lamia and Cameron

	Day 1	Day 2	Day 3	Day 4	Day 5
Lamia	Red 1 to Red Warp	[Red Warp to Blue Warp]	Blue Warp	Blue Warp to Blue Boss 2	Blue Boss 2 to Green 1
Cameron	[Red 1 to ?]	[? to Green Boss 2]	Green Boss 2 to Yellow Boss 2	Yellow Boss 2 to Purple Boss 2	Purple Boss 2 to Orange Boss 1

Generally, Cameron moved faster, but from what we can tell, other game measures looked similar. Two specific game play measures we checked are average number of attempts per level and average trial time. Average attempts records how many times a player attempted a given level, how many trials they had, or in other words, the number of times they hit the lever to simulate their choices. Average trial time records the average amount of time a given player takes to place their forces for each trial they have, across all the levels they've played. The differences between these two girls on each of these measures were not significant. So, in at least those two ways, they played similarly.

In general, the game actions Cameron and Lamia took looked similar, except that Cameron arrived at levels days before Lamia played the same level. In this way, speed of progression might be an indicator of frustration or perception of difficulty. In fact, the starkest difference between the engagement responses of these players is the question "Would you play again?" While Cameron "strongly agrees" she would play again, Lamia "strongly disagrees." Given her apparent frustration and perception of *SURGE* as a "learning game," it is hardly surprising. However, an additional question to disentangle from these findings is whether Lamia's perception of the game impacted her interactions, which impacted her learning, or whether getting stuck on lower levels impeded her experience with different types of Newtonian dynamics, which impeded her learning.

Again, because of these players' categorical similarities, and as shown here, their similarity in game actions (other than speed of progression), we suggest the difference in experience might be due to the players' perceptions of what they're doing—as either game or school. We aim here to understand how the players saw the task they were interacting with, and how that may be reflected in their engagement. After looking at quantitative data of players' pre- and posttests and logged game data without finding clear divergence in experience, we look to player talk to better understand the nuance of how their engagement with *SURGE* developed from the beginning to the end of the experience, and how perception of what they were doing impacted their game play. Specifically, we posit that Cameron interacted with *SURGE* as a gamer who saw what they were doing as beating a game, while Lamia played as a gamer who saw *SURGE* as, simply, a learning game.

CAMERON "BEAT THE GAME"

Here we describe what Cameron's play looked like and provide evidence of how she interacted with the design *as a gamer who squarely saw her task as beating a game.* Our overall conjecture is that one of the key differences in the girls' experiences is that Cameron saw *SURGE* as a game, while Lamia did not.

During the first days of the study, while Cameron played alone and wasn't exceptionally vocal, she described what she was doing as "a game" to classmates multiple times. For example, in rejecting a bid for conversation, she said, "I really want—I really want to finish the game, ok?" Soon after, when talking to a neighboring peer, she reiterated this label, indicating, "Watch, I'm going to beat the game." Cameron also appeared to be highly attuned to her own and others' progress. After asking another student what level he was on, she placed her cursor over the star map to search where his current level was relative to her own. Likewise, soon after, when asked by a member of the research team, "What level is this?" she responded, "The one that everyone's stuck on—Purple Boss 2." Notably, her naming of the level included an allusion to its difficulty, indicating her awareness of others' progress and the perceived arduousness of Purple Boss 2. As previously noted, gamers often pay attention to competitive elements of gaming, especially as higher levels are reached.

One key difference in Cameron and Lamia's game play must have been their reaction to difficulty, since both of them rated *SURGE* as difficult, but Cameron seemed to enjoy the experience, and progressed very far, while Lamia did not. Cameron sometimes appeared to apply systematic strategies to solving difficult levels. For example, when her ship blew up along the trajectory and she couldn't figure out the problem after multiple attempts, she continued filling in forces later in the trajectory before returning to test the problem area. Also, she often replayed the simulation at each step, solving the puzzle piece by piece rather than trying to solve it as a whole. Cameron's core game actions, like placing accurate forces, didn't appear notably different from what other players did. However, her overall enthusiasm for game play, and her persistence in response to difficulty, looked quite different from other students, particularly Lamia, who often became frustrated. It seemed that Cameron's learning and enjoyment of the game cannot only be understood to be a result of the microactions she took *in* the game, but also as her reactions and talk in the context of the game, or the metagame.

Cameron saw her task as a game and appeared to use systematic strategies for beating levels. We also know that she enjoyed what she was doing, despite finding it difficult. Her verbal reactions show what her ratings of perceiving game difficulty and success looked like during actual game play, as someone who believed they were successful at a very difficult game task. For example, as she noticed her ship successfully heading toward the exit portal, she announced, "I only have three more! Three more levels! I AM SO HAPPY." In another instance, she pleaded with the game, saying "Come on. . . . come on. . . . please please." Lamia pleaded similarly, but in a more forceful tone ("I'm going to hit you!"), which makes sense, since both players rated the game as being difficult. Cameron also squeaked excitedly when a switch on the screen turned blue, indicating that a fuzzy has been thrown to its intended target and she would pass the level.

Illuminating Cameron's high engagement and attachment to the game were her visible emotion and verbal outbursts when solving higher levels, but also a final instance when she learned that she couldn't save, re-enter, or continue the game further at home, due to our research constraints. At the end of the final day, when a researcher announced that it was time to sign out, Cameron continued playing, saying, "I'm doing this! I'm finishing this. I'm finishing this." As one of the researchers prompted the students to sign out another time, she uttered, "PLEASE. I am so close." After she eventually signed out, she asked a researcher, "When we go home and get on the game, do we have to create a new account?" When the response was "Yes," she let out a loud gasp, and then asked many questions challenging why creating a new account was necessary. Cameron was the only participant to have such a substantial emotional reaction within the course of the study, and in truth, in our work in multiple schools. However, Cameron's anxiety about losing her accomplishments is not uncommon to gamers. Many gamers need to play games frequently in order to build up their game characters, so they become more powerful. To do this, gamers spend a lot of time and effort to achieve their gaming status and achieve accomplishments, and one mistake within a game may lead to a loss of earned resources and gamers' anxiety may grow as they progress to ever higher game levels (Bringula et al., 2015). This was clearly the case for Cameron and supports the claim that she saw *SURGE* as a game.

LAMIA "THE GEEK" PLAYED A "LEARNING GAME"

Lamia's case illustrates *a gamer who sees what she's doing as a learning game—* she appeared to immediately associate the task with school. Her discussion during the game illuminates Lamia's frustration and discontent with academic identity, and how it was at odds with her self-described gamer characteristics. In fact, Lamia described herself as a "geek" and elaborated her definition of "someone who isn't good at school but likes sci-fi." Lamia showed similar characteristics to the case studies who were less successful, as measured by our posttest, including a general frustration with the levels of the game and lack of enjoyment. While we contrast Lamia with Cameron because we claim that a game is an ecological experience, we don't posit that Lamia performed *badly*, or worse, in playing *SURGE*. Instead, the game was less successful *for Lamia*, and here, we reflect up why certain affordances weren't perceived and acted upon.

Lamia's experience depicts how someone who is a gamer might see an educational game as not a game at all, but associated with academics. When a person doesn't see herself as academically inclined, this may actually create frustration and impede both enjoyment and learning. In fact, Lamia labeled *SURGE* as a learning game multiple times, drawing a bold line between academics and play, articulating that *SURGE* was clearly NOT a game as players can't "quit" or "cheat." When asked what she would change the game as the designer, she suggested two solutions for her frustration:

> What I would change is, if you lose, after one time you lose, there's a superguide to do the whole thing for you! Or . . . I'd make, when you complete a level, there'd be a non-learning game, so somebody would look forward to completing it.

When the researcher asked what about *SURGE* made her think it was a learning game, she said, "The questions it tells you at the end of the level. The QUIZ questions!" Even here, she used academic language, calling the review questions "quiz" questions. When her friend suggested that it must be a learning game because they're required to do it, she agreed and elaborated on the idea:

> Yes, because school doesn't let us play any for real games. Plus, if I'm at home, and I can't pass a level, of ANYTHING, video games or any game in particular, Google is always helpful. Google. Type in the game, and cheat, and done. I'm awesome. And plus, when I get my laptop back, maybe this weekend, because of my good grades, I might be able to have my own laptop to where nobody can touch it. And I'll make sure to be good this time, and not have any social media websites.

Along with labeling *SURGE* as a learning game, she articulated her disengagement with school by labeling herself a "geek" but also made sure to distance that word from academic achievement. Toward the end of day 4, Lamia and her friends at her table arranged definitions and a hierarchy of geek/dork/nerd words as they played. She explained, "Geeks and dorks are completely different. Geeks are a lower level. No, actually a geek is higher, because that doesn't mean you're so good in school, that basically means you like sci-fi a lot." Later she reiterated the same idea, "Geek is the lowest class [the least stigmatized class]. That means—you just like sci-fi. You're not good at school, basically. Dweeb would be next. I would consider myself as a geek." Here, through her talk, Lamia discusses her identity as a game player and sci-fi fan alongside her academic identity. She places her own game play somewhat at odds with academic success and her own place as player. Next, when asked how she can tell how well she's doing (in the game), she said "If I keep failing." Here she was saying that failure (blowing up) on the screen was connected to low performance, but, oddly, she extended the explanation by associating the word "failing" in the game to academic failure, continuing, "'Cause now that I'm in 7th grade, I can't fail a single class."

Lamia's perceptions about both the game as a "learning" game and herself as a "geek" influenced how she played *SURGE*. Lamia's perception of the game as academic, and herself as disillusioned with school, may have influenced her perception of game affordances and her own choices about what to do. Given her frustration with the game, it is perhaps not surprising that Lamia's engagement ratings for *SURGE* were low, reporting that she didn't enjoy what she was doing, found it difficult, and did not feel capable of playing well. We suggest the experience was, in part, influenced by her disillusion with school and her perception of the task as academic in nature.

DO PLAYERS OF EDUCATIONAL GAMES
SEE A "GAME" OR "SCHOOL"?

Up to this point, we have presented the substantive differences between Cameron and Lamia with respect to their perceptions of the educational game they were playing, their talk, their enjoyment of the game, and ultimately, their learning. Given our discussion, it appears that players' perception of the game as academic (school-like) or playful (game-like) may influence game interactions, game engagement, and learning. For Lamia, perceiving the game as more school-like (and intertwined with her self-proclaimed "geek" identity) appeared to undermine enjoyment and subsequent learning of the game. But that is not to say that such a perception might be consistent for all students; Lamia perceived the game as being school-like and did not have a strong academic identity, which put success in the game at odds with her own stated identity. Of course, students who were affiliated with school and who perceived the game as school like might have had very different experience with and enjoyment of the game.

Expanding from Cameron and Lamia to look at other participants in the study, we examined how other players categorized *SURGE*, and how specific game affordances were linked to "games" or "school." On the second day of game play, case study students who were present were asked: "Does what you're doing feel more like a game or like school?"

Drawn from players' comments, the qualities or affordances that attune players to the game-like nature of *SURGE* are superficial qualities of the platform (i.e., "the fact that we're on a computer"), the look of the space, the storyline, but also its interactive nature. Participants defended its game-like qualities using phrases like it was "just fun," "you play," and there were "different concepts than you would see on a test." The things reported that make it more like school are its passive nature, and that it's telling information, but also that it includes intellectual work, because it "makes you think," is like a "brain teaser" and requires the process of "trying to figure it out." It asks questions of players and is an individual intellectual task because "you have to do it yourself." These users of *SURGE* saw what they were doing as a combination of these named affordances. We did refer to "the game" when framing the activity of *SURGE*, which may have influenced players' perception of context. At the same time, they were playing *SURGE* in their classroom, and game play was preceded by a somewhat traditional pretest.

The players who squarely saw a game after they were introduced to *SURGE* described how game play felt like figuring out a puzzle and contrasted the format of game play to books and worksheets, typical of school:

> A game . . . the spaceship, and the um . . . it kind of felt like a pattern. That's what it kind of feels like. It's like a pattern, when you know the number, you know what comes next.

> It really feels more like a game to me. The whole . . . presentation. It's not a book.

> Like a game, I guess. I guess the looks of it, and because you are on a laptop and not like in a workbook . . .

> The fact that it's on a computer and we're interacting with stuff [makes it count as a game]

While medium (being on a computer and not a workbook) seemed important for many players, another player, when asked what made *SURGE* feel like school, responded definitively, "the questions that it asks of me." The questions at the end of the warp levels appeared to signal school to this girl, and others, as well as contributing to a certain level of frustration, as these levels halted progress for many players until they reached the minimum warp score.

However, *most* players saw *SURGE* as a mixture of game and school, articulating what made it count as each.

> For me, it kind of feels like a mixture of both. It's a game, but it's sort of like school, in that you have to figure it out. And also because of the speed and such, it sort of ties into science. So, to me it's kind of a mixture. It's like science class in the form of a game . . . [researcher asks what makes it game like]. How you can control the ship . . . and kind of like the storyline, and what the missions, and what you're trying to do.

It's like a brain teaser, so it kind of ties in with school, but it's like a game that helps you with school, so it's kind of both . . . I think the school part of it is that you have to guess at which size or speed and which direction it's going, so that makes you think. And I think the game is like playing the computer game, and trying to have fun and get the thing to the other side.

Well, it's kind of somewhere in between, because it shows you the walkthrough videos, but you have to do it yourself. So, in that aspect it's more like school, but then it's just a game because, you know, it's a game, so it's different concepts than you would see on a test, so I'd probably say somewhere in between. The parts that made it more like a game was the detail. So, the ship is sort of like this, so you know where the things are based on—and it's in space, but there's no correlation to it, so it's more like a game.

The diversity in players' characterization of the game offers a compelling example of why the player must be considered in analyses of games, as a player's perception of the task matters, in conjunction with players' experience, both with the content of the game (in school or otherwise) and with gaming in general, seems likely to influence their attunement to elements of the game and the likelihood of them acting on those elements. Given this, it is necessary to consider multiple factors within the ecology of game play that impact player experience, two of these being (a) what the player perceives themselves as doing (e.g., school or a game), and (b) the player's perception related to what they're doing, impacted by previous attunement in either school or game play. One could imagine quadrants of possible players based on their perception of *SURGE* (or any game) as being a game or school and their affinity to games or school. We discussed two of those hypothetical quadrants here.

CONCLUSIONS

This analysis arose from a desire to better understand the role of the player in the ecology of game play. Although we were prepared, in our analyses, to look for and document the complexity and diversity of player experience, we did not initially anticipate the significant role that the perception of the task would play. More specifically, the framing that students brought to the experience appeared to significantly influence players' expectations and reactions during game play, and therefore their enjoyment and learning. Based on this analysis, we conjecture that the experience of an educational game is, in part, rooted in whether players see the task they're engaged as academic or playful. Here we present two players who identify as heavy gamers—though one sees the activity as a *real* game and one does not. Cameron represents a gamer who sees an educational game as a game and treats it as such in her interactions. The dedication and ease of interaction she may have from her game experience is leveraged in her educational gaming. Cameron had a relatively high learning gain after her play experience, and she rated that she enjoyed it as well. Contrasting this, Lamia presents a case of a gamer who is very vocal about her popular game experience and dedication to it, yet sees an educational game as simply a "learning game. " Lamia was less successful with *SURGE*, with respect to enjoying the game and learning from game play. Further, she appeared to experience a lot of frustration, and other than taking short breaks, was unable to use her typical gaming strategies of "quitting" and "cheats."

Drawing from the experiences of Cameron and Lamia, one overall conclusion may be that framing of an educational game is of great importance (as in the study of Lieberoth, 2014), as well as paying attention to how particular game mechanics might signal "school" or "game" to potential players. More and more teachers are using digital games in their teaching; a recent survey (Fishman, Riconscente, Snider, Tasi, & Plass, 2014) found that 57% of survey respondents used digital games in their classrooms at least once a week, and over 80% say they are moderately comfortable using games in their classrooms. Given this, the framing of educational games in an educational context is a legitimate topic for discussion, as well as how students' previous perceptions of games may impact their learning. Clearly, a classroom of students is not made up entirely of heavy gamers. Parallel to these two cases, players who see the game as primarily academic but who are academically successful and are able to apply their academic attunement to game play may learn and enjoy the experience. Lastly, someone who is academically successful but sees the activity as a game may become frustrated by the indirect and playful nature of educational game play (as opposed to a lecture or other direct instructional method; Squire, 2005).

LOOKING FORWARD

Games are not perceived and interacted with in the same way by any particular user because a game is not simply a set of static affordances—rather, it's an interactive ecological tool. The thesis of this chapter is that player experience is driven by more than simply superficial categories of player characteristics, including and especially ecological factors that relate player to game. Namely, we suggest that player perception of game affordances matter, but more ecological factors may be identified and understood. We do not claim that categorical player characteristics don't matter, but these might factor into the ecological experience: players of a particular gender or SES background might perceive game affordances in a particular way. These relationships must also be understood to intentionally design educational games for all learners. Further, the impact of context in which games are played must be further understood. Educational games balance along a fence of being *game-like* and (often) taking place *in school*. Additional work should look into how context frames both game play and learning. In other words, users of the same game might perceive different affordances within the game when interacting within a classroom or leisure context.

REFERENCES

Appel, M. (2012). Are heavy users of computer games and social media more computer literate?. *Computers & Education, 59*(4), 1339–1349.

Bahr, C. M., & Rieth, H. J. (1989). The effects of instructional computer games and drill and practice software on learning disabled students' mathematics achievement. *Computers in the Schools, 6*(3–4), 87–101.

Barab, S. A., Gresalfi, M. S., Dodge, T., & Ingram-Goble, A. (2010). Narratizing disciplines and disciplinizing narratives: Games as 21st century curriculum. *International Journal for Gaming and Computer Mediated Simulations, 2*(1) 17–30.

Bringula, R. P., Lugtu, K. P. M., & Aviles, A. D. (2015). "How do you feel?": Emotions exhibited while playing computer games and their relationship to gaming behaviors. *International Journal of Cyber Society and Education, 8*(1), 39–48.

Caleb, L. (2000). Design technology: Learning how girls learn best. *Equity & Excellance in Education, 33*(1), 22–25.

Chen, J. A., & Pajares, F. (2010). Implicit theories of ability of Grade 6 science students: Relation to epistemological beliefs and academic motivation and achievement in science. *Contemporary Educational Psychology, 35*(1), 75–87.

Christou, G. (2013). A comparison between experienced and inexperienced video game players' perceptions. *Human-Centric Computing and Information Sciences, 3*(15). doi:10.1186/2192-1962-3-15

Clark, D. B. (2011). *SURGE Fuzzy Chronicles*. Nashville, TN: Vanderbilt University. Retrieved from http://www.surgeuniverse.com/home/game/fuzzy-chronicles-1

Clark, D. B., Tanner-Smith, E. E., & Killingsworth, S. S. (2015). *Digital games, design, and learning: A systematic review and meta-analysis. Review of educational research.* Menlo Park, CA: SRI Education.

Cone, C. (2001). Technically speaking: Girls and computers. In P. O'Reilly, E. M., Penn, & K. de Marrais (Eds.), *Educating young adolescent girls* (pp. 171–187). Mahwah, NJ: Erlbaum.

DiSessa, A. A. (1993). Toward an epistemology of physics. *Cognition and instruction, 10*(2–3), 105–225.

Entwistle, N., & Tait, H. (1995). Approaches to studying and perceptions of the learning environment across disciplines. *New directions for teaching and learning, 1995*(64), 93–103.

Fishman, B., Snider, R., Riconscente, M., Tasi, T., & Plass J. L. (April, 2014). *How teachers use digital games for formative assessment: Exploring gaps between design and practice.* Poster presented at the Annual Meeting of the American Educational Research Association (AERA), Chicago, IL.

Gee, J. P. (2003). *What video games have to teach us about learning and literacy*. New York, NY: Palgrave Macmillan.

Gibson, J. J. (1986). *The ecological approach to visual perception*. Boston, MA: Houghton Mifflin.

Gresalfi, M. S. (2015). Designing to support critical engagement with statistics. *ZDM: The International Journal on Mathematics Education, 47*(6), 933–946.

Gresalfi, M. S., & Barnes, J. (2015). Designing feedback in an immersive video game: Supporting student mathematical engagement. *Educational Technology Research and Development, 64*(1), 65–86.

Gross, E. F. (2004). Adolescent Internet use: What we expect, what teens report. *Journal of Applied Developmental Psychology, 25*(6), 633–649.

Harteveld, C. (2011). *Triadic game design: Balancing reality, meaning and play*. London, England: Springer.

Ke, F. (2008). Computer games application within alternative classroom goal structures: Cognitive, metacognitive, and affective evaluation. *Educational Technology Research and Development, 56*, 18.

Lenhart, A., Kahne, J., Middaugh, E., Macgill, A. R., Evans, C., & Vitak, J. (2008). Teens, Video Games, and Civics. Pew Internet and American Life Project. PEW Internet & American Life Project.

Lieberoth, A. (2015). Shallow gamification testing psychological effects of framing an activity as a game. *Games and Culture, 10*(3), 229–248.

Lowyck, J., Elen, J., & Clarebout, G. (2004). Instructional conceptions: Analysis from an instructional design perspective. *International Journal of Educational Research, 41*(6), 429–444.

Lucas, K., & Sherry, J. L. (2004). Sex differences in video game play: A communication-based explanation. *Communication research, 31*(5), 499–523.

Marsh, J. (2011). Young children's literacy practices in a virtual world: Establishing an online interaction order. *Reading Research Quarterly, 46*(2), 101–118.

Mäyrä, F. (2007). The contextual game experience: On the socio-cultural contexts for meaning in digital play. In *Proceedings of DiGRA 2007* (pp. 810–814). Tokyo, Japan: DiGRA.

Nacke, L., Drachen, A., Kuikkaniemi, K., Niesenhaus, J., Korhonen, H. J., Hoogen, W. M., . . . & De Kort, Y. A. (2009). Playability and player experience research. In *Proceedings of DiGRA 2009: Breaking New Ground: Innovation in Games, Play, Practice and Theory*. London, UK.

Orvis, K. A., Horn, D. B., & Belanich, J. (2008). The roles of task difficulty and prior videogame experience on performance and motivation in instructional videogames. *Computers in Human behavior, 24*(5), 2415–2433.

Passig, D., & Levin, H. (2000). Gender preferences for multimedia interfaces. *Journal of Computer Assisted Learning, 16*(1), 64–71.

Salomon, G. (1984). Television is "easy"' and print is "tough": The differential investment of mental effort in learning as a function of perceptions and attributions. *Journal of Educational Psychology, 76*(4), 647–658.

Shuell, T. J., & Farber, S. L. (2001). Students' perceptions of technology use in college courses. *Journal of Educational Computing Research, 24*(2), 119–138.

Steeves, V., & Kerr, I. R. (2005). Virtual playgrounds and buddybots: A data-minefield for tweens. *Canadian Journal of Law & Technology, 4*(2), 91–105.

Squire, K. D. (2003) Videogames in education. *International Journal of Intelligent Games & Simulation, 2*(1).

Squire, K. (2005). Changing the game: What happens when video games enter the classroom. *Innovate: Journal of Online Education, 1*(6).

Squire, K., Barnett, M., Grant, J., & Higgenbotham, T. (2004). Electromagnetism supercharged! In *Proceedings of the 2004 International Conference of the Learning Sciences* (pp. 513–520).

Squire, K. D., & Jan, M. (2007). Mad city mystery: Developing scientific argumentation skills with a place-based augmented reality game on handheld computers. *Journal of Science Education and Technology, 16*, 5–29.

Tawfik, A., He, Z., & Vo, N. (2009, December). Impact of video game experience and gender differences in educational video games. In *Pervasive Computing (JCPC)*, 2009 Joint Conferences on (pp. 715–720). IEEE.

Vandercruysse, S., Vandewaetere, M., Cornillie, F., & Clarebout, G. (2013). Competition and students' perceptions in a game-based language learning environment. *Educational Technology Research and Development, 61*(6), 927–950.

van Eck, R., & Dempsey, J. (2002). The effect of competition and contextualized advisement on the transfer of mathematics skills in a computer-based instructional simulation game. *Educational Technology Research and Development, 50*, 23–41.

Volman, M., & van Eck, E. (2001). Gender equity and information technology in education: The second decade. *Review of educational research, 71*(4), 613–634.

CHAPTER 6

ASK NOT WHAT YOU CAN DO FOR BADGES; ASK WHAT BADGES CAN DO FOR YOU

Peter Samuelson Wardrip
Children's Museum of Pittsburgh

Samuel Abramovich
University at Buffalo–SUNY

Two of the most important pedagogical goals for teachers looking to develop high-quality instruction and improve student learning experiences are (a) increased student engagement and (b) the use of data to address student learning needs on-the-fly and in real-time (Ball & Forzani, 2009; Grossman, Hammerness & McDonald, 2009; Windschitl, Thompson, Braaten, & Stroupe, 2012). One way to reach them is to develop assessments (Wiliam, Lee, Harrison, & Black, 2004) that are both engaging and instructionally informative (Cooper, 2014). By engagement, we mean the extent to which a learner is attentive, interested, and curious during a learning activity in school (Fredricks, Blumenfeld, & Paris, 2004). Traditional school grades (e.g., A+, B–, C+, F) are quality assessments; a teacher can use grades as an assessment that will increase student engagement by providing recognition

Exploding the Castle, pages 117–137
Copyright © 2017 by Information Age Publishing
All rights of reproduction in any form reserved.

(e.g., an A on a report card). Assessments can also generate formative and summative feedback that informs the learners on what they still need to learn while also providing data that a teacher can act upon. For example, a quiz can let both a student and the teacher know if the learning goal has been achieved or if additional instruction is necessary. Frederiksen and Collins (1989) referred to this as an element of "transparency" for the learning and assessment process.

Advocates of *digital badges*—one subset of game-based assessment tools—suggest that they function as evaluative measures capable of supporting learner engagement and enabling data-informed instruction beyond traditional quizzes, tests, and homework (Wardrip, Abramovich, Kim, & Bathgate, 2016). Assessment research reinforces this suggestion, with badges appearing to motivate learners through specific badge-driven learning experiences (Casilli & Hickey, 2016; Finkelstein, Knight, & Manning, 2013) and increase student engagement by recognizing learners for demonstrating mastery of some skill or knowledge (i.e., students earn badges for displays of proficiency or growth). Digital badges also offer instructors the opportunity to curate robust records of learner growth and accomplishment, providing reference information that can later be used to craft individualized learning trajectories or pathways toward future learning goals (Finkelstein et al., 2013). Traditional assessments, by contrast, do not typically motivate or act as robust records of growth or proficiency.

But, even in the presence of digital badge-enabled resources, good teachers tend to utilize *non*-badge assessments to generate data and engage some students (Anthony, Hunter, & Hunter, 2015). One possible reason is that digital badge usefulness is limited by the quality of student engagement and growth/proficiency data a badge or badge system can yield (i.e., "Do badges yield higher quality outcomes than existing systems?"). This is why determining whether or not a given technology—badge or otherwise—can facilitate engagement or lead to actionable data is challenging at best (Cuban, 1990): Even if badges have the potential to engage students or more effectively generate data than other types of gamification, there remain substantial confounds to empirically verifying their broader value (e.g., environment, teacher skill, prior knowledge, student preference; see Chapter 12—"The Inevitability of Epic Fail: Exploding the Castle with Situated Learning").

To address this dilemma, we suggest researchers and developers apply a more situated cognition-oriented lens to their work—that is, treating digital badges as means to explore how particular objectives can influence individual learning within particular educational contexts (formal or informal). This isn't a wholly new idea: Evidence suggests that beyond supporting learner motivation (Abramovich, Higashi, Hunkele, Schunn, & Shoop, 2011; Abramovich, Schunn, & Higashi, 2013; Abramovich & Wardrip, 2016; McDaniel & Fanfarelli, 2016; Reid, Paster, & Abramovich, 2015; Wardrip,

Abramovich, Bathgate, & Kim, in press; Yang, Quadir, & Chen, 2015) and capturing evidence of learning (Casilli & Hickey, 2016; O'Byrne, Schenke, Willis, & Hickey, 2015; Wardrip et al., 2016), badges generate new opportunities to study how motivation and instructional feedback interact *in situ*. Because they can be designed to match a particular learning opportunity or the needs of a particular learner, they function as a highly granular motivator and record of meaningfully authentic experience. Researchers can examine artifacts like these to better understand if and what learning has occurred, implying that the educational value of a digital badge comes not from asking what a learner can do for a badge but instead what a digital badge can do for the study of individualized motivation and data-informed instruction.

To illustrate the types of research and instruction opportunities afforded through badge use, we will spend the first portion of this chapter summarizing emergent theory and research on digital badges—this will ground our situated cognition argument by establishing how badges can and should function in dynamic instructional contexts. Then, we will share results from two studies of a badge implementation that created research opportunities for studying motivation and feedback, specifically. We will conclude with implications and next steps for researchers who see badges as a resource for more in-depth studies of human thinking and learning. While the ideas presented herein may seem like simple advocacy for badge development and implementation, we believe them to be much more: a cautious (but optimistic) statement about the way digital badges can enhance our collective ability to understand learning phenomena under particular environmental and individual constraints.

A BIT OF BACKGROUND

Before addressing how digital badges can support the study of motivation and data-informed instruction, we first provide some background on digital badges for learning. In general, they are defined as "a symbol or indicator of an accomplishment, skill, quality or interest" (Mozilla & P2PU, 2011, p. 3). They "represent skills, interests, and achievements earned by an individual through specific projects, programs, courses, or other activities" (Mozilla, 2013, p. 2) and often function as public representations of what someone has learned, accomplished, and experienced (Plori, Carley, & Foex, 2007). For this reason, a badge's value as a visual representation of growth or proficiency boils down to whether and how the badge is visible to others through an online social networking portal or some other platform.

Of course, badges and badging are not a new construct—medals signifying a soldier's experience and accomplishments have been used in the military for centuries (Halavais, 2012; Ostashewski & Reid, 2015). Most contemporary badge literature characterizes badges as digital or inhabiting digital spaces, but we know they can also have tangible, real-world counterparts (Halavais, 2012). One of the most common referents for badges are the physical merit badges awarded to members of the major American scouting associations, the Boy Scouts of America and the Girl Scouts of America. These merit badges are regarded as proficiency markers in aviation, cooking, computer programming, and more, and they are granted only after boys and girls have engaged in particular demonstrations of skill or knowledge. While there may not appear to be noteworthy differences between digital and physical badges, the extent to which a digital badge can be "information rich" with data cataloguing the badge-earner's experience, expertise, interests, and accomplishments is worth considering (Casilli & Hickey, 2016; O'Byrne et al., 2015). Said information can provide the badge's audience (e.g., teachers, prospective employers, supervisors, friends, family) with a clearer context of the badge earners' learning endeavors, including time frames, instructors, or especially interesting activities and outcomes.

WHAT ARE DIGITAL BADGES GOOD FOR?

While digital badges have their roots in recording accomplishments and experiences, some designers and researchers view digital badges as an educational technology that can facilitate motivation. From a behaviorist perspective, badges are generally designed to serve as external motivators. For example, in creating an achievement system to accompany a photo-sharing web application, Montola, Nummenmaa, Lucero, Boberg, and Korhonen (2009) defined badges as a "secondary reward systems that have been developed for digital games" (p. 94). These rewards represent deeper levels of engagement and experience as more badges are earned (De Paoli, De Uffici, & D'Andrea, 2012) and scaffold user movement/behavior in the virtual environment. Assuming users find value in earning digital badges, the virtual environment effectively becomes a perpetual motivation machine (i.e., regularly offering new badge-earning opportunities that are aligned with particular behavioral learning objectives).

If this setup sounds familiar, it is because it's one of the more popular ways to develop and utilize badges: *gamification*. Organized in the form of achievements (e.g., Microsoft's XBox Network) or trophies (e.g., Sony's PlayStation Network), gamification runs parallel to gameplay (Deterding, Sicart, Nacke, O'Hara, & Dixon, 2011; Zichermann & Cunningham, 2011) and is defined as the application of game mechanics and other elements of game design to nongame situations (McGonigal, 2011). Although all game mechanics are designed to elicit a particular user response, gamification uses specific elements of a game (e.g., points, in-game activities) to enhance the human reaction (e.g., motivation, fun, patience) that would be elicited through play alone. In this context, badges shape the way a particular learner *interacts* with a particular game (or educational) goal.

But gamification is not the only design option. As badge advocates have suggested throughout the last decade, there are a variety of other reasons and ways to use badges in classroom, museum, and home environments (Barker, 2013). They can provide a more detailed view of what the badge recipient has learned (compared to traditional report cards and diplomas), and they can signify learning in informal instructional environments (Selingo, 2012). Antin and Churchill (2011) refined these powerful (if somewhat vague) badge affordances into five highly specific badge functions to support optimal clarity and granularity in outcome data (i.e., transparency in credentials; Goligoski, 2012). These include: (a) goal setting, (b) instruction, (c) reputation, (d) group identification, and (e) status/affirmation. Below, we explore each role and establish its relevance to game-based instruction.

The first, *goal setting*, refers to mileposts that can be set for learners or participants as they proceed. Perhaps an intuitive aspect of badges, identifiable goals motivate and impact learner effort within a learning activity (Belenky & Nokes-Malach, 2012; Elliott, 1999). Achievement goal theory (Elliot, 1999; Elliot, Shell, Henry, & Maier, 2005) proposes that goals can influence a learner's engagement in an activity by the extent to which they seek to perform or master a skill, or the extent to which they avoid performing or demonstrating underperformance. For example, a scout may seek to earn a programming badge as a means to master a particular programming language, while another scout may avoid that badge because he does not want to show how little he knows about programming. Goals, in this context, refer to design features of computer-based learning environments that assume users can and will learn through participating in activities designed to help them reach a given benchmark or outcome (Schank, 1994; Schank, Fano, Bell, & Jona, 1994). This is where our situated cognition lens comes in handy: Goals and motivators are elements of one's context that are foregrounded or backgrounded depending on their importance and relevance to the learner (Nolen, Horn, & Ward, 2015). Although learners may not seek to fulfill educational goals on their own (if, for instance, those goals don't align with the learner's individual intentions), the capacity to earn badges has the potential to *induce* goal adoption and thus bridge the gap between learners, instructors, and content, ultimately making instruction more effective.

Instruction refers to the way developers and instructors use badges to define content value within a given context. Zimmerman (2004) referrs to such instruction parameters examples of "operational rules" or "completion logic" that delineates player goals—for example, using badges (or "achievements," as they are often called in games) to highlight specific features, mechanics, or pathways within a system (Montola et al., 2009). Likewise, as badges can point participants to different aspects of a learning, work, or recreational activity, they can be used to highlight and/or affirm different roles that participants can adopt within a given system or learning experience. One analysis of Barnstars—the Wikipedia badging system—revealed that digital badges granted on the site's back-end encouraged users to go beyond simple editing by inducing adoption of specific goals related to the site's social support and administrative tasks (Kriplean, Beschastnikh, & McDonald, 2008). This reaffirms the notion that badges can potentially lead users toward designer-preferred behavior (i.e., participation in activities or trajectories with high community value) and influence them to complete the unappealing but necessary work of site/community moderation.

Reputation, in badging terms, refers to the ways in which badges can capture badge earners' interests, experiences, and skills. In the Boy Scouts, badges serve not only as a public symbol of what a scout has done but also the badge earner's relative level of expertise (e.g., number of badges related to outdoor skills) and their relative level of engagement in Boy Scout-related activity (e.g., total number of badges earned). In game contexts, the number and quality of earned achievements is largely considered representative of ability—the more achievements earned and the higher quality they are, the more likely a player is proficient at particular kinds of game-related tasks (i.e., earning more badges reinforces a player's skill, begets new extra-game rewards, and earns the player an elite reputation within the community). Importantly, not all achievements need be displayed the same way or at the same time—badge earners often enjoy and see social benefit from cultivating personalized images of themselves using achievement-linked badges. *Team Fortress 2* players, for instance, showcase achievement by dressing their avatars in special clothing (e.g., hats) that represent fulfillment of certain skill-based objectives (Bjork & Holopainen, 2005; Moore, 2011). *Hearthstone* players similarly use special card backs to display in-game achievements to friends and opponents (e.g., finishing challenging heroic adventures, reaching legendary status in ranked play).

Group identification refers to the way badges can be used to define membership within a given community. For the Boy Scouts, merit badges are emblematic of scout affiliation and recognizable to both in- and out-group observers. They create a sense of solidarity among group members and define a shared set of community standards (Antin & Churchill, 2011). Gold and platinum trophies earned in video games like *Dark Souls* are similar insofar as they represent community membership, although the relative value assigned by out-group observers is different than it is for the Boy Scouts (simply by virtue of the communities' respective structures; i.e., a formal institution vs. a loose congregation of individuals sharing a common interest). Together, the two illustrate the symbolic power of badges to convey potentially substantial or complex information about an individual's background and experience through simple (digital or physical) iconography.

Finally, *status/affirmation* refers to a badge's perceived value among badge earners, grantors, and surrounding community members. Generally speaking, greater status is apportioned to individuals with higher numbers of badges or who have earned especially difficult-to-earn badges (Antin & Churchill, 2011). Accumulation across a wide area of content or skillsets positively affirms the earner's growth, proficiency, and experience over time, not unlike a collection of trophies that serve as a reminder of one's past accomplishments.

Unlike other portions of Antin and Churchill's badge framework, however, status/affirmation combines multiple variables (i.e., status, affirmation, and reputation) into a general concept of *recognition*. If badges serve as recognition for prior accomplishments, then that recognition is a kind of credentialing currency (Mozilla, 2011). This is useful with respect to underresearched microskills that are seldom captured by "blunt" credentials like educational degrees, transcripts, or certificate programs. For instance, Stackoverflow—a website that facilitates question-and-answer interactions between professional and amateur computer programmers—allows users to participate as questioners, answerers, and/or moderators. In these roles, they develop a reputation score that provides (a) a shorthand estimate for a questioner's/answerer's programming expertise and (b) a means of tracking relative user reliability within the Stackoverflow community. Not only does this highlight microskills that might be overlooked in a traditional educational environment, but it provides a measurement that can be easily understood by external observers (Gibson, Ostashewski, Flintoff, Grant, & Knight, 2013). Put another way, badges make complex, rhetorically useful constructs like collaboration and playfulness quantifiable (Wardrip et al., in press) and—depending on the granting organization—can signify earner credibility to parents, administrators, potential employers, or others (Hickey, Itow, Rehak, Schenke, & Tran, 2013).

The degree to which Antin and Churchill's (2011) five functions support student learning is now the biggest question badge research seeks to answer, and the investigation has not been entirely smooth thus far. Whether or not badge earning should be optional is an area of contention, with little empirical research suggesting that either option is more effective than the other (although, as Hamari and Eranti [2011] argued, badging makes the most sense as an optional activity given that participants tend to have divergent goals and prefer agency over forced action). There is a similar dearth of information about the way badges affect knowledge and behavior in the social spaces that surround them (the "meta" metagame). If we are not careful to think multilaterally about the way badges are studied, gaps in knowledge may ultimately make or break them as an educational innovation.

One way to improve our approach is to think of badges as a unique educational technology that can be deployed in communities that struggle to understand or lack high-bandwidth access to online environments. Like email and the Internet in general, the infrastructure underpinning badge use is remarkably open and simplistic—enough so that any determined user with basic access to the web (say, through a mobile device) could create and award his or her own badges. The website Credly, for example, uses Mozilla's open badge framework to support the creation and distribution of personalized badges. This openness allows educators to issue badges as motivators, a means of highlighting a specific learning trajectory, or as a mark of proficiency in any formal or informal learning environment. Likewise, it simplifies assessment procedures (used in conjunction with rubrics) and encourages reflection on when and how to provide feedback.

Badging is currently the only assessment technology capable of achieving near-universal access and the ability to generate data-rich evidence of growth and performance. Teachers can issue badges for learning that occurs in a classroom; parents can issue them for learning at home; and religious leaders, coaches, and social assistance programs can issue them for learning in their respective domains. Because badges can be issued by anyone for any purpose, they effectively democratize assessment. What was once the province of just formal educational organizations now belongs to anyone with the need to engage, provide feedback, and credential.

BADGES WITHIN IN A LEARNING CONTEXT

Because digital badges are readily available to so many learners and educators across a variety of settings and platforms, we contend that they hold unique potential to inform our understanding about motivation and its role within complex systems. Here, complex systems refer to classrooms, museums, businesses, hospitals, and other institutions wherein learning opportunities are intertwined with individual learner engagement, social interaction, and the historical, intellectual, and material resources available as part of the learning space (Greeno, 1998). Being a scalable, low-cost assessment tool, badging is one of the few ways researchers can get a realistic picture of how such factors interact to generate engagement, learning, and achievement in context.

This, of course, does not change the fact that a substantial amount of badge research conducted thus far (including studies cited in this chapter) tends to oversimplify badging, largely treating it as a single variable that exists in a vacuum instead of one piece of a much more complicated puzzle. That is why the remainder of this chapter focuses on studies of interactivity between badges, earners, grantors, and community dynamics. Here, we hope to draw a line between what others have done and what we believe must be done in order for badging to work (instructionally) as part of any learning ecosystem.

Before getting ahead of ourselves, we should briefly address the relevant assumptions about our situated badging perspective (specifically as they relate to tools of assessment). First, we assume that the context and activities in which people learn are fundamental to what they learn (Greeno, Collins, & Resnick, 1996). Second, digital badges interact with the learner (and vice versa) as part of the learning process. For example, badging systems can be organized to let individuals choose badges they want to earn and amass learning artifacts that demonstrate proficiency of a badge-related skill OR design badges of their own (aligned with learning goals) that they can work toward at their own pace. This makes agency—the extent to which a learner is empowered to act as they wish—an integral part of the learning environment (Greeno, 2006). Finally, digital badges blur the line between *assessment* and *learning* (Hickey, 2015) by defining one's community membership as a function of one's demonstrable knowledge and skills (Greeno, 2003; Lave & Wenger, 1991).

As you will see in the coming section, these assumptions are part and parcel of badge scalability and integration. While it might be possible to work around them, doing so can only serve to narrow our understanding of how and why badging works—or doesn't—at the individual learner and learning environment level.

BADGES AS A MEANS OF UNDERSTANDING LEARNING

The majority of literature on digital badges for learning argues that the primary reason instructors should implement badges is to enhance the learning experience. This can mean providing new and different goals for learners to engage with or simply using badges to measure long-term learner growth. Badges, after all, are known to give learners a reason to persist in their efforts, and they provide rich information about what students have accomplished in the past. Such data visualization makes it easier for students to recognize when they have "levelled up" at the edge of their zones of proximal development, and it enables them to move toward higher-level learning goals that better align with their advancing skills and knowledge.

It is this multithreaded, spiraling functionality that makes badging a valuable tool for studying the role of motivation and data-informed instruction on the learning process. Viewing badges as part of a broader context, we begin to see how an individual learner's motives within that context are distributed across other learners, resources, and even the badges themselves.

A TALE OF TWO STUDIES

The badge program we describe below—a case study in badging—was implemented at a small, Jewish school serving kindergarten through grade 8 students in the southeastern United States. The program grew out of a collaborative effort between the school's teachers, students, administrators, and an educational nonprofit looking to support the development of knowledge and skills for 21st century participatory culture (Jenkins, Purushotma, Weigel, Clinton, & Robison, 2009). During the two years that we followed this school's work, students were given the option to earn one of several different badges across multiple domains, including information literacy, collaboration, acceptance, and empowered learning. In accordance with the school's core mission, each of the badges was aligned with a distinct aspect of Jewish cultural identity.

The objectives used to define the badging system targeted specific skills that (a) could facilitate learning in both *formal* and *informal* learning environments and (b) improve the likelihood of long-term success in various 21st-century educational and career paths. Because badge-aligned objectives were not traditionally part of the school's formal curricula, they were seldom accompanied by any type of traditional assessment (e.g., quizzes, tests). The badging program addressed this issue by clarifying student learning goals and making it easier for students, teachers, parents, and administrators to track student growth and proficiency across domains.

Participation was entirely voluntary, and no grades or other traditional assessments were tied to performance in the badging system. Individuals choosing to participate were tasked with selecting a goal (i.e., a particular badge they wanted to earn) and, over a period of months, complete three distinct learning activities related to the chosen badge: Recognize It, Talk About It, and Do It. With badges being chosen in the late fall/early winter and the program running through the end of the school year, students had roughly six months to document evidence of their learning (and thus earn their target badge).

The Recognize It learning activity required students to outline their understanding of specific knowledge and skills associated with the badge they had selected. Once it was clear they understood the learning objective, the Talk About It activity required students to provide evidence of content fluency based on their ability to successfully communicate about badge-related knowledge and skills. Finally, as part of the Do It activity, students were asked to compile digital artifacts evidencing badge-related knowledge and skill mastery.

The school's teachers served as the primary arbiters of evidence quality and were responsible for judging whether or not a student had "passed" each badge phase. To maintain alignment in evaluative decision making, they received professional development seminars run by an external provider with the support of lead teachers (this leveled the playing field with respect to how badges work and the way they would be implemented at this school, specifically). Additional monthly meetings were scheduled so participating teachers could request support as needed, and, as a matter of gauging artifact quality (and thus determining who had successfully earned their badges), participating students were expected to schedule meetings with their teachers to review submitted artifacts and badge-specific rubrics (see Appendix).[1]

Upon completing each of their three badge-related learning activities (i.e., Recognize It, Talk About It, Do It), students were rewarded with special events and tangible emblems of mastery. These included ceremonies where individual student experts would receive a wearable version of their badge, nontangible in-school privileges such as unsupervised computer time or the ability to leave class to work on another badge activity, and out-of-school privileges like badge-related fieldtrips. The student-submitted artifacts of learning used to assess mastery were stored in digital archives for students, parent, and teachers to review as desired.

Over the course of two years of program implementation, we interviewed participating educators and students, collected artifacts, and surveyed participating students. The resultant data have us thinking about two overarching questions:

- What, exactly, is the relationship between student motivation and assessment with respect to participatory skills?
- Does the use of a badge-based assessment system influence teachers' instructional practices?

BADGES AS A MEANS OF UNDERSTANDING MOTIVATION

By investigating learner motivation via engagement in a digital badging system, we managed to surface some key points. First, badge rhetoric—namely, arguing that badges are a reliable motivator—needs to be much more nuanced. The way individual learners perceive and value badges is highly personal, meaning that designed experiences (i.e., those leading to badge earning) can and will only motivate some students, not all. Second, despite the fact that badges are often referred to as a "rewards" system, the badging system we studied featured badges as much more than a reward. Rather, the system was built to add several theoretical and practical dimensions to the learning environment beyond behavioral reinforcement. For example, students frequently cited nonreward learning opportunities they found interesting and engaging when discussing their motivations for participation (e.g., independence recognition, values, personal connection). These dimensions theoretically link to two subcategories of self-determination theory: expectancy value theory and cognitive evaluation theory (see Wardrip et al., in press).

In Table 6.1, we indicate five dimensions emergent from our data that relate to student interest and participation in the badging system. The evidence column provides summary statements drawn from student and teacher interview responses. One noteworthy aspect of these findings is that—despite the program specifically emphasizing badge earning—student responses suggest the designed system successfully influenced student reflection on nonbadge concepts. These include ways in which participation held some personal relevance, recognition of the activity's (relative) novelty, and how multiple technologies can be integrated with an educational badging system (giving us a deeper look into teacher–student interaction and student motivation as it relates to badge-aligned activities).

TABLE 6.1 Relationship of Students' Interests and Badge Participation	
Aspect of Interest	**Evidence Within the SBBS**
Enjoyment and Independence	1. Students perceived badges as fun. 2. Students liked having choices in terms of the type and level of their participation.
Recognition	1. Students indicated a preference for badge-based recognition for work that extended beyond their typical academic activities.
Values	1. The novelty of the SBBS was attractive to the students. 2. The learning associated with earning a badge was seen as beneficial to short- and long-term goals.
Personal Connection	1. The SBBS allowed for students to connect out-of-school activities with their academic pursuits. 2. Students chose badges that had personal relevance. 3. Student earned badges through methods that were selected based on appeal.
Rewards	1. Students valued rewards for earning badges based on the direct appeal of the reward. 2. Students indicated appeal of school-based and out-of-school benefits.

BADGES AS A MEANS OF UNDERSTANDING
DATA-INFORMED INSTRUCTION

Beyond student participation and motivation, we looked at the second part of this investigation as an opportunity to explore teacher pedagogy in badge-supported learning environments. That meant evaluating evidence of student performance/achievement and how teachers use such information to inform their instructional practice.

The data revealed two interesting trends. First, although the school had a relatively small student population, the corresponding student–teacher ratio made it easier for teachers to build relationships with their students and learn new, potentially useful information about how they navigate the learning process. Second, teachers tended to modify their instruction to incorporate newfound knowledge of individual student strengths (e.g., creative talents), difficulties (e.g., struggles with specific content or ways of thinking), and interests (e.g., *Doctor Who*). This may not be surprising given that best practice generally involves gathering and applying formative assessment data to improve pedagogy, but it's quite common for assessment researchers to assume instructional changes are a consequence of standardized assessment data, attendance records, and written evaluations (e.g., report cards) rather than student–teacher interaction (i.e., a teacher understanding his or her students' backgrounds and the way they frame their individual goals). That is, personal student information is rarely considered part of the data corpus in data-driven instruction literature (e.g., Marsh, 2012) even though statements from and the behavior of teachers in our study suggest badge-based student data gives teachers a means of better understanding students as individuals.

The benefits of knowing individual student strengths, goals, and challenges seem obvious given the amount of communication and contact time we expect of students and teachers, but participating teachers emphasized how competing goals sometimes caused them to overlook individualized student details. Focusing on and engaging with student interests allowed them to make better curricular choices like—for example—introducing a Dalek Project graphic novel to engage a reluctant reader. In other classrooms, knowledge of student strengths helped teachers recognize and position particular students as skill leaders. One educator in particular spoke to the benefits of knowing which students are most tech-savvy (for the purposes of resolving technological issues during class time). For us, this reaffirms the importance of continually seeking information and, accordingly, refining instruction. Data enable us to make better decisions, and the better informed our decision making, the higher the likelihood of improved instruction. We can see examples of this in Table 6.2.

TABLE 6.2   Digital Badge System Impacts on Instruction

Badge Informed Instructional Practice	Examples
Teachers learned new aspects about students through the badging system.	Students' interests, students' strengths, students' difficulties, facts about students' lives outside of school
Teachers adapted instruction based on what they learned about the students.	Teachers adapted curricular choices or positioned students as help

We want to stress that findings from this portion of the study are less about how digital badge systems (as a technology) intersect and potentially support instruction than how new kinds of student data can and do shape practicing educator pedagogy. In some cases, data may be closely aligned to what the teacher expects (e.g., a student working toward the informational literacy badge may demonstrate an interest and competence with computers), but in others, the teacher may get a chance to learn about a student's favorite television show, what synagogue she attends, or that he plays soccer every Tuesday and Thursday. This gives teachers a new way to connect with and engage learners, and it gives us—the research community—a new way to track how knowledge emerges in student–teacher interactions, whether or not the information learned is considered relevant by the teacher, and if/how teachers modify their instructional practice based on student–teacher interaction (i.e., how they interpret the new information and if/how its incorporated into regular instruction).

IMPLICATIONS

Since the rise of gamification in the mid-2000s, digital badges have received a fair amount of attention. Some badge advocates have sought to emphasize ways in which digital badges may support engagement, learning, and the communication of competence for learners across settings. Others, like ourselves, have sought to leverage digital badging systems as the foundation for new research directions, explained below.

The utilization of badging systems to further our understanding of human thinking and learning is an intended shift from the way educational technologies are usually treated in a learning environment. After all, tools already exist to assist teachers with student assessment and evaluation (Heffernan & Koedinger, 2012; Pellegrino & Quellmalz, 2010). But digital badging systems are an inquiry-based resource for teachers, enabling them to dig into how and why their students engage with schoolwork (or don't) in the first place. They position students to engage with domain content in novel, in-depth ways (i.e., a deep, inquiry-driven dive). And they position researchers to do granular studies of motivation, learner goal fulfillment, and so-called "breach experiments"—perturbations of the daily, lived experience of research participants (sometimes unwitting) that disorient them to a point where an active reset of their rhythms and expectations of daily experience becomes necessary (Garfinkel, 1967).[2]

As Crabtree (2004a) argued,

> [We] have seen the emergence of a range of technological innovations that have little or no grounding in existing practice. Instead, these technologies create entirely new possibilities, but practices for their use have yet to emerge. How, then, are disciplines that take practice as their object of inquiry and study to proceed in the *absence* of practice and, furthermore, to support innovation in design? (p. 1)

Crabtree's proposed solution is "treating technological innovations in an experimental fashion" (p. 59)—that is, use technological innovations like badge systems to help participants codify their desires and expectations through organic detection of technology affordances and purposing of those affordances toward sensible ends (i.e., learners perceiving a tool, recognizing its affordances for action, and acting upon those affordances to alter or maintain a given learner–technology–environment interaction state). This is why we advise a long-term situated cognition framework for badge design: The relationship between motivation and learning is defined by our understanding of individual intentions and goal adoption. There's a distinct difference between student motivation to *engage* in an activity and student motivation to *learn* within an activity (Edelson & Joseph, 2004)—it's our job to identify where one interaction state ends and the other begins.

We should add that as the badge community benefits from a situated cognition framework, so too does the situated cognition community benefit from continued exploration of digital badging systems. The bidirectional link between badges and ecological psychology offers a rare opportunity to integrate individualized data from multiple, disparate sources by connecting badging systems with other data sources currently in use among K–12 and institutions of higher learning. Interoperability of data systems has been a significant goal of school improvement efforts (Collins & Fruth, 2007; Fox, Schaffhauser, Fletcher, & Levin, 2013), and we see this as one area—of potentially many—where situated cognitivists and game designers could benefit from collaboration.

CONCLUSION

As research moves forward, digital badging not only gives us the opportunity to explore motivation within a context of distributed resources and social practices but also facilitates potential changes within that context. Design experiments that use digital badges as a target for iterative revision may help the field refine explanatory theories of motivation in context. Rather than treating digital badges as an isolated variable (as many of the studies cited throughout this chapter), experimental designs can target the coconstitutive nature of motivation, context, and personal connections that beget different levels of engagement. In other words, taking a situated cognition perspective on badging can help us understand how individual motives for learning emerge across people, programs, and contexts.

We end by reiterating our belief that digital badging represents a unique opportunity for games researchers and learning scientists alike. As stated previously, we approach badges with cautious optimism for what they might add to the field in terms of improving assessment and increasing engagement. There is potential in the study of digital badging systems—We just need to remember it is not about what we can do for them, but what they can do for us.

APPENDIX 6.1 Sample Rubric—The Sergey Brin Information Literacy Badge

	Exemplary Performance	Proficient Performance	Partially Proficient Performance	Poor Performance
Recognize It Phase	Clearly and consistently recognizes the skill when it is enacted. Can accurately differentiate between high and low skill levels and between this and other skills.	Often recognizes the skill when it is enacted. Occasionally differentiates between high and low skill levels.	Sometimes recognizes the skill when it is enacted. Occasionally differentiates between high and low skill levels.	Does not recognize the skill when it is enacted. Cannot differentiate between high and low skill levels.
Talk About It Phase	Accurately talks about the skill. Can state multiple examples of when it is enacted. Articulates importance or value of the skill.	Accurately talks about the skill. Can state examples of when it is enacted.	Can talk about the skill in a basic way, sometimes inaccurately. Provides weak examples of when it is enacted.	Cannot talk about or abstract the skill. Fails to state examples of when it is enacted.
Do It Phase	Clearly identifies what information is needed to address research questions. Intentionally uses and modifies search strategies that yield relevant information. Evaluates quality of sources for credibility and effectively selects credible sources. Gathers sources and information highly pertinent to research questions. Creatively designs an original product organizing and presenting information from multiple sources. Synthesizes content from multiple sources to make larger arguments.	Identifies most of the information needed to address research questions. Uses and sometimes modifies search strategies that yield somewhat relevant information. Sometimes evaluates quality of sources for credibility and somewhat effectively selects credible sources. Gathers sources and information mostly pertinent to research questions. Designs a product organizing and presenting information adequately. Synthesizes multiple sources to support argument.	Identifies few of the pieces of information needed to address research questions. Uses search strategies that yield little relevant information. Rarely evaluates the quality of sources and does not effectively select credible sources. Gathers sources and information with little relevance to research questions. Designs a basic product that poorly conveys content. Rarely integrates multiple sources into argument.	Fails to identify what information is needed to address research questions. Uses search strategies that yield no relevant information. Never evaluates the quality of sources and often uses inaccurate sources. Gathers sources that are irrelevant to research questions. Copies or relies on others for product design, merely repeats information provided; denies evidence without adequate justification, fails to communicate content accurately or effectively.

NOTES

1. The majority of student–teacher badge interactions were conducted in person, but a supplemental online badging platform was made available to encourage social engagement regarding artifacts and teacher feedback. Because it was seldom used during implementation, however, we have chosen to focus on more instructionally useful portions of the study.
2. Following on an argument from Dourish and Button (1998), Crabtree (2004a, 2004b) suggested that researchers could and should use technology to design breach experiments given their unique ability to induce in-the-moment, on-the-fly behavioral responses.

REFERENCES

Abramovich, S., Higashi, R., Hunkele, T., Schunn, C., & Shoop, R. (June, 2011). *An achievement system to increase achievement motivation.* Paper presented in the 7th annual conference, Games Learning and Society, Madison, WI.

Abramovich, S., Schunn, C., & Higashi, R. M. (2013). Are badges useful in education? It depends upon the type of badge and expertise of learner. *Educational Technology Research and Development, 61,* 217–232.

Abramovich, S., & Wardrip, P. S. (2016). The impact of badges on motivation to learn. In L. Muilenburg & Z. Berge (Eds.), *Digital badges in education.* New York, NY: Routledge.

Anthony, G., Hunter, J., & Hunter, R. (2015). Prospective teachers' development of adaptive expertise. *Teaching and Teacher Education, 49,* 108–117.

Antin, J., & Churchill, E. F. (May, 2011). *Badges in social media: A social psychological perspective.* Paper presented at the SIGCHI conference on Human Factors in computing systems, Vancouver, BC, Canada.

Ball, D. L., & Forzani, F. (2009). The work of teaching and the challenge of teacher education. *Journal of Teacher Education, 60,* 497–511.

Barker, B. S. (June, 2013). *Digital badges in informal learning environments.* Paper presented at ICIW: The Eighth International Conference on Internet and Web Applications and Services. Rome, Italy.

Belenky, D. M., & Nokes-Malach, T. J. (2012). Motivation and transfer: The role of mastery-approach goals in preparation for future learning. *Journal of the Learning Sciences, 21*(3), 399–432.

Bjork, S., & Holopainen, J. (2005). *Patterns in game design.* Boston, MA: Cengage Learning.

Casilli, C., & Hickey, D. (2016). Transcending conventional credentialing and assessment paradigms with information-rich digital badges. *The Information Society, 32*(2), 117–129.

Collins, L. & Fruth, L. (2007). The right data to the right people at the right time: How interoperability helps America's students succeed. PESC white paper. Data Quality Campaign, Washington, DC.

Cooper K. S. (2014). Eliciting engagement in the high school classroom: A mixed methods evaluation of teaching practices. *American Educational Research Journal, 51*, 363–402

Crabtree, A. (August, 2004a). Design in the absence of practice: Breaching experiments. *Proceedings of the 2004 conference on Designing interactive systems: processes, practices, methods, and techniques*, 59–68.

Crabtree, A. (2004b). Taking technomethodology seriously: hybrid change in the ethnomethodology–design relationship. *European Journal of Information Systems, 13*(3), 195–209.

Cuban, L. (1990). Reforming again, again, and again. *Educational researcher, 19*(1), 3–13.

De Paoli, S., De Uffici, N., & D'Andrea, V. (2012). Designing badges for a civic media platform: reputation and named levels. In *Proceedings of the 26th Annual BCS Interaction Specialist Group Conference on People and Computers* (pp. 59–68). London, England: British Computer Society.

Deterding, S., Sicart, M., Nacke, L., O'Hara, K., & Dixon, D. (2011, May). Gamification: using game-design elements in non-gaming contexts. *Proceedings of the 2011 annual conference extended abstracts on Human factors in computing systems* (pp. 2425–2428). New York, NY: Association for Computing Machinery.

Dourish, P., & Button, G. (1998). On "technomethodology": Foundational relationships between ethnomethodology and system design. *Human-Computer Interaction, 13*(4), 395–432.

Edelson, D., & Joseph, D. (June, 2004). *The interest-driven learning design framework: Motivating learning through usefulness.* Paper presented at the international conference on the learning sciences. Los Angeles, CA.

Elliot, A. J. (1999). Approach and avoidance motivation and achievement goals. *Educational psychologist, 34*(3), 169–189.

Elliot, A. J., Shell, M. M., Henry, K. B. & Maier, M. A. (2005). Achievement goals, performance contingencies, and performance attainment: An experimental test. *Journal of Educational Psychology, 97*(4), 630.

Finkelstein, J., Knight, E., & Manning, S. (2013). *The potential and value of using digital badges for adult learners.* Washington, DC: American Institute for Research.

Fox, C. Schaffhauser, D., Fletcher, G., & Levin, D. (2013). *Transforming data to information in service of learning.* State educational technology directors association (SETDA), Washington, DC.

Frederiksen, J., & Collins, A. (1989). A systems approach to educational testing. *Educational Researcher, 18*(9), 27–32.

Fredricks, J. A., Blumenfeld, P. C., & Paris, A. H. (2004). School engagement: Potential of the concept, state of the evidence. *Review of Educational Research, 74*(1), 59–109.

Garfinkel, H. (1967). *Studies in ethnomethodology.* Englewood Cliffs, NJ: Prentice-Hall.

Gibson, D., Ostashewski, N., Flintoff, K., Grant, S., & Knight, E. (2013). Digital badges in education. *Education and Information Technologies, 20*(2)1–8.

Goligoski, E. (2012). Motivating the learner: Mozilla's open badges program. *Access to Knowledge: A Course Journal, 4*(1), pp. 1–8.

Greeno, J. G. (1998). The situativity of knowing, learning, and research. *American Psychologist, 53*, 5–26.

Greeno, J. G. (2003). On claims that answer the wrong questions. *Educational Researcher, 26*, 5–17.

Greeno, J. G. (2006). Learning in activity. In R. K. Sawyer (Ed.), *The Cambridge handbook of the learning sciences* (pp. 79–96). New York, NY: Cambridge University Press.

Greeno, J. G., Collins, A. M., & Resnick, L. B. (1996). Cognition and learning. In D. C. Berliner & R. C. Calfee (Eds.), *Handbook of educational psychology* (pp. 15–46). New York, NY: Macmillan Library Reference.

Grossman, P., Hammerness, K., & McDonald, M. (2009). Redefining teaching, reimagining teacher education. *Teachers and Teaching: Theory and Practice, 15*, 273–289.

Halavais, A. M. (2012). A genealogy of badges: Inherited meaning and monstrous moral hybrids. *Information, Communication & Society, 15*(3), 354–373.

Hamari, J., & Eranti, V. (2011). Framework for designing and evaluating game achievements. *Proc. DiGRA 2011: Think Design Play, 115*(115), 122–134.

Heffernan, N. T., & Koedinger, K. R. (May, 2012). *Integrating assessment within instruction: A look forward in invitational research symposium on technology enhanced assessments.* The center for K–12 assessment & performance management at ETS, Washington, DC.

Hickey, D. T. (2015). A situative response to the conundrum of formative assessment. *Assessment in Education: Principles, Policy & Practice, 22*(2), 202–223.

Hickey, D. T., Itow, R. C., Rehak, A., Schenke, K., & Tran, C. (2013). Speaking personally—With Erin Knight. *American Journal of Distance Education, 27*(2), 134–138.

Jenkins, H., Purushotma, R., Weigel, M., Clinton, K., & Robison, A. J. (2009). *Confronting the challenges of participatory culture: Media education for the 21st century.* Cambridge, MA: MIT Press.

Lave, J., & Wenger, E. (1991). *Situated learning: Legitimate peripheral participation.* New York, NY: Cambridge University Press.

Kriplean, T., Beschastnikh, I., & McDonald, D. W. (2008, November). Articulations of wikiwork: Uncovering valued work in Wikipedia through Barnstars. In *Proceedings of the 2008 ACM conference on Computer supported cooperative work* (pp. 47–56). New York, NY: Association for Computing Machinery.

Marsh, J. A. (2012). Interventions promoting educators' use of data: Research insights and gaps. *Teachers College Record, 113*(11), 1–48.

McDaniel, R., & Fanfarelli, J. (2016). Building better digital badges: Pairing completion logic with psychological factors. *Simulation & Gaming, 1*, 30.

McGonigal, J. (2011). *Reality is broken: Why games make us better and how they can change the world.* New York, NY: Penguin.

Montola, M., Nummenmaa, T., Lucero, A., Boberg, M., & Korhonen, H. (2009). Applying game achievement systems to enhance user experience in a photo sharing service. In *Proceedings of the 13th International MindTrek Conference: Everyday Life in the Ubiquitous Era* (pp. 94–97). New York, NY: Association for Computing Machinery.

Moore, C. (2011). Hats of affect: A study of affect, achievements and hats in Team Fortress 2. *Game Studies, 11*(1), pp. 1–14.

Mozilla Foundation. (2013). *Expanding education and workforce opportunities through digital badges.* Washington, DC: Alliance for Excellent Education.

Mozilla Foundation and Peer 2 Peer University, in collaboration with The MacArthur Foundation (2011). *Open badges for lifelong learning.* Mountain View, CA: Author.

Nolen, S. B., Horn, I. S., & Ward, C. J. (2015). Situating motivation. *Educational Psychologist, 50*(3), 234–247.

O'Byrne, W., Schenke, K., Willis, J. E. III, & Hickey, D. T. (2015). Digital badges recognizing, assessing, and motivating learners in and out of school contexts. *Journal of Adolescent & Adult Literacy, 58*(6), 451–454.

Ostashewski, N., & Reid, D. (2015). A history and frameworks of digital badges in education. In T. Reiners & L. C. Wood (Eds.), *Gamification in education and business* (pp. 187–200). New York, NY: Springer International Publishing.

Pellegrino, J. W., & Quellmalz, E. S. (2010). Perspectives on the integration of technology and assessment. *Journal of Research on Technology in Education, 43*(2), 119–134.

Plori, O., Carley, S., & Foex, B. (2007). Scouting out competencies. *Emergency Medicine Journal, 24*(4), 286–287.

Reid, A. J., Paster, D., & Abramovich, S. (2015). Digital badges in undergraduate composition courses: Effects on intrinsic motivation. *Journal of Computers in Education, 2*(4), 377–398.

Schank, R. C. (1994). Goal-based scenarios: A radical look at education. *The Journal of the Learning Sciences, 3*(4), 429–453.

Schank, R. C., Fano, A., Bell, B., & Jona, M. (1994). The design of goal-based scenarios. *The Journal of the Learning Sciences, 3*(4), 305–345.

Selingo, J. (2012). Colleges need some big ideas to drive change from within. *Chronicle of Higher Education, 58*(7), A1–A12.

Wardrip, P. S., Abramovich, S., Bathgate, M., & Kim, Y. J. (in press). A school-based badging system and interest-based learning: An exploratory case study. *International Journal of Learning and Media.*

Wardrip, P. S., Abramovich, S., Kim, Y. J., & Bathgate, M. (2016). Taking badges to school: A school-based badge system and its impact on participating teachers. *Computers & Education, 95*, 239–253.

Wiliam, D., Lee, C., Harrison, C. & Black, P. (2004). Teachers developing assessment for learning: impact on student achievement. *Assessment in Education, 11*, 49–65.

Windschitl, M., Thompson, J., Braaten, M., & Stroupe, D. (2012). Proposing a core set of instructional practices and tools for teachers of science. *Science Education, 96*(5), 878–903.

Yang, J. C., Quadir, B., & Chen, N. S. (2015). Effects of the Badge mechanism on self-efficacy and learning performance in a game-based English learning environment. *Journal of Educational Computing Research, 54*(3), 371–394.

Zichermann, G., & Cunningham, C. (2011). *Gamification by design: Implementing game mechanics in web and mobile apps.* Newton, MA: O'Reilly Media.

Zimmerman, E. (2004). Narrative, interactivity, play, and games: Four naughty concepts in need of discipline. In N. Wardrip-Fruin & P. Harrigan (Eds.), *First person: New media as story, performance, and game* (pp. 154–164). Cambridge, MA: MIT Press.

CHAPTER 7

AN ECOCENTRIC FRAMEWORK FOR GAME-ENABLED IMPACT

Lessons Learned From the Quest2Teach Project

Sasha Barab and Anna Arici
Arizona State University

This chapter draws from design work on a series of 3D immersive game curricula, *Quest2Teach*, designed specifically for teacher education using cutting-edge gaming technologies and the transformational play theory to inform its impact design. Quest2Teach is a series of bounded games, gamified professional network, lessons plans, and suite of professional development services designed specifically for teacher education to help bridge between educational theory and its application into the field. In the designed games, preservice teacher candidates create their professional avatar, play out roles, solve realistic problems, fail safely, and reflect on the impact of their individual decisions and trajectories, while gaining experience and

Exploding the Castle, pages 139–177

fluency in these theories-in-action. Game meters and other in-game analytics are pulled into a real-world network homepage, reflecting their growth over time and semester coursework. Foremost in our work is a distinction between treating games for impact as "bounded products" whose capacity for impact lies within the technical structures, from the more expansive "game-enabled impact" perspective being advanced here. In this chapter, we argue that games for impact, or game-enabled impact, should not be thought of as product-centric innovations focused on developing specific student learning outcomes, but rather should be treated as one component of an ecosystem framework in which implementation partners (whether system administrators, classroom teachers, or the players themselves) are enabled to reinterpret core lessons in terms of their local needs.

LAYING A FOUNDATION

The video game industry has emerged as one of the most powerful influences of the 21st century, generating billions of hours of highly engaging entertainment and surpassing the film industry in terms of worldwide revenues—$99.6 billion USD to $35.9 billion, respectively, in 2013 (Newzoo, 2016). A growing body of research is also highlighting the enormous potential of games to help address some of the most pressing social, cultural, scientific, and economic challenges of the 21st century. Digital games are different from other media in that they are interactive, participatory, and highly engaging. Well-designed games and game-infused experiences offer a delicate balance of challenges and rewards that can drive deep levels of engagement and time-on-task, enabling players to advance at their own pace, fail in a safe and supported environment, acquire critical knowledge just-in-time (vs. just-in-case), iterate based on feedback, and use acquired knowledge to develop mastery.

Moreover, role playing and narrative games enable players to step into different roles (e.g., scientist, explorer, journalist, inventor, political leader), confront problems, make meaningful choices and explore the consequences of these choices (Barab, Gresalfi, & Ingram-Goble, 2010). Games can make learning engaging, social, and relevant. They can give students real agency in ways that static textbooks, or even real-world experiences such as field trips, simply cannot. Additionally, well-designed affinity spaces (Gee & Hayes, 2010) and surrounding communication infrastructures (Steinkuehler, 2006) can provide rich mentoring frameworks that facilitate ongoing literacy development, interest-driven participation and 21st-century communication skills as learners collaborate with each other and with adults. However, when it comes to using games for impact, we are still an emerging field with much fragmentation and often inconsistent results

(Stokes et al., 2016). While there are emerging "best practices" and case examples that can be drawn upon from the impact sector, there is a need to bring together these efforts, and to identify productive frameworks, assumptions, and methods for advancing impact goals.

Foremost in our work is a distinction between treating games for impact as "bounded products," whose capacity for impact lies within the technical structures of schools, from the more expansive "game-enabled services" perspective being advanced here. Viewing games for impact as a component of enabled services (versus bounded products) affects what we design, how we design, the way we prioritize budgets, when we consider the work complete, who is responsible for the impact and ultimately, the types of impact we are likely to bring about. As further elaboration, it is quite common to treat designed innovations, especially those built using a strong logic model, as containing a solution that has the potential to produce transformative outcomes *on the individual*—that is, a technological fix (Sarewitz & Nelson, 2008). In contrast, we argue that a more productive view is to understand any potential outcomes as achieved *in collaboration with* those individuals and systems to be impacted, not simply produced by the designers in the studio. The latter focus, what we refer to as a node-centric or ecological framework, is based on the assumption that the innovation lives in the edges, at the implementation sites themselves, rather than being bound up in the core product and pushed out.

Taking a lesson from the tech-enabled services industry, we see a movement where companies are positioning their brand in the experiences they enable, not simply the designs they produce. For example, while Nike advertisements include their designed products, the real focus is on what users can do and become with their products—those transformative outcomes users are able to achieve with their products. As another example, Intel changed their tagline from "Intel inside" to "*We create amazing experiences.*" Starbucks, a company who produces a great cup of coffee, refers to their employees as partners and views their brand as jointly distributed among the products they offer, the partners who prepare these products, and the way that customers view these products as advancing their goals (Schultz & Yang, 1999). Such a view is consistent with the agile startup movement (Maurya, 2012; Ries, 2011), in which the emphasis even during the design phases is on customer development, rather than merely on product development.

Here, we are suggesting that games for impact, or game-enabled impact, should not be thought of as product-centric innovations focused on outputs, nor simply as service-centric invitations, but we need to enlist them as one component of an ecosystem framework in which implementation partners (whether system administrators, classroom teachers, or the players themselves) are enabled to reinterpret core lessons in terms of their local needs. This view is further consistent with Toyama's (2015) notion of the amplified self, based on over a decade of research with the Microsoft Corporation in which he found that the most successful initiatives were those that focused on amplifying and unlocking existing capabilities and capacities rather than introducing a new capacity or "whole-cloth" solution. The design intent is to push the responsibility for impact out to the nodes (i.e., in each of the players and their ecosystems) by leveraging existing potentials and capacities, as opposed to seeing all capacity coming from that which was developed by the designer and placed within the product. This process requires the player to "lean-forward" and take ownership for her own transformation, finding opportunities to apply the content to achieve great things in her world—not simply in the designed products. The challenge is in how our designs share agency and meaning, allowing the player to codetermine structure and impact with our system, with each other and with the contexts of implementation. The goal here is not that the system "adapts" to player choices, but that the choices that players are making are motivated towards a goal in which they are invested.

To further ground our discussion of game-enabled impact as a node-centric phenomenon that is distributed across the designed innovation, the implementation service, those who are to be impacted, and the work it does in the world, we will draw on illuminative examples from the *Quest2Teach* game-based curriculum. *Quest2Teach* is a series of bounded games, gamified professional network, lessons plans, and suite of professional development services designed specifically for teacher education to help bridge between educational theory and its application into the field. Pre-service teacher candidates (university students) evolve their professional identity and capacity through a variety of narrative-based 3D role-playing scenarios, each with a particular academic focus, and embedded within a larger experience-based curriculum and professional network. The goal here is not to validate *Quest2Teach*, but instead we will leverage data from observations of over 40 separate implementations with over 2,500 pre-service teacher candidates across two years to further illuminate the argument by highlighting data related to three transformative outcomes: identity shifts, applied theory, and meaning construction.

THE POWER OF GAME-BASED LEARNING

At the core of our theory of change model is that learning is not simply the acquisition of content knowledge, but it involves user-directed participation in which learners apply their emerging competencies within a situation in which they have agency and consequentiality to accomplishing something they value (Barab et al., 2012; Brown, Collins, & Duguid, 1989; Bransford,

Brown, & Cocking, 1999). Such positioning transforms the teacher from an individual responsible for following our procedural rules to an *agentic and empowered partner* who is leveraging a powerful tool to realize a shared vision. This sort of positioning is consistent with Gresalfi and Barab (2011), who discussed the implications of different forms of engagement: procedural, conceptual, consequential, and critical engagement. Most relevant here is the distinction between *procedural engagement* (using procedures accurately but without a deeper understanding of why one is performing such procedures) and *consequential engagement* (recognizing the usefulness and impact of disciplinary tools; that is, being able to connect particular solutions to particular outcomes). In fact, we argue that the distinction is quite relevant when leveraging, for example, gamification mechanics in that one could leverage these to apply "external" control over a player's behaviors or invite the player to "make sense" of the scores as they deconstruct their meanings with the ultimate outcome of inspiring players to unlock "more advanced" versions of themselves; that is, positioning the gamification mechanics and scores as feedback to players on goals that they are invested and not as a means of having scores take external responsibility for what needs to be investment motivated by the meaningful work that the score represents.

This distinction between using scores or practices to cause behavioral changes and conceptual understanding versus providing data and consequential feedback from which players are "compelled" or "invited" into their own transformation is a key challenge in building all curricula, let alone leveraging game mechanics. In our work as impact designers, we refer to this as orchestrating a "dance of agency," in which we as designers are making claims on the player at the same time we are inviting the player into using our learning challenges and emergent data as well as insights generated with peers to make their own claims on what matters. This notion of shifting learners, whether students or teachers, from procedural engagement to consequential engagement, is motivated in part by our belief that the latter is more likely to cultivate the underlying dispositions or "ways of being" necessary to thrive in the real world—not simply on the fictional scenarios that we designed for them. Especially powerful in bringing out real-world gains is the integration of what Gee (2013; 2013 personal communication) refers to as small "g" games with big "G" infrastructures (Steinkuehler, 2006).

Small "g" Games

To elaborate, small "g" games are bounded experiences; they are self-contained and finite, preoptimized to introduce, cover, or re-enforce a particular lesson and well suited for learning in a safe, simulated, and structured environment. In other words, when we embed a fictional scenario into a set of interactions that the player experiences, there are choices and consequences designed into the scenario even though it requires players for the story to unfold. When we develop a "virtual park in a box" for middle-school students to learn about water quality as they endeavor to save virtual fish, the small "g" game is heavily structured by the designed experience as opposed to, for example, gamifying their investigation of a real park. The former, because the choices and consequences are created by a designer, are optimized towards learning gains, as opposed to the real park, which has many competing scenarios and complex interactions that are not conducive to, or potentially detract from, learning the targeted content. Importantly, even in such bounded games, players do not simply empathize with someone else's story but rather adopt a projective stance, participating in the role of a game character (an avatar) to interrogate and impact the game dynamics. In this manner, games enable players to step into different roles (e.g., scientist, explorer, journalist, inventor, political leader), confront problems, make meaningful choices, and explore the consequences of these choices. And, while small "g" games are bounded, they remain quite powerful in part because the way they position learner, content, and context as fundamentally integrated; creating a place in which what you know is directly related to what you are able to do and, ultimately, who you become.

As one example, in our previous work we advanced a theory around transformational play, a threefold theory that argues for the positioning of *person with intentionality*, the *content with legitimacy*, and the *context with consequentiality* (Barab et al., 2010; Barab, Zuiker et al., 2007) (see Figure 7.1). The idea of transformational play highlights relations among the three interconnected elements of person, content, and context. In these games, learners become protagonists who use the knowledge, skills, and concepts

Figure 7.1 Mystery of Taiga River, where youth take on role of scientist to save a park through inquiry.

of the educational content to make sense of a situation and then choices that transform the play space and the player—they see how the world changed because of their efforts (Barab, Arici, & Gresalfi, 2009). Such play is transformational in that it changes the context in which play is occurring, while at the same time transforming the player and his or her potential to interact with the world. Here, the important affordance of the game is that the designers have built a world in which the player is required to leverage disciplinary concepts to understand (make sense of) and make choices that transform the gaming environment. By creating a bounded world that is designed to operate in a manner that requires the player to productively leverage disciplinary tools is quite powerful for learning about those concepts.

Further, by leveraging embedded assessments, pedagogical scaffolds, game consequentiality, and teacher dashboards, these experiences can provide an important learning tool through which experiential learning can occur and be effectively managed by a teacher in the context of actual classrooms. Key genres of small "g" games include, among others, (a) *adventure* (optimized for enabling students to take on identities and solving problem in an engaging, narrative context); (b) *simulation* (optimized for students to experience real-world scenarios that contextualize learning vs. optimized for pure fidelity itself); (c) *strategy* (optimized for students to solve complex problems balancing multiple variables to accomplish desired outcomes); and (d) *toolbox* (optimized for students to create content with powerful tools to realize diverse goals and develop new media literacies). The small "g" games have proven to be particularly effective at creating high levels of student engagement and enable students to work independently (both in class and at home) with teachers able to monitor their work through a dashboard offering clear guidance as to when and how a student needs a direct engagement with the teacher (Barab et al., 2010). The design of the game itself embeds the scaffolding and feedback for students to advance at their own pace and requires critical competencies to be developed in order to finish the game.

However, small "g" games do have limitations. They are bounded, cover a constrained range of content, and can be more difficult to optimize—for example, they do not always fit seamlessly into prescribed state and local class scope and sequence. Even if they do capture the goals of the local experience, they fail to be open to extensions and personalization beyond the immediate precrafted design. To help address these limitations, there is much that can be learned from the commercial game franchises, which often have significant communities and nongame service components that reach beyond the core gameplay experience. These games have expanded beyond their design experience to bring players together in affinity spaces, video tutorials, resource guides, peer mentorship frameworks, and larger communities. Through these metagame affinity spaces, players interact socially around games—discussing them, often requiring extensive reading and writing, playing them cooperatively or competitively, and even potentially modifying them.

Big 'G' Games

Metagame interactions that take place outside of the game all act as extensions of the original design, providing the game a larger life and impact than initially developed. This metagame experience is what James Paul Gee refers to as the big "G," and it acts as a force multiplier on the engagement level of games. Big "G" game infrastructures are open-ended and seamlessly integrate the small "g" games into a larger, flexible "metagame" structure and affinity space that fosters user-driven extensions and adaptations in support of real-world goals and outcomes. It is with the big "G" components that we transform individual experiences within a game into a dynamic social interaction to enable learning to be applied and extended beyond the classroom walls.

In fact, Gee and Hayes (2010) argued that the most powerful learning happens around the game, not simply within the game. When applying this in the context of our designed learning journeys, these big "G' elements that unite, deepen, and extend the learning experience include, among others: (a) learning and management platform (easily customizable and optimizable platform for hosting and managing learning trajectories within and across the multiple game-infused experiences); (b) data and analytics dashboard (that allow teachers, students, and other key stakeholders to not only see data, but also interact with the game and optimize the learning experience based on this data); (c) social communities and affinity spaces (a framework for engaging in discussion, comentoring, tutoring, critique, reflection, theory crafting, and designing); (d) achievement-based framework and gamification layers (carefully designed extrinsic reward systems and intrinsic motivators to focus attention, motivate action, and provide a trajectory of advancement); (e) metagame identity (framework for personalized avatars, meta storylines, and open APIs that unite small "g" and real-world experiences); (f) smart tools (tool systems that can be used as templates for real-world applications and move learning beyond the classroom walls); and (g) modding tools (powerful tools, opportunities, and support structures so students and teachers can extend, shape, and augment the core platform). While individual small "g" game experiences can and do achieve learning success, we believe the deeper learning outcomes come through the seamless integration of the small "g" games with a big "G" infrastructure that both connects and extends each of the individual learning modules.

The argument and need for big "G" infrastructure when striving for impact is consistent with what we have learned from the meta-research studies on the power of games for impact. A meta-analysis conducted by Wouters, van Nimwegen, van Oostendorp, and van der Spek (2013) found multiple studies in which games were more effective than traditional methods in terms of achieving impact goals (usually at the output level), especially when (a) they were supplemented with other instruction methods, (b) multiple training sessions were involved, (c) players worked in groups. A separate meta-analysis conducted by Clark, Tanner-Smith, and Killingsworth (2016) found numerous studies indicating that digital games were associated with significantly better competency outcomes relative to comparison conditions but that (d) certain value-added game structures were more or less effective for certain outcomes, underscoring the point that "games" as a medium come in many different types each leveraging particular mechanics and affordances that should be thoughtfully aligned to the particular learning goals.

It is quite common to become enamored with the game as product and forget that when we are leveraging the power of games for impact the focus is on how the game enables the player to engage the core impact focus beyond the game experience into the real world. This involves letting the game mechanics do what they do well and support the impact goals with additional curriculum, but do so in ways that support peer interaction and if available leverage the expertise of a prepared facilitator. A prepared facilitator is an individual who has (a) played the game and appreciates how the mechanics work; (b) connected the game experience into other curricular goals; (c) identified shortcomings and misconceptions, even building supplemental curriculum and activities; (d) has access to, and is capable of, providing actionable feedback in response to player data; (e) uses strategies for ensuring players are collaborating with each other around game choices; (f) aligns implementation strategies to the theoretical assumptions underlying the design; and (g) has defined meaningful outcomes in terms of local ecosystem needs, with a commitment to optimizing these rather than simply moving players through the game. What is important here is an acknowledgement that games are one component of a broader system, and that if we want the impact of the game to extend beyond the designed experience then we need to prepare facilitators to engage the bounded play components within a larger infrastructure that collectively becomes the game-infused experience or, as we have argued, game-enabled services.

Integral to our theory of change for the power of games is our assumption that game-infused experiences are most effective when created as services that are integrated, managed, and continually optimized for ecosystem integration, ongoing sustainability, and scaled impact—as opposed to products that are released and remain static. A successful rollout includes processes and technologies (e.g., teacher dashboards), and especially pro-fessional development, to enable local adaptations in a manner that main-tains implementation fidelity and allows for local optimization of products and services to maximize sustainable and scalable outcomes. Building a game-infused ecosystem that is likely to leverage the game effectively is, we argue, a key feature of shifting the impact from local outputs to sustainable and scalable outcomes—regardless of the product design. On one level, the ecosystem includes the life trajectory of the player, and the "game" should be introduced at a point in which it is connected to existing or possible life goals that the player once realized. At another level, ecosystem integration involves the broader network of peers available and enthusiastic to decon-struct and apply the lessons, helping to localize the core ideas in relation to local ecosystem needs.

In places where the community uses the designs with support from a trained facilitator such as a staff member or a teacher, there exists even more potential to position the game as a service as part of a larger ecosystem. The effectiveness of the facilitator can be enhanced through training in terms of best implementation practices, but also in terms of the facilitator's disposi-tion to position the game as a service or potential, which can be unlocked in collaboration with motivated and invested players. In this framework, stakeholders are viewed as partners who, when properly empowered, have the potential to be force multipliers in terms of maximizing potential and value out of the game-enabled service. In this model, the power of the game lies in the potential of the external nodes (whether players, facilitators, ad-ministrators) to bring forth the desired outcomes with the game serving as one component of the larger ecosystem in which outcomes are produced in collaboration. Again, the "dance of agency" between the player and the game is key, with each having a shifting role, with moments in which the game is making "claims" on what the player can become and moments in which the players are making claims on what is the potential of the game, taking responsibility for their own becoming.

UNDERLYING THEORY OF CHANGE

The *Quest2Teach* university initiative that we studied was situated within and supported by an innovative teachers college embracing the tenets of a New American University (Crow & Dabars, 2015), and occurring at a period where faculty and students were eager to integrate technology into their learning and teaching practices. What is significant here, and consistent with the game-enabled services framework we are advancing, is an appre-ciation that the potential of a designed intervention is bound up within a complex set of interactions, as represented in a theory of change, and optimized during implementation for a particular ecosystem. Therefore, at a high level, our strategy for achieving the desired results involves the integration of bounded games with a professional network, embedded within existing curricular goals, supported by trained facilitators, connected to just-in-time learner needs, and within a culture in which game scores are treated as facilitative of conversations and not declarative claims on ability or mastery. Below, we characterize this framework as a logic model, illustrating our theory of change in terms of problem, inputs, outputs, outcomes, strategies, assumption, community needs/assets, and influential factors (Kellogg Foundation, 2004).

This framework, or logic model (see Figure 7.2), facilitates designer and stakeholder alignment in terms of the relations among the inputs, outputs, and outcomes (Alter & Egan, 1997; Alter & Murty, 1997; Dugan & Hernon, 2002; Julian, 1997). Elaborating on the components, one starts with the problem or issue that the program, broadly conceived, will address. It is important to acknowledge here that it is not always about addressing a known problem, and sometimes it is more about pursuing what Pendleton-Julian and Brown, 2011) refer to as a "visionary pursuit" in which one is attempting to engineer a new possibility that makes existing processes seem problematic or less useful. Even when engaging a pursuit that is not directly tied to one community problem, it is still useful to have an appreciation for existing community needs/assets that make one's pursuit significant. Central to the logic model is the articulation of one's desired results, whether conceptualized as outputs, outcomes, or impact more generally. Consistent with the argument here, one's desired results will fundamentally change the rest of the model, a belief that is captured in the assumptions portion of the logic model. In our case, we desire that the work goes beyond learning outputs (i.e., content-specific, declarative-level test scores, focused only on the learning experience) to realize more transformational outcomes (i.e., issues of identity, transfer of theory to actual practice).

How one accomplishes these goals is captured in the strategies portion of the logic model. These strategies should be in the service of the desired results based on one's assumptions and those influential factors that are likely to impact the success or even hinder program success. While being clear about these individual components is important, the power of the logic model characterization is in defining the interrelations among the strategies that one employs, the assumptions one has about why and how those strategies operate, and the desired results that one hopes to achieve with the employed strategies. It is in this way that one's identified problem, desired results, core assumptions and developed strategy all become interrelated, with the idea that success is more likely if they consider community needs and assets. Whereas logic models have been used successfully in many projects across multiple disciplines (see Kellogg Foundation, 2004),

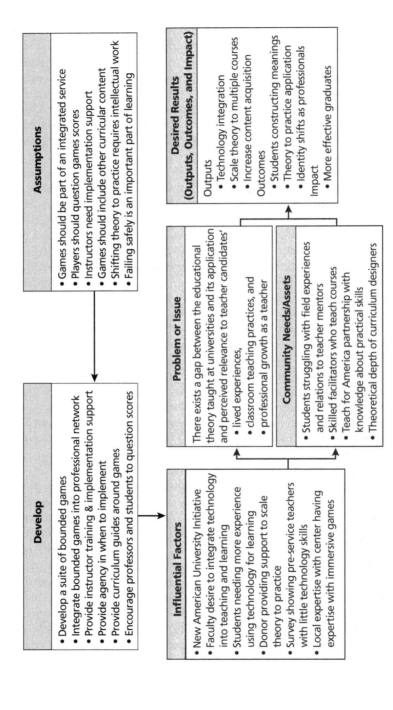

Figure 7.2 Kellogg Foundation logic model template applied to *Quest2Teach*.

Millar, Simeone, and Carnevale (2001) argued that following a sequence from the inputs through to the outcomes could limit one's thinking to the existing activities, programs, and research questions. Instead, their recommendation, which resonates with our own work, is that the logic model should focus activities on the intended outcomes of a particular program, but the overriding question that must be continually asked needs to be "what needs to be done?" not "what is being done?" This is, in part, because of our core belief that impact is a shared accomplishment, leveraging what is known, but adapted in response to those being impacted and what constitutes productive translations for achieving the desired impact.

QUEST2TEACH AS A GAME-ENABLED SERVICE INITIATIVE

Quest2Teach is a series of bounded games, gamified professional network, lessons plans, and suite of professional development services designed specifically for teacher education to help bridge between educational theory and its application into the field. In the designed games, pre-service teacher candidates create their professional avatar, play out roles, solve realistic problems, fail safely, and see the impact of their individual decisions and trajectories, while gaining experience and fluency in these theories-in-action. Game meters and other in-game analytics are pulled into their real-world network homepage, reflecting their growth over the semester and not simply within the game. The network utilizes badges (see Chapter 6: "Ask Not What You Can Do for Badges; Ask What Badges Can Do for You") to validate and extend teachers' digital experiences into their real lives, and unlock new learning trajectories, within a network of supportive colleagues. Having demonstrated expertise in the games, players earn the ability to endorse their colleagues in the network for their meaningful contributions. In this way, game achievements are translated into a social currency that is used to applaud and encourage other players as they reflect on, craft, and evolve their impact stories in the real world.

Currently, there are four small "g" games, each bounded and able to be completed in 2–3 hours, along with a big "G" open-ended infrastructure; a socio-professional network (see Figure 7.2) integrating small "g" games into a larger whole, with student driven extensions, teacher smart-tools, affinity spaces, a 3D hub; and a professional identity that evolves over semesters from in-game analytics, reflections, and real-world experiences. Across the bounded games, teacher candidates engage with important skills and literacies, including (a) professional competencies ("Pursuit of Professionalism" game, Figure 7.2), (b) student conferencing ("On the Write Track" game, Figures 7.1 and 7.3), and (c) data-driven decision making ("Diving into Data" game, Figure 7.4), with a fourth game providing an orientation

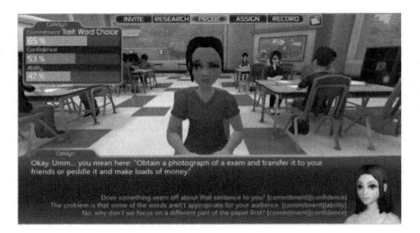

Figure 7.3 Screeshot from student conference in the *On the Write Track* game.

experience. Research was carried out over five semesters of design-based implementation research to investigate and innovate the learning, engagement, identity shifts, and other theories at play in these player–game curricular interactions (Arici & Barab, 2016). Specifically, we implemented the 3D immersive game across more than 80 preservice teacher field experience courses over three years with our design-based research including more than 3,500 preservice teachers in a large Southwestern teacher preparation program. Approximately 75% of students were women, with the vast majority of them Caucasian, and self-identified as nongamers with only "average" technology experience and "below average" gaming experience, as compared to national averages for their age and gender. Only 9% played even 1–5 hours of games a week, and only 5% of them identified themselves as "gamers."

Over the three years of design and data collection we carried out indepth observations, collecting field notes and video observations, of at least 50 classrooms with others involving members of our team helping with technology issues. Additionally, workshops were run once in the summer and again in December to prepare course instructors using the game and network technologies—focused on both communicating the underlying theory, particular game mechanics, and managing a class through the facilitator toolkit. For this reporting, we also drew on data from a comparison study with 98 students and further implementations as part of the larger design-based implementation research project. Reported here are illuminative cases selected opportunistically to offer "plausible interpretations" and "plausibility proofs" (Bruner, 1990, p. xiii) with the intention of building grounded possibility insights rather than using exhaustive analysis and

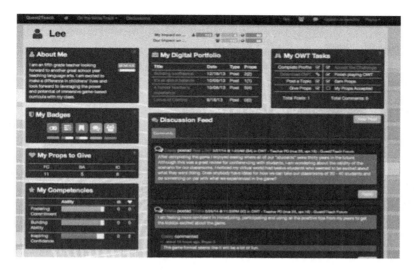

Figure 7.4 Screenshot from professional network with meters that represent in-game world progress.

positivist causal explanations to warrant particular claims. Our results over the four semesters consistently revealed pre/post learning gains on targeted concepts, as well as high levels of engagement. A comparison study showed that students in game-based classes reflected on their learning as a first-person protagonist, and spoke of learning "skills" and "language" in those theories, rather than reflecting passively of "learning about" the theory, as reported by control groups. Additionally, after completing a single game curriculum, many students reported higher levels of confidence in their future teaching ability, had increased commitment to teaching as a career, and showed a shift in their identity from viewing themselves as students to seeing themselves more as professional educators. While it was clear that the games, even with minimal facilitation, were having a positive effect on learning outcomes, it was these latter benefits around player-owned meaning making, transfer from theory to practice, and identity shifts in how they perceived themselves as professionals that, in the spirit of grounded theory, became our research focus as reported here.

OUTCOME 1: MEANING MAKING

Meaning making refers to the fact that it is a quite different phenomenon when learners participate in the *making-of-meaning* from a first-person perspective rather than simply receiving r*eady-made meanings* to be discussed as objects from a third-person perspective (Latour, 1987). Such a view is grounded in what we know about how people learn (Bransford, Brown, & Cocking, 1999), in a shift from acquisition to participation metaphors (Sfard, 1988), in an emphasis on students as producers (not simply consumers) of literacy (Jenkins, 2004), on distributed sense making (Pea, 1987) and connected learning frameworks (Ito et al., 2009), and on a situated perspective of what it means to know (Gee, 2003; Greeno, 1989). The key here is an active learner, working with others and leveraging theory to make sense of and act productively within the context of situations in which he or she is invested and that provide copious feedback about the use-value of choices in ways to illuminate the underlying theories to be learned. In this way, theories become embodied tools useful for addressing situations (Brown et al., 1989), with meaning being produced in relation to the work that the tools do or don't do in relation to the situation in which they are being applied.

The Professionalism game, as one example, places players in an immersive world where they are having a professional difference of opinion with their mentor teacher in regards to pedagogical approaches. The goal of this game was to help players go beyond professional mannerisms and conduct and engage them in applying the soft skills regarding communication and interpersonal relationships that are often overlooked in coursework and only learned through experience. To base this in formalized concepts, we incorporated the Teaching as Leadership Curriculum for Professionalism (Farr, 2010) as a means to create authentic and nuanced narratives for students to explore and play out issues of professional communication, dynamics, and relationships. The players learn to handle potential disagreements between their views and those of their mentor teacher professionally,

Figure 7.5 Screenshot from the professionalism game.

partly through engaging professional competencies such as interpersonal awareness, suspending judgment, and asset-based thinking—displayed as meters that grow and contract based on their in-game choices (see Figure 7.5). One pilot study (Arici, Barab, & Borden, 2016) provided insight into how games do their work; more than statements that students must remember, in the professionalism game students make choices about which responses are most appropriate as they struggle with simulated situations.

Prior to implementation, the preservice teacher candidates in both conditions had overly simplistic and superficial notions of what it means to be a professional, with common descriptions of "professionalism" including: "how to dress," "not being 'buddies' with students," "not talking slang," "being punctual." Post-implementation, definitions of professionalism were expanded significantly in both conditions to include facets such as: "Trying to see good things in others," "Thinking about how others would view my actions," "Not judging somebody by their cover," and "Taking responsibility when I make mistakes." Where more interesting differences emerged was in how they described what they learned, with students in the curriculum condition using phrases (emphasis added) such as: "this unit made me more *aware of* my actions" and "it taught me *about* a lot of different professional situations." In contrast, students playing the professional game used phrases (emphasis added) such as:

> Candidate 1: "This experience *gave me the language* to approach new and challenging situations in my professional career. It taught me that I should not listen to other people's judgments and I should instead face the situation with an open mind."

> Candidate 2: "I now realize that the professional *choices I make affect my students,* and I need to slow down and consider many perspectives."

The game-based student responses were often richer and more nuanced, frequently including more specific lessons learned, or a greater fluency and sophistication in the content domain not frequently found in the control classroom responses (Arici et al., 2016).

We credit these differences in part to the active and experiential nature of learning when using games, where one is embedded within a situation in which one has to make choices and gain feedback on the experiential utility of that choice in bringing out desired consequences (Barab et al., 2010; Dewey, 1938). Central to the thesis being advanced here is that transformative outcomes are rarely "acquired" or "transmitted," but instead involve active participation on the part of the learner. Consistent with this sentiment, games often position players as "learning protagonists," having to actively make choices that advance the game forward (Squire, 2006). In doing so, they unlock or, in some cases, produce meanings even if they were built into the dynamics by the game designer (Jenkins, 2004). When a player perceives the preconditions in which the choice was made and appreciates why the particular outcomes came about, they are engaged in what Salen and Zimmerman (2004) referred to as *meaningful choice.* The perceived relationship and, importantly, the driving meaning that connects the two allows for an act of "sense making" that the cultural psychologist Jerome Bruner (1986) referred to as essential for human learning. In this case, even the "designed" meanings are not simply acquired but rather are built out of meaningful relationships and consequences to be engaged by the learner.

> Candidate 1: "I now realize that the professional choices I make affect my students, and I need to slow down and consider many perspectives."
>
> Candidate 2: "The game gives you an option that was a better way to phrase it. It was great just reading the various options and seeing there are a lot of different ways to approach it."
>
> Candidate 3: "I loved that I could mess up and say the wrong thing here, in a safe place, rather than saying the wrong thing later when I'm teaching and the consequences would be more serious."
>
> Candidate 4: "This unit made me more aware of my actions."
>
> Candidate 5: "I think the options are nice, because . . . personally I don't think I was ever taught those social skills, of how to react to someone. So maybe I would say something, but then it'd give you an option that was a lot better way to phrase it.

In these cases, the game is affording if not prompting the player to make consequential choices, and then making claims about the meaning of that choice. A key benefit of these types of designed spaces is that they allow for consequences without the real-world consequences associated with reaching a failure state. At the same time, they can create overly simplistic interpretations of quite problematic and complex consequences, obfuscating the potentially damaging impact of real-world consequences.

To the extent that the player can replay or simply interrogate the conditions of failure, it has the potential to be what Kapur and Bielaczyc (2012) referred to as *productive failure.* We view in these moments that it is essential that players have an appreciation for the "anatomy of choice," a precondition to meaningful choice in which the player is clear on what conditions led to the choice and what were the implications of the choice, and they are able to discern why these conditions came about. In another game, Diving into Data, the player is working to determine why the lesson failed, exploring the school looking for data from which he or she will draw inferences and use them to align to particular arguments (described more below). At one point they meet a teacher game character who blames it on kids today being difficult. If the player agrees, they reach a game stopper moment, where their virtual mentor appears and suggests that this choice is not a very productive one. The impact of agreeing with the NPC, failing the level, conversing with the NPC, and having to replay was articulated by one candidate:

> The aha moment for me was when the teacher (in the game) was blaming the kids for the classroom chaos, and how "they just don't care." Which is exactly what I hear at my school site. All the teachers around me, and even the principal, say that there's really nothing we can do because our students are so challenging. And in the game I found myself agreeing with that teacher, that "it's the kids' fault."

> But then the game stopped me and my [in-game] mentor popped in to explain that there are a lot of things I can do, and within my control. I was so used to "It's the kids, it's the kids, it's the kids," but now, after experiencing this [game], it makes me want to go back and try something new with my students. I'm starting to wonder if it really could be all the kids as a collective, or if we as teachers need to do something different.

It is one thing for the game to make the claim, and it is quite another when the players make the claim.

Given Gee's (2013) argument that the true impact of games lies in the conversations around the game, not simply within the game, we emphasize the importance of a prepared facilitator, as discussed above, who supports players deconstructing particular game moments—even highlighting particularly salient ones in the teacher toolkit to support classroom conversation. Further, we built the Diving into Data game in a manner that encourages the player not simply to accept the predesigned scores, but actually to create their own. This occurs in relation to the "smart tool" in which players bring their collected inferences and aligns them to one of four possible causes (i.e., lesson planning, classroom management, student investment, checking for understanding) for their lesson going so poorly, to determine which one is best supported by the available data (see Figure 7.6). For each piece of collected data and subsequent inference, students receive a score depending on how well it supports that particular cause. Each time a candidate places an inference into one of these categories, they get a score attached to corner of that inference, between 0 and 3, to say how well this data interpretation supports the need to work on this facet of their practice. While the score provides meaningful feedback based in experts' interpretations, in order to empower players and push them beyond consequential feedback and towards critical, we designed an opportunity for players to challenge the game's scoring mechanisms, as an embedded and explicit feature of the product and not simply an opportunity for those who feel motivated to raise these challenges in class conversations.

Figure 7.6 Screenshot from the data-driven decision making game.

After a few initial rounds of feedback scores are given on fairly straightforward choices, the in-game principal explains to the candidates' avatar that others have questioned the in-game scoring mechanisms. If they have a good argument for why they disagree with a score or rationale, they can now flag that instance and leave a note to explain their own interpretation. These notes from candidates are then available to the course instructor to review and leverage for further in-class discussions. Classes in which we observed instructors leveraging the facilitator dashboard to highlight these notes, rather than simply what claims the game made on players (treating their game scores as representing lessons learned), gave rise to conversations in which candidates proactively connected the game experience to their own views as a means of evolving their views and biases. The important point is that players were able to dive deeper into their constructed interpretations about what is meaningful, rather than simply consuming the assumptions and claims as they were coded into the game. While a powerful design trope, in our observations, the most powerful meaning making occurs when the classroom engages in dialogue, usually supported by a trained facilitator, around the game. Here, the game play experiences become boundary objects (Cole & Engeström, 1993), providing common reference points with which to engage meaningful conversations. In fact, even where student questioning the game dynamics was built into the game, the most powerful implementations of this feature occurred when the teacher formulated lesson activities simply by sharing and discussing students "claims" on which scores they questioned as recorded in the teacher toolkit and available to the teacher.

OUTCOME 2: CONNECTING THEORY TO PRACTICE

One of the classic challenges that has faced preservice teacher education, if not academia more generally, is how to bridge theory to practice, and numerous efforts in teacher education have attempted to bridge this divide (Barab, Barnett, & Squire, 2002; Cochran-Smith & Lytle, 1999a, 1999b; Guskey, 2002; Kagan, 1992; Putnam & Borko, 2000; Stein & Smith, 1998; Wineburg & Grossman, 1998). Whereas some teacher education programs view teacher education as progressing in a fixed development path toward an expert state, others have critiqued such preparation programs as imposing a monistic framework on a complex, situated, and individualistic process that cannot be reduced to the mastery of a set of specific skills (Grossman, 1991). Cochran-Smith (1991) argued: "The power to liberalize and reinvent notions of teaching, learning, and schooling is located in neither the university nor the school but in the collaborative work of the two" (p. 284). In this way, theory and practice are linked through student participation in actual K–12 school contexts, but with common reference points to develop the necessary critical lenses associated with best practices. *Quest2Teach* is one attempt to bridge the divide by offering what others have called a third space in which students can practice and fail safely and then use professional network tools to further connect theory and practice.

As one example, in another *Quest2Teach* game, "On The Write Track," teacher candidates engage in an immersive curriculum around student conferencing, both one-on-one and peer-led, as they inspire revisions in the Writers Workshop. The game itself has the potential to afford meaningful practice as players mentor four individual virtual students, by first reviewing each of their digital portfolios, using in-game tools to identify the literacy trait on which to focus, then engaging the virtual student in a dialog around his or her work. Rather than simply focusing on the identification of the problem in the work (i.e., which of the literacy skills is lacking from grammar to voice to audience), candidates are tasked with mentoring students in such a way that increases his or her *ability*, while balancing the feedback in such a way to also encourage students' *confidence* and *commitment* to their work, all three of which are meters in the game (see Figure 7.3).

One candidate discussed how the game reflectively increased her own confidence and commitment, in response to a Q2T Network post to one of her classmates:

> I haven't seen student conferences in any classroom, which made me feel very nervous about them, because I felt like I couldn't do something that I have never experienced. Thanks to this game I feel more confident about leading

student conferences. Also, after reading about them I still was not too sure that this was something that I could implement in my own classroom, but now I think that I am committed.

This comment highlights the notion that the game experience provided a commitment to student conferences that this student was unable to get through "reading about them." This brings up a key point; these game curricula were not meant to replace reading, or any other classroom learning experiences, and rather serve as a bridge to help extend that theory into real-world practice. More related to the notion of identity, what is so powerful in these games is the interrelations among what one knows, what one does, and who one becomes both in the game world (Barab et al., 2010) and, fundamental to the argument here, in the real world. With respect to the latter, where a game fits into one's professional trajectory is essential.

Early gameplay implementations made it clear that students often strived to score perfectly in these game meters and "get it right." Thus we emphasized in teacher training and curriculum guides to not use the game scores as grades, and instead encourage mastery, to allow students to fail safely. One instructor supported this by saying; "Don't worry about your score, as you can keep practicing and improving with different students until you feel good about your mentoring." As evidence of this framing, one student shared in her post that she was able to grow through multiple mentoring opportunities in the game (see Figure 7.7 for screen shot showing multiple students to select for student conferences). She posted this to her Q2T Network, and received subsequent replies from classmates:

Figure 7.7 Screenshot from the On the Write Track game; the player is selecting for a writers workshop conference.

Candidate 1: Sometimes I felt I was telling the student the correct answer during the conference, but would end up hurting their feelings. So it took me a couple conferences to be able to do a whole conference without saying anything that would upset the student, and it became more natural.

Candidate 2: I wasn't too sure on the correct way to approach the students or offer feedback either, but the game was such a realistic and helpful tool. I felt as though I was in the teacher's position and it has helped build my confidence for my future students.

Candidate 3: I also enjoyed playing the game. However, the peer-led review was a bit of a challenge for me, but after going through the scenario the game was able to explain to me (when talking to the principal) what I did wrong and what I needed to improve on. I was happy to learn this through the game though. So now I will be more attentive to what happens when I do a peer review in the classroom.

The positioning by the instructor and the game gave the candidates listed above the opportunity to fail safely and grow ability without real-world consequences. However, whether the safety of the designed space transferred to real-world situations was sometimes successful, and other times seemed to stay in the "magic circle" that defines the fictional boundaries of the game (Salen & Zimmerman, 2004). Our observations have led us to the belief that much of the variance in whether this occurred was based on how the instructor connected the game experience to broader classroom activities and especially to conversations around real-world placement situations.

No game can prepare for the local context and candidates better than an instructor, to extend these learning experiences from outputs to outcomes. The importance of the instructor creating the right context for the games was evident when we observed a literacy faculty lead her classes in rich theoretical preparation to contextualize the "On the Write Track" game. By the day of game play, the candidates had read the relevant chapter of theoretical grounding, taken instructor-led notes in class, discussed a YouTube video of student mentoring step by step, and engaged in role-play scenarios of student conferencing in small groups. We were uncertain what additional benefit the game would provide beyond her excellent coverage in her existing curriculum. Observations, interviews, feedback, and network posts revealed that the candidates felt the game provided the missing link that allowed them gain real-world practice and language, with the ability to fail safely, and not harm any real students in the process. As one student commented in a post-interview:

Teacher Candidate: "It definitely created a place where I could test it out and feel okay with it, because it wasn't real. Because if I had to do this with real students and not have gone through this experience, I would have so much anxiety, I wouldn't be able to stand it! Because there's a difference between just observing other teachers do it and take notes, and then actually being able to interact, myself. So I really enjoyed it and it made me feel a lot better about being able to go talk to students now about their work."

Another student added that the virtual game mentoring felt "more real" than the role-play, as he knew more or less how his classmates would act and respond. The game characters have infinite possible reactions, with expressive faces that show hurt emotions in the face of negative mentoring, and thought bubbles that make apparent their inner feelings. These game affordances gave candidates the ability to see immediate consequences and impact of their choices on their students.

> Teacher Candidate: "I enjoyed being able to jump in to a virtual situation where we are given ideas of comments and questions to make. I thought it was more helpful, because of my inexperience, to provide possible responses rather than me having to create responses; I found it important to see those examples to better be able to derive my own responses in real world situations. As I navigated through the game, I found that I related well and was drawn to the responses that would boost confidence, and therefore build ability in my students."

Many of the observed candidates become caught up in these mentoring exchanges, in the in-world characters they managed, and invested in the impact they were having on their virtual students, much more so than acting these out in person.

In a contrasting class observation, we arrived to find a new instructor had only recently been hired and was unfamiliar with the game. While we facilitated the introduction to gameplay for her, she naturally wasn't able to tie the game into their past class experiences, and further, she openly expressed her stress in her new job with students at the start of class. Interestingly, the only time we heard outwardly negative feedback was within this session. There was a markedly different feel to the class, which was quiet compared to other implementations, with some visibly uninterested, and one girl even stating, "I'm bored," in sharp contrast to the enthusiasm we usually encountered. These students still demonstrated learning gains on targeted content; however, the negativity and lack of curricular contextualization limited this implementation from reaching larger outcomes. In contrast, the literacy faculty mentioned previously embedded the game in a meaningful context within her curriculum that allowed extensions into the candidates' practice and even served as an extension into future classes and new theories of focus.

Later classroom observations revealed that for the teacher who integrated the game experiences with our other curriculum, the four virtual students continued to "live on" in the class conversations. When candidates entered new chapters, the faculty member referenced these NPCs in novel ways, saying, "Remember when you worked with Jaime," referring to an in-game character, "and remember how he was struggling with…" She recognized that these virtual students could serve as touchstone experiences, where all her candidates had interacted with and taught the same virtual students, and she extended her course discussions to these characters and their strengths and needs in new theoretical applications. We also observed positioning the game experience as an ongoing resource for continued PD, with one candidate stating, "I will play this game again to give myself more practice on conferencing with students." The important point is that the learning culture (c.f. Brown, 1992) the teacher created and the connections to the real-world placements elevated the game experience beyond its simply being another assignment to be completed, and a new service to be used both in class and in their own lives.

Similar bridging from theory to practice was observed for the professionalism game, in part because of the "embodied" ways in which narrative games position theory. Here, rather than disembodied facts, even the theory is lived and experienced, rather than described. For example, one candidate shared, "This game allowed me to *practice* how to be respectful in a disagreement, it gave me *skills* in interpersonal relationships and *how to work better* with others" (emphasis added).

Such enacted positions contributed to the perceived "use-value" of the theory for achieving desired outcomes, as opposed to the more common "exchange-value" positioning in which knowing content can be exchanged for a grade (Lave, 1997; Lave & Wenger, 1991). In part, what made *Quest2Teach* so powerful, however, was the seamless positioning of the small "g" games and the big "G" gamified infrastructures with the goal of *thrivifying* player learning to help them apply ideas in their placements as opposed to simply gamifying their engagement with the learning content. In *thrivification*, the goal is not to simply increase time on task, but to motivate players in experimenting with how application of the theory in practice allows them to achieve great things. This was most evident in the professional network posts, where candidates shared reflections of how the theory introduced through the bounded games related to their field placements:

> There was a moment in my internship class where a student came up to me to talk about how to spell "mystery." I sat with her for a second because I know she is a great student, but she is very shy; it was strange to me that she even came up to ask a question. When I asked her to sound out the word, I told her this one was a little tricky and might need extra attention, but I didn't want to give her the answer right away. When she turned to me confused, I told her, "I know you can do it." She replied, somewhat excited, "Oh! There must be a y!" I gave her a smile that let her know she got it and she was so happy with herself! She walked away and went back to her seat with such a

huge smile, it made me feel as if I gave her the confidence and ability to work on her spelling.

In response, another player who earned "props" then awarded the maximum number in response to the above post, acknowledging her peer's meaningful application of theory to practice at the same time gaining further contextualized insight on her own theory to practice application.

> I think that's awesome that you took so much time to make sure that she spelled the word on her own. I've seen far too often that teachers get frustrated and decide to just tell the student how to spell the word. I will definitely try your approach some time in my own class.

This affordance of game mechanics provides what Sawyer (2014) referred to as "seductive ubiquitous interfaces" in that they are available just-in-time when they are needed through, for example, smart phones.

OUTCOME 3: PROFESSIONAL IDENTITY SHIFTS

Within the context of this chapter, we are treating identity as distributed, situated, and continually evolving set of experiences, beliefs, and potentials that form one's sense of who they are and what they want to become in relation to a profession (Eccles et al., 1983; McDermott, 1993). We find it productive to view one's professional identity as an ever-growing and fluid set of convergences, an identity system (Engeström, 1987; Leont'ev, 1974; Nardi, 2000), which continuously evolves over the course of one's lifetime in relation to new opportunities and accomplishments. Such a dynamic and ecological view of self (Bronfrenbrenner, 1978; Eisenhart, 2002), one that treats professional identity as a distributed accomplishment shifting over time and space (Pea, 1993), is more empowering then views that position identity as fixed property primarily residing within an individual (Barab & Plucker, 2001; Pepper, 1970). In fact, part of the power of games is the different roles on offer that a learner can take on over the course of the game, and from a theory of change perspective, what one knows, what one does, and who one becomes all become interrelated. In fact, a key transformational potential of games is that through play they create possibility for all, allowing players to experience what it means to be "head above themselves" even if the identity feels quite distal in the real world (Vygostky, 1978).

It is in this sociocultural framing of identity as coconstructed, distributed, and as a situated set of opportunities that could be available to all (Sternberg, 2007) where we see games as capable of producing a third type of transformative outcome. As Gee (2003) argued, the line between me as real-world player, me as in-game avatar, and me as player-avatar quickly becomes blurred through meaningful play. Therefore, in terms of a learning medium, games create a truly transformative medium for helping people grow their professional selves, even if in the real world it feels less possible. The goal from a game designer's perspective is to enable meaningful person–environment couplings, creating and inviting players into identity claims through which they can evolve their sense of who they are as a professional. One student, referring to the Professional game, stated:

> This was a significant shift out of not being a student anymore, you know? We are in the professional world now, and we need to see ourselves as teachers. This game was like a shift into "the real life," and other people can relate to that struggle.

Another student, reacting to the consequentiality she experienced in the On the Write Track game, posted in the network:

> I never felt that way when I had conferences with my English teachers. From my experience, it's led me to want to be the teacher that builds up the confidence for each of my students and this game has helped me get to do that.

Another student responded to her post, acknowledging who she was becoming as a professional:

> Tamara, I think because you have had a negative experience with your writing, you will really go the extra mile to encourage your students to be confident in theirs. It is so important to lift our students up and I am confident that you will do that as a teacher!

It is important to note that it was not the game, nor the game plus the network, but each of these in relation to the teacher, and especially where the experience fits into the player life trajectory that allows it to become an identity experience. Further, it is essential to remind the reader that these quotes are opportunistically selected in order to advance a proof existence, and should not be read as representative of all players—although we did hear numerous statements of this type, especially in those classes where the instructor connected the game to other classroom activities and to field placement discussions.

While different types of game mechanics offer different affordances for learning, and in our work 3D immersive role-playing games where students create an in-game self, embody it within a designed avatar, and then make real-world connections by combining accomplishments of their in-game performance with, for example, giving props to peers based on real-world performance is potentially transformative. As further elaboration, teacher candidates begin each of the games by creating avatars to represent themselves as the protagonists in the narrative, and most individuals typically select features to represent themselves. It is here where they first engage in project play, building a representation that is them and not them, and developing a playful disposition to the game mechanics, which we argue is an important part of learning through games:

> **Researcher:** So did you put much thought into what you're wearing?
> **Student 1:** We did! We wanted to go with like, tan professional pants, with matching shoes and shirt. [laughing]
> **Student 2:** And buttoned down, and wedges—so they're not flats, or biker boots.
> **Student 3:** And the different colors of shoes. We liked that, so we could coordinate our shirt with our shoes. [more laughing]
> **Student 1:** And I teach 2nd grade, so no skirts! I need to be able to get down on the floor with my students.
> **Student 3:** Exactly! [laughing]

We even observed instances in which players who were assigned game play during class and had to share computers would create avatars and make choices that were hybrids of both players (see Figure 7.8 for screen shot of avatar creator). For example, one pair from different backgrounds and of different genders, created a shared account who was male (i.e., as was the Asian male candidate), but who had long hair and brown skin (i.e., more similar to the Latino candidate). At one point in the game they had prepared

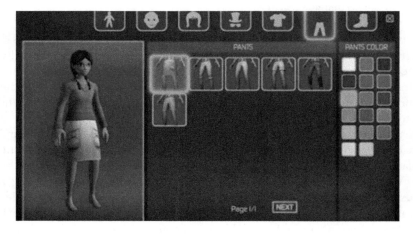

Figure 7.8   Screenshot of the avatar builder.

their lesson and the male candidate wanted to go out with friends, to whom the female responded that she had a child and could not just go out.

> **Male:** What do you mean? He doesn't have a kid. [referring to the game character]
>
> **Female:** [emphatically] I do have a kid. And some of us can't just go party as we have to work and go to school.
>
> **Male:** [with a look of surprise, stated] What do you mean . . . wait, you have a kid?
>
> **Female:** Yup, have all year, and even did last year. Why do you think I am so tired?
>
> **Male:** [somewhat shamefully] Wow! But, I was talking about the game choice. Our game avatar doesn't have a kid. I mean, I didn't think he did.

We highlight this interaction simply to show the blurring of the in game and the real, and additionally to illuminate how the game interactions create a space for real-world interactions that had not occurred previously.

The teacher candidates use this avatar to navigate and negotiate through this immersive narrative, with each decision point changing their trajectory in the game. They travel between their virtual apartment, where they prepare their lesson plans and can discuss their problems with their roommates (who are also student teaching), to the school, classroom, and teachers' lounge, where they are met with a variety of opportunities to act professionally as they interact with their mentor, their students, and other teachers, many of whom would love to engage in gossip, and others who offer sound advice. An important part of the challenge in designing these games is to represent what has been referred to as the "quantified self," capturing the notion that in games many of the interactions and even personal identities are assigned a value. Clearly, if the game is not positioned effectively, failure could be quite traumatic, and it is so important that the players use their game play to make claims on their self as opposed to the game making problematic claims that undermine player confidence and sense of themselves as professional. An important strength of these games is in how they force the designer, and the player, to make implicit biases explicit. This becomes an important part of the design opportunity in that it is not simply the player identity that is quantified, but also the design of the game characters create further opportunities to advance productive and problematic identities and to understand who others grow and even positioning them as role models for observational learning (Bandura, 1986). This is because academic content, in the context of the game, is not simply decontextualized concepts but embedded characters who have emotions and personalities, and who respond accordingly—for example, having player statements

Figure 7.9 Screenshot of the game character internal reaction to player's dialogue choice.

or actions affect game characters based on their professional identity (see Figure 7.9 for screenshot of character reaction). But, again, it is our belief that these events are made much more transformational when the game is situated in relation to player life trajectory, and to local interactions that leverage these opportunities for deepening one's understanding and sense of self.

The game was initially available to first-semester teacher candidates to prepare them for their initial classroom observations. However, when implemented this early in their field experience, we were surprised by choices and comments from the teacher candidates. One student's comment was representative of many students' inexperience, when she said, "I would never have a conflict with my mentor teacher. I'm just going to roll over and do whatever she says!"

In contrast, another instructor asked to have her student teachers (three semesters ahead of the previous group) to play this same Professionalism game that semester. One student teacher articulated the importance of grounding this game in experience by stating, "I don't think if we played this last semester or last year, any one of us would have taken it as seriously, but now we know, this is for real!"

This contrast highlights the difference in what we call "just-in-time" versus "just-in-case" learning, and the experience of ecosystem integration if the innovation is going to support transformative outcomes.

Players in their first semester of teacher preparation lacked the context and experience to make sense of the game and its complexities. They enjoyed the game and learned the core concepts of professionalism as demonstrated on applied tests, but the larger experience, relevance, and impact was lacking. In contrast, when student teachers played the same game curriculum with three semesters more experience in the field, they found it engaging and relevant, with many students even asking for a transcript so they could review and practice the language for saying things professionally. When players engaged the game curriculum "just-in-time," they had the context and experience from which to draw, engage, and transform the game transactions. Further, their reflections posted in their class's Q2T professional network postgame were more nuanced with rich connections to their real-world practice, serving as shared resources for improving practice (outcomes), as opposed to in the "just-in-case" implementations where the ideas were simply concepts to be memorized and posts were more declarative in nature.

We made an interesting design choice based on these contrasting findings and experiences. In balancing the college's need to prepare the new students in the professionalism competencies, yet understanding the richer impact of contextualized game play, we decided to have students play the game twice, once at the end of their first semester (to allow several months of field experience for context), and again 2 years later during their student teaching as a refresher before entering job interviews and their careers and as a reflection activity around their growth as a professional. In the iterative process of design-based implementation research, the same students who found the Professionalism game somewhat irrelevant when placed too early in their program later used their game play to validate the professional growth they had indicated previously as being irrelevant. One student shared:

> The last time I played this game, I have to admit, all the [dialog] choices looked the same to me. I was like, "I guess I'll just click this one and see what happens!" But this time I was like, "Wow! This is really common sense!" I could tell I had grown as a professional.

Another candidate added a related and interesting facet of reaction by saying:

> The first time I played the game and my mentor [in the game] didn't like my lesson plan I quickly backed down and said, "Oh, I'm sorry! I'll change it, or just go with yours." This time around though, I had the confidence to stand up for myself, and even the experience to say how I felt the students were learning well with my plan. I was able to choose professional ways to support my own plan.

In this case, the game provided data from which the player was able to critically assess her own professional growth, and to illuminate how she had changed during the course of her matriculation.

The "enabling ecosystem" within this game-based curriculum is fundamentally the teacher candidates' life trajectory and where the game fits into that larger experience. Ironically, the game, and one's projection into a virtual character constructed primarily out of bits and bytes, allowed the curriculum to become deeply tied to their real-world identity, creating a space for reflecting on what it means to be a professional beyond academic content knowledge:

> Last time around I was totally academically based, choosing only to work on my lesson plan and email my mentor the night before my teaching. This time I felt accomplished enough to say, I'm prepared now, I can go relax with my friends. That's part of professionalism to me, once you've prepared, also taking time for yourself, and realizing that's also pivotal for your development. And that realization was new to me this time around.

The point here, however, is that in initial gameplay, teacher candidates lacked the field experience to make sense of the game curriculum beyond domain-specific outputs. However, in the later gameplay, they had experience enough to learn the targeted content and contextualize that within a framework of personal relevance and even self-assess and recognize specific traits in their identify shift to that of a professional educator. Placement of these immersive experiences quickly became less about convenience or scheduling and more about uncovering the optimal context and experience, which were key for these identity shifts to take place.

REFLECTING ON LESSONS LEARNED

We have built an argument that the potential of games to cultivate transformative impact is less about how powerful games are and more how they can be integrated as part of a suite of products and services that enable players to thrive in their life. And unlike traditional video games, it is less about what the player can do and become in the game designer's world, and more how the game can enable players to be great in their world. This argument is not meant to undermine the power of a strong design, especially when it helps the player level up with usable knowledge, storied achievements, life connections, scaffolded successes, local ownership, and supportive peers. However, the goal in these designs is less about bringing the players into the designer's world and more about supporting the players in more effectively engaging constructs and practices in their world. More generally, we are suggesting that games for impact need to raise the question of where and with whom fidelity resides. In the game-enabled services thesis, fidelity is less about staying true to the designer's goals or even to the meaning being advanced in the product, but instead it lies in the ways the ecosystem, the facilitator, and/or the player is able to leverage and integrate the experience to meaningfully affect their personal goals and their implementation contexts, even if that is a departure from the original design intentions. Designing for such a partnership involves a deep belief in all people's potential to thrive when provided the right inputs, with a key role of the game being to invite, inspire, and unlock a potential, with the player having the responsibility of stepping into the opportunity.

A fundamental assumption underlying this work is that while demonstrating immediate outputs tightly coupled to the content as presented in the learning innovation is straightforward, building transferrable outcomes often requires a different type of learning experience. The key to unlocking transformation must be turned by the player, and it is here where we see impact as invitational and residing at the nodes. It is here, we argue, where one's relationship to the learning situation and to how one learns is so important, and it is here where we believe that player intention (motivations for learning), content application (use-value of the content), and ecosystem integration (contextual relevance and fit) are essential. We believe that unlocking this transformative and expansive potential within human beings is both an art and a science. Just as we tend to critique "dissemination" models of learning as being too top-down, we need to question models of impact that do not enable those being impacted to have an essential role in realizing its potential. It is within those individuals who operate at the implementation nodes, where fidelity belongs, with the focus being on how they are able to productively re-define structures in ways that realize their needs (Baker & Sinkula, 2002; Siedman, 2007).

Game designers have a rich tradition of creating game worlds that invite the player in to do great things. At first blush, this creates a powerful vision, and in our previous work it was our core goal to bring the reader into our designed worlds where we could allow even a ten-year-old to become a successful environmental scientist who could save a park (Barab, Zuiker, et al., 2007). However, when designing games for impact that are focused on what we have referred to as transformative outcomes, it is more about how our games integrate into their worlds. In other words, *it is less about what players unlock in our designs, and more about what our designs unlock in them and for them*; the competition that matters in games for impact is not a game score, but instead it is how the designed and facilitated suite of products and services inspire players to compete with their better selves. In a very real way, we are promoting a view that it is the players themselves who produce the impact and not our games, even though our designs have an important role in inspiring, visualizing, challenging, connecting, and scaffolding players in meaningfully and enthusiastically engaging this work.

Sadly, however, for many there are too few opportunities to engage in consequential experiences where they matter in positive ways. This has resulted in many finding agency, belonging, and a sense that they matter in transgressive or destructive causes and movements, from bullying to reckless disregard for our surroundings or selves, or at an extreme, joining movements such as ISIS. Clearly, we have an ethical responsibility in terms of creating stories and illuminating perspectives as part of what the "game as product" accomplishes. We need to remain deeply reflective in deciding what narratives live within our designs, or what perspectives our game mechanics and gamification meters bias. There are many issues that need to be illuminated, and it is our opportunity, if not responsibility, to determine the places our game could take the player and be reflective of why we think it is appropriate. There are many places that people wouldn't go without games, whether we are talking about an inner-city Latino youth believing he can become an engineer, or a Muslim woman believing she can start a business, or an Alaskan Native storyteller believing that his cultural stories could be globally resonant.

Good game designers can help make the unreal become real, and it is our challenge to make what feels real within the confines of our virtual worlds unlock possibilities for players in the other worlds in which they inhabit. We need to ensure that the designs we create are engaging and are of high quality, or our messages won't scale. At Games for Change a couple or years ago, games scholar James Paul Gee made clear that the power of games both as entertainment products and for impact lies in what happens around the game. This coincides with other gamification efforts and with notions that designers need to expand the construct of "game," and consider "seductive ubiquitous interfaces" that follow players through multiple contexts, increasing real-world behaviors, as part of our available toolkit. For us, gamification already has much historical baggage, and we are seeking different terms for characterizing our goal in supporting game-enabled impact. For example, "thrivification" conjures up a very different focus then gamification, less about the game features and more about the goal of inciting a passion that respects the agency and humanity of the player, and that invites (not simply reinforces) player choice. Thrivification, when used in this context, is not about what we design, nor how teachers were trained to support the implementation, but what the learner was able to do as a result of their engagement with the design.

Gamification without deeper meaning runs the risk of undermining true impact, even while there are powerful examples where players operating within carefully designed gamification systems accomplish great things. Consistent with our theory of change, thrivification is about lighting an internal passion and building within each one of us the agency and capacity for change—both individually and collectively. The power of games like Foldit resides within the protein folding recipes produced by the community, and Minecraft is so powerful because of the possibilities it affords, and, more importantly, how players have realized these affordances—not in following the rules or acquiring the knowledge and meanings the designer created. Games provide "possibility space for action," but they need a player who acts on these possibilities—impact asks for a bit more from the player. In other words, sustainable impact and even transformative outcomes lie within the communities' or players' hands, and we need to have faith in the potential of people to take act on these opportunities, and at the same time building designs that inspire them to reach for more.

IMPLICATIONS FOR THE FIELD

In the end, when it comes to real-world impact, the potential to achieve transformative outcomes lives within those whom we hope to impact—not the designer or the product. Ultimately, our impact lies within the potential of each player to take up the unlocked possibilities in their lives. Arizona State University president, Michael Crow, has argued that talent is equally distributed across zip codes, but opportunity is not. It is our responsibility to leverage the power of games, in its many forms, to create opportunities for players to unlock their potential, and we must ensure that our designs are optimized to support this unlocking: partly as products, partly as services, and fully by human beings who want to achieve great things. Ultimately, the success of our designs is bound up in human potential, not game mechanics, and the mark of a masterful designer can be seen in his or her ability to give up control and create spaces and structures for others to achieve great things.

This is a paradigm shift for most individuals and organizations who treat impact as something one does to another, and who position expertise as something that resides in the hands of a few core individuals. Instead, we are arguing for a human-centric framework that fundamentally provides and acknowledges the agency of and respect for those being impacted. Beyond simply the player, we are positioning those who are often responsible for implementing the innovation as needing to have agency in how owning how they enable the innovation. We see these individuals as codesigners, managing the fit and re-architecting local meanings that will have more resonance to their context. We believe that the lessons learned in our work are applicable across multiple fields and could provide a methodological framework that has resonance with many initiatives in multiple domains working towards scaling impact.

More generally, while the notion of a theory of change, of a logic model, and even the distinction between outputs and outcomes is known by many, how we leverage particular models and frameworks in ways that will lead to transformative outcomes is less clear. Here, we are arguing that such impact is an internal or invitational process that requires the innovation to empower the nodes—those supporting and being impacted. More generally, what is needed is a more systematic and cross-disciplinary examination and application of diverse models in order to build a science of impact, or what might be thought of as *impact sciences*. In this chapter we draw on models and best practices that have usefully informed our work on using games for impact. We view these models and our lessons learned as applicable beyond games and encourage the reader to find these connections in their work for impact. We also hope to see the emergence of a broader field focused on advancing impact—a field that is deeply rooted in the needs of our planet but that leverages methodological routines and scholarly debates in a way that results in a stronger sense of how to cultivate sustainable and scalable outcomes.

ACKNOWLEDGEMENTS

Special thanks to Denny Sanford for his generous donations to the Mary Lou Fulton Teachers College, to Dean Mari Koerner for entrusting us with this support, and to I-Teach AZ for integrating these into their courses and field placements. Also, special thanks to Ryen Borden and the Sanford Inspire program team who worked tirelessly with us to continually iterate the game, and for their patience as we integrated the larger theory of change to inform the work.

Special thanks to the Gates Foundation for their generous support in funding the development of the ARX game engine. Thanks to Adam Ingram-Goble, Kathryn Dutchin, Lee McIlroy, E-Line Media, and the other designers and implementation team that supported us in developing and iterating these games.

Correspondence should go directly to Dr. Sasha Barab, Professor in the School for Innovation and Society and Executive Director at the Center for Games and Impact.

REFERENCES

Alter, C., & Egan, M. (1997). Logic modeling: A tool for teaching critical thinking in social work practice. *Journal of Social Work Education, 33*(1).

Alter, C., & Murty, S. (1997). Logic modeling: A tool for teaching practice evaluation. *Journal of Social Work Education, 33*(1).

Arici, A., & Barab, S. A. (2016). Producing sustainable and scaled impact: A human-centric framework. In L. Lin & B. K. Atkinson (Eds.), *Educational technologies: Challenges, applications, and learning outcomes* (pp. 142–168). Hauppauge, NY: Nova Science.

Backer, T. (2001). *Finding the balance: Program fidelity and adaptation in substance abuse prevention. A state-of-the-art review.* Rockville, MD: SAMHSA.

Barab, S. A., Gresalfi, M. S., & Ingram-Goble, A. (2010). Transformational play: Using games to position person, content, and context. *Educational Researcher, 39*(7), 525–536.

Barab, S. A., Zuiker, S., Warren, S., Hickey, D., Ingram-Goble, A., Kwon, E-J., & Herring, S. C. (2007). Situationally embodied curriculum: Formalisms and contexts. *Science Ed., 91*(5), 750–782.

Brown, J. S., Collins, A., & Duguid, P. (1989). Situated cognition and the culture of learning. *Educational Researcher, 18*(1), 32–42.

Bruner, J. S. (1990). *Acts of meaning* (Vol. 3). Cambridge, MA: Harvard University Press.

Cochran-Smith, M. (1991). Learning to teach against the grain. *Harvard Educational Review, 61*(3), 279–311.

Cochran-Smith, M. & Lytle, S. L. (1999a). Relationships of knowledge and practice: Teacher learning in communities. In A. Iran-Nejad & P. D. Pearson (Eds.), *Review of research in education* (pp 249–305). Washington, DC: American Educational Research Association.

Cochran-Smith, M., & Lytle, S. L. (1999b). The teacher research movement: A decade later. *Educational Researcher, 28*(7), 15–25.

Crow, M. M., & Dabars, W. B. (2015). *Designing the new American university*. Baltimore, MD: John Hopkins University Press.

Dewey, J. (1938). *Experience & education*. New York, NY: Collier MacMillan.

Dugan, R. E., & Hernon, P. (2002). Outcomes assessment: Not synonymous with inputs and outputs. *The Journal of Academic Librarianship, 28*(6), 376–380.

Eccles, J. S., Adler, T. F., Futterman, R., Goff, S. B., Kaczala, C. M., Meece, J. L., et al. (1983). Expectancies, values, and academic behaviors. In J. T. Spence (Ed.), *Achievement and achievement motivation* (pp. 75–146). San Francisco, CA: Freedman.

Engeström, Y. (1987). *Learning by expanding*. Helsinki, Finland: Orienta-konsultit.

Greeno, J. (1998). The situativity of knowing, learning, and research. *American Psychologist, 53*(1), 5–26.

Gee, J. P. (2003). *What video games have to teach us about learning*. New York, NY: Palgrave.

Gee, J. (2013). *The anti-education era: Creating smarter students through digital learning*. New York, NY: Palgrave Macmillan.

Gresalfi, M., & Barab, S. A. (2011). Learning for a reason: Supporting forms of engagement by designing tasks and orchestrating environments. *Theory into Practice, 50*(4), 300–310.

Grossman. P. L. (1991). Overcoming the apprenticeship of observation in teacher education coursework. *Teaching & Teacher Education, 7*(4), 345–357.

Guskey, T. R. (2002). Professional development and teacher change. *Teachers and teaching, 8*(3), 381–391.

Ito, M., Baumer, S., Bittanti, M., Cody, R., Stephenson, B. H., Horst, H. A.,...& Perkel, D. (2009). *Hanging out, messing around, and geeking out: Kids living and learning with new media*. MIT press.

Jenkins, H. (2004). The cultural logic of media convergence. *International Journal of Cultural Studies, 7*(1), 33–43.

Julian, D. A. (1997). The utilization of the logic model as a system level planning and evaluation device. *Evaluation and Program Planning, 20*(3), 251–257.

Kagan, D. M. (1992). Professional growth among preservice and beginning teachers. *Review of Educational Research, 62*(2), 129–169.

Kapur, M., & Bielaczyc, K. (2012). Designing for productive failure. *Journal of the Learning Sciences, 21*(1), 45–83.

Kellogg Foundation. (2004). *Logic model development guide: Logic models to bring together planning, evaluation & action.* Battle Creek, MI: W.K. Kellogg Foundation.

Latour, B. (1987). *Science in action: How to follow scientists and engineers through society.* Milton Keynes, England: Open University Press.

Lave, J, (1997). The culture of acquisition and the practice of understanding. In D. Kirshner & L. A. Whitson (Eds.), *Situated cognition: Social, semiotic, and psychological perspectives* (pp. 17–36). Mahwah, NJ: Lawrence Erlbaum Associates, Inc.

Lave, J., & Wenger, E. (1991). *Situated learning: Legitimate peripheral participation.* New York, NY: Cambridge University Press.

Leont'ev, A. (1974). The problem of activity in psychology. *Soviet Psychology, 13*(2), 4–33.

Maurya, A. (2012). *Running lean: Iterate from plan A to a plan that works.* " O'Reilly Media, Inc."

Millar, A., Simeone, R. S. & Carnevale, J. T. (2001). Logic models: A systems tool for performance management. *Evaluation and Program Planning, 24*, 73–81.

Nardi, B., (2006). *Context and consciousness: Activity theory and human-computer interaction.* Cambridge, MA: The MIT Press.

Newzoo. (2016). 2016 annual report of Newzoo on the Global Games Market. Retrieved from http://www.newzoo.com/infographics/global-games-market-report-infographics

Pea, R. (1993). Practices of distributed intelligence and designs for education. In G. Salomon (Ed.), *Distributed cognitions: Psychological and educational considerations* (pp. 47–87). Cambridge, England: Cambridge University Press.

Pendleton-Jullian, A., & Brown, J. S. (2011). *Design unbound: Evolving design literacy pathways of efficacy.* Draft manuscript, Charleston, SC.

Pepper, S. C. (1970). *World hypotheses.* Berkeley, CA: University of California Press.

Putnam, R. T. & Borko, H. (2000). What do new views of knowledge and thinking have to say about research on teacher learning? *Educational Researcher, 29*(1), 4–15.

Ries, E. (2011). *The lean startup: How today's entrepreneurs use continuous innovation to create radically successful businesses.* Crown Business.

Salen, K. & Zimmerman, E. (2004). *Rules of play.* Cambridge, MA: MIT Press.

Sarewitz, D., & Nelson, R. (2008). Three rules for technological fixes. *Nature, 456*(7224), 871–872.

Schultz, H., & Yang, D. J. (1999). *Pour your heart into it: How Starbucks built a company one cup at a time.* New York, NY: Hyperion.

Seidman, D. (2007). *How: Why how we do anything means everything…in business (and in life).* Hoboken, NJ: John Wiley & Sons.

Sfard, A. (1998). On two metaphors for learning and the dangers of choosing just one. *Educational Researcher, 27*(1), 4–13.

Squire, K. (2006). From content to context: Videogames as designed experiences. *Educational Researcher, 35*(8), 19–29.

Stein, M. K., & Smith, M. S. (1998). Mathematical tasks as a framework for reflection: From research to practice. *Mathematics teaching in the middle school, 3*(4), 268–275.

Steinkuehler, C. A. (2006). Why game (culture) studies now? *Games and Culture, 1*(1), 97–102.

Sternberg, R. J. (2007). Who are the bright children? The cultural context of being and acting intelligent. *Educational Researcher, 36*(3), 148–155.

Stokes, B., O'Shea, G., Walden, N., Nasso, F., Mariutto, G., Hill, A., & Burak, A. (2016).*Impact With Games: A Fragmented Field*. Pittsburgh, PA: ETC Press. Retrieved from http://gameimpact.net/reports/fragmented-field/

Toyama, K. (2015). *Geek heresy: Rescuing social change from the cult of technology*. New York, NY: PublicAffairs.

Wineburg, S., & Grossman, P. (1998). Creating a community of learners among high school teachers. *Phi Delta Kappan, 79*(5), 350.

Wouters, P., van Nimwegen, C., van Oostendorp, H., & van der Spek, E. D. (2013). A meta-analysis of the cognitive and motivational effects of serious games. *Journal of Educational Psychology, 105*(2), 249–265.

CHAPTER 8

EDUCATING DIGITAL NATIVES

Possible and Prospective Futures of Students in Learning Ecologies

W. Ian O'Byrne and Nenad Radakovic
College of Charleston

> *All education springs from the images of the future and all education
> creates images of the future. Thus all education, whether so intended or not,
> is a preparation for the future. Unless we understand the future
> for which we are preparing we may do tragic damage to those we teach.*
>
> —Toffler, 1974, p. 3

The Internet has become the one of the major defining technologies for literacy and learning in the 21st century (Friedman, 2005; International Reading Association, 2002; Partnership for 21st Century Skills, 2004). Literacy, as a sociocultural practice (Street, 1984, 1993), is rapidly shifting from paper to screen, to hybrid models of learning that value different ways of meaning making, including literacies influenced by multiple digital technologies (Lankshear & Knobel, 2002; New London Group, 1996, 2000). Regarding Internet literacy, for example, one sixth of the world's population—1.3 billion individuals—now uses the Internet to read, write, communicate, learn, and solve important problems (Internet World Stats:

Exploding the Castle, pages 179–197
Copyright © 2017 by Information Age Publishing

Usage and Population Statistics, 2008), and the number of Internet users has increased by nearly 300% over the last seven years (Internet Live Stats, 2015). Assuming Internet access rates continue to grow at this pace, more than half of the world's population will be using the Internet by 2023, and there may be universal access in as little as 10 to 15 years.

Such universality—living in a connected world where the web affords unprecedented learning opportunities—has made information plentiful and put experts, figuratively speaking, at our fingertips. New, ubiquitous mobile technologies have made the promise of improved access a realistic, achievable goal. And crucially, our web-enabled landscape has prompted a new vision for education, demonstrating the value of learning anywhere, anytime, and with equal access as a fundamental human right (UNESCO, n.d.). Never in the history of civilization have we seen such a potentially transformative literacy technology adopted by so many in so many different places in such a short period of time (Leu, Kinzer, Coiro, & Cammack, 2007). That leaves the current generation of educators, researchers, and policymakers with the critical responsibility to help facilitate a cultural transition during this period of profound change, ensuring a successful and positive move from print to digital resources (Merchant, 2007). Additionally, it will force us to address print-to-digital shifts in a manner that guarantees equity for all learners across the globe.

This chapter features a series of future studies intended to assist with the identification and cataloguing of possible, critical game and game-based literacy resource affordances for K–12 and higher education (Hicks, 2006, 2012; Slaughter, 2003). We have provided three constructed cases set in classrooms existing just a few years ahead of present and positioned them as a context for (a) identifying contemporary research of value to educators, researchers, and others, and (b) pointing to what we believe is the optimal pathway toward a brighter educational future. Though it is more a thought experiment than researched study of existing school settings, we have integrated multiple lines of research from related fields (e.g., web literacy, digital gaming, badges, open learning, hybrid/blended learning environments) in hopes of pinpointing opportunities to move learners from simple consumers of digital literacies to curators of content and creators and remixers of digital media.

Before forging ahead, we should clarify our *deictic* perspective on technology and literacy (Leu et al., 2004), meaning that the role and the nature of technology and literacy keeps changing as new communication and information technologies emerge. The illustrative case studies (Datta, 1990; Davey, 1991) presented in this chapter were constructed on the assumption that emerging technologies afford the creation of novel digital spaces for literacy learning, something Coiro, Knobel, Lankshear, and Leu (2008) described as "continuously new, multiple, and rapidly disseminated" (pp. 5).

We believe this will provide special insight into important variations (Davey, 1991) in student knowledge, skills, and dispositions as they engage in literacy and technology practices.

OUR STUDY OF THE FUTURE: METHODOLOGY AND CAUTION

We build our cases using a combination of elementary, middle, and high school contexts, which we believe will demonstrate the value of games and game mechanics across a variety of learning environments. As we begin this thought experiment, we acknowledge the challenges and opportunities that exist in future studies (Slaughter, 2003; Voros, 2008). The overall approach relies upon the utilization of theoretical perspectives and personal experiences to critically and creatively propose paths to and predictions about events to come (Bell, 2010). Importantly, though, future studies are not empirical analyses but instead attempts to consolidate ideas about the future and serve as a basis for actions in the present capable of empowering individuals by providing them with opportunities to create, enact, and re-envision their preferred futures (Dator, 2005). Our perspectives in this work are framed by four goals (Hicks, 2012):

- Enabling individuals to understand the links between their own lives in the present and those of others in the past and future.
- Increasing understanding of the economic, social, political and cultural influences that shape individuals' perceptions of personal, local, and global futures.
- Developing the skills, attitudes, and values that encourage foresight and enable individuals to identify possible probable and preferable futures.
- Working toward the achievement of a more just and sustainable future in which the welfare of both people and planet are of equal importance.

Future studies may include four orientations that guide our determination and prognostication of future educational contexts (Gidley, 2004): probable, possible, preferred, and prospective. The probable perspective is defined as being primarily a global or ecological analysis of trends. The possible perspective is defined as being imaginative and utilizing creative ideas and permitting for flexibility. The preferred perspective is defined as including a values position that is critical and perhaps ideological. The prospective perspective is identified by a will to act and includes themes of self-reliance and empowerment. In this chapter, we have primarily focused on possible and prospective orientations, given that our approach is primarily speculative in nature and focuses on collaborative dialogue between researchers.

Of course, there is ample reason to be cautious as we reflect, as demonstrated in the 1967 film *1999 AD* (Philco-Ford Corporation & Madden, 1967). The story depicts life in the year 1999 from the perspective of a small, nuclear family consisting of a husband, wife, and their eight-year old son. Although the movie is set in "the future," the 1960s family structure remains intact with the husband stereotypically serving as the family's sole financial provider and his wife acting as a doting homemaker and spender of her husband's money.

Their son, Jamie, is homeschooled and "much of his education is carried in a quite specious educational center within their home" (Philco-Ford Corporation & Tom Thomas Organization, 1967, n.p.). The narrator tells us that Jamie's "assignments are programmed into a home computer and fed into the teaching machines which allows him to progress as rapidly as his awakening mind can absorb the audio-visual lessons" (n.p.). The computer is shown to give an assessment in terms of true/false questions about the history of astronomy, offers the results, and, upon recognizing Jamie's poor outcome, suggests a lecture review. Jamie transitions to a module that offers an audio lesson on the primary test topic, but he quickly loses interest, turns on a different monitor, and begins watching a cartoon. Importantly, Jamie is alone in the room, and there is no evidence of collaboration with any peers.

Clearly, the film's writers foresaw a future rooted in direct instruction based on remediation and regurgitation of fact rather than education initialized (and meaningfully engaged with) by the student. It reveals as much about 1967 (if not more) than about 1999, including societal beliefs and expectations, gender norms, national aspirations (e.g., space research), and technological advances. The entire pedagogical model hinges on learning as teacher-centered and deficit-based. Despite the fact that he is learning in no one's company but the machine's, little of Jamie's experience can or should be considered autonomous.

This example illustrates some of the difficult-to-avoid shortcomings associated with future studies like ours. According to Slaughter (2003), many approaches to scenario building may have a tendency to ignore underlying social structures and (inadvertently) take them for granted. Even a quick glance at *1999 AD* highlights how its authors overlooked the potential for mid-20th-century gender and societal norms to evolve by the turn of the 21st century. By failing to make the defining paradigms of their worldview transparent, the movie's educational future could not account for any shifts away from the top-down, transmission model of education. The purpose of describing this particular film is to illustrate the shortcomings of the future case studies and not to offer the outline of history of future studies. The challenge, then, is to make our assumptions as transparent as possible to avoid the same future study trap.

THEORETICAL PERSPECTIVES

We have identified a series of theoretical perspectives that we believe can help us optimally understand and construct these illustrative case studies of prospective students of the future. In this we identify preferred future approaches to teaching and learning. These include resources and tools with origins in seven distinct fields of study: web literacy, open education, digital badges, gaming, play and learning, collaborative learning, and hybrid/blended learning. For each, we have framed contemporary thinking as it relates within and across subject matter and explained how it directly aligns with our investigation. Please note, however, that the selected fields and schools of thought they represent are not exhaustive, do not include all possible connections made as students learn and teachers teach, and represent just one attempt at explaining how and why learning happens *in situ*. Each field is a distinct ecosystem in and of itself, and new properties and affordances will always emerge dependent on the life-worlds of those who engage with and around them.

Web Literacy

The World Wide Web has become a defining technology for literacy learning and development among millennial learners. It provides access to a seemingly unlimited volume of information via a participatory learning space. Accordingly, multiple theories and years of research have examined literacy practices in these online and hybrid spaces. Yet, in spite of being early adopters, history's first generation of "always connected" individuals often lack the knowledge and skills necessary to critically explore, build, and connect online. They are in desperate need of opportunities to practice web literacy for to the purposes of reading, writing, and positively participating in Internet-based environments (McVerry, Belshaw, & O'Byrne, 2015).

Clearly, there is a need for our 21st-century educational system to educate all students in the effective and authentic use of technologies for academic and personal uses that permeate society to prepare them for the future. Educational institutions have previously (and consistently) emphasized the use of traditional tools like textbooks, chalkboards, overhead projectors, ring binders, and composition books, but over the last two decades, we have collectively embraced new and dynamically changing media that do not necessarily overlap with those of the past. To truly prepare learners for the challenges of everyday life in the modern world, we must make intentional instructional decisions that empower students to encode and decode meaning through the dualistic producer/recipient, or reader/writer nature of online informational contexts (O'Byrne, 2014). Understanding the computational concepts upon which digital applications run can offer them the opportunity to move beyond simply reading such media by becoming more discerning end users—and potentially innovative writers of new media—themselves.

Multiple educational technology pedagogical frameworks (e.g., those focused on digital literacy, media literacy, information literacy) emphasize complex thinking skills as required for effective web use. However, researchers and instructors in these areas have attempted to teach web functionality and use through direct instruction and metaphor in place of activities that capitalize on explicit affordances of the web as a networked medium. Bringing these varied perspectives into one area as identified as web literacy allows for the consideration of the pedagogical opportunities of technology as a literacy.

Open Education

Open learning (sometimes called "open education") is defined as "a set of practices, resources, and scholarship that are openly accessible, free to use and access, and to re-purpose" (Graham, LaBonte, Roberts, O'Byrne, & Osterhout, 2014, p. 418). Educators who support the open learning/education movement have frequently argued that (a) knowledge should be free and that anyone should be able to access an education and (b) this approach encourages teachers and learners to collaborate, create networks, and connect new forms of knowledge in ways that are not always possible in traditional, face-to-face educational environments (O'Byrne, Roberts, LaBonte, & Graham, 2014).

Some have taken this belief a step further, suggesting that educational resources—not simply subject matter—should also be open source. This means movement toward the creation and support of "learning materials licensed in such a way as to freely permit educators to share, access, and collaborate in order to customize and personalize content and instruction" (Bliss & Patrick, 2013, p. 2), or teaching, learning, and research tools that exist in the public domain and/or have been released under an intellectual license that permits use and repurposing by others (Hilton, Wiley, Stein, & Johnson, 2010). They can include full courses, learning modules, textbooks, streaming videos, tests, software, and other resources, materials, or tools used to scaffold learners (Atkins, Brown, & Hammond, 2015) intended to improve proliferation of content on the Internet and allow individuals to create, share, connect, and learn with other like-minded learners around the globe (Greenhow, Robelia, & Hughes, 2009; McVerry, Belshaw, & O'Byrne, 2015). Of course, the use of OER in the classroom can pose challenges for educators who want to integrate them into their lessons. Some of these challenges include privileging of paid materials offered by publishers as opposed to materials freely available online. Another challenge is that educators may not know how or where to identify and secure OER materials online while evaluating their credibility and relevance. Given these concerns, OER provides the opportunity to utilize a variety of teaching and learning materials from a variety of perspectives without access constraints.

Digital Badges

For our purposes, digital badges are defined as web-enabled tokens of accomplishment that are backed by well-defined assessments/evaluations of skill and circulate in social network communities through which badge issuers and earners connect and collaborate (Knight & Casilli, 2012; see also Chapter 6: "Ask Not What You Can Do for Badges; Ask What Badges Can Do for You"). Much like traditional scout merit badges, digital badges are visual representations of proficiency with the added benefit of linking to artifacts capable of fully demonstrating what and how the earner has learned (e.g., reflections, journal entries, created projects). They usually consist of an image and relevant metadata (e.g., badge name, description, criteria, issuer, evidence, date issued, standards, and tags) that make it possible for viewers to click on the badge to see which goals have been met and map out a learning trajectory toward badges yet to be earned (O'Byrne, Schenke, Willis, & Hickey, 2015).

Badging technology may be able to help educators break open existing economies for skill and achievement recognition not currently found in more traditional letter and number grades. They are often used in teacher education (Metha, Hull, Young, & Stoller, 2013), online professional networking communities (Gamrat, Zimmerman, Dudek, & Peck, 2014), commercial/industry training environments, and Massively Open Online Courses (MOOCS; Oliver & Connors, 2013) to represent new ways of recognizing and assessing learning.

Gaming

Gaming can be viewed as a "system in which players engage in artificial conflict, defined by rules, that results in a quantifiable outcome" (Salen &

Zimmerman, 2004, p. 80). Digital games in particular (i.e., those unfolding in virtual spaces) also necessitate the incorporation of sophisticated computer technology. Simulations, augmented reality, virtual reality, and traditional video games generally fall within this category assuming they generate quantifiable outcomes. "Gamification," on the other hand, emphasizes the use of gaming mechanisms and mechanics (e.g., leader boards, point systems, badges) to motivate or reward participants (i.e., a strictly behaviorist approach). There are a variety of specific, beneficial properties that provide opportunities to engage and motivate learners in K–12 (Slota & Young, 2014). This in turn provides opportunities to re-envision and recreate pedagogical opportunities for learners.

The benefit of employing games for educational purposes is that they can provide tightly controlled opportunities for practice and mastery. Many times in a gaming environment, failure is an integral part of learning, can scaffold reengagement with misunderstood or entirely missed content, and is not immediately rejected as a kind of punishment (Gee, 2009; Groff, Howells, & Cranmer, 2010; Ke, 2009). Games also provide immediate feedback and clear goals to guide the user(s), and they serve as continuous, formative assessments that encourage strategy refinement as players work toward any and all victory conditions (Dickey, 2005). This feedback loop allows students to improve their work on the fly and fosters a dialogue between the game and player via actionable, constructivist feedback (Black & Wiliam, 1998).

Play & Learning

Play is defined as any activity that is freely chosen, is directed by the individual player, and arises from intrinsic motivation (Miller & Almon, 2009). It permits children to apply their creativity while engaging several areas of school readiness, including—but not limited to—academic competency, social-emotional development (Bergen, 2002; Bredecamp & Copple, 1997), neurological development (Perry, Hogan, & Marlin, 2000), physical development (Rees, 2009; Stover, 2009), and literacy development (Perry et al., 2000; Zigler, Singer, & Bishop-Josef, 2004).

As children ascend through the education system, they quickly discover how the "game" of school is played and learn to suppress spontaneous creativity (Malone & Tranter, 2003; Sternberg, 2006). The same restrictions seldom exist at home, on digital platforms, or in the context of ill-defined problems that require creative manipulation to resolve (Ito et al., 2009; Tharp & Gallimore, 1991). In general, playful and play-oriented instruction afford teachers the chance to embed opportunities for creative thinking and open exploration in the classroom (Cremin, Burnard, & Craft, 2006; Starko, 2013). Such pedagogical structuring supports the development of improved cognitive flexibility and helps students learn to cope when faced with novel and unprecedented challenges (Grabinger & Dunlap, 1995; Koehler et al., 2011).

Collaborative Learning

Collaboration can be viewed as a productive interaction between two or more individuals facing a common challenge and working in a unified, organized fashion to reach a satisfying and appropriate solution (Lawson, 2004). This requires a certain amount of balance and compromise as individuals are forced to negotiate personal wants and needs with the overall success of the collective whole. In education, specifically, collaborative learning is a pedagogical approach through which student groups or teams are tasked with exploring a shared question and creating a work product together (Barron & Darling-Hammond, 2008). It can also be used to support other pedagogical models in which knowledge is actively coconstructed by a group of learners who share and/or complement one another's experience sets, areas of expertise, and preferred group roles (Hmelo-Silver, 2004; Paavola, Lipponen, & Hakkarainen, 2004).

Through the integration of new and digital literacies, computer-supported collaborative learning (CSCL) identifies a pedagogical approach in which this collaboration—or the social act involved in learning—takes place using a computer or the Internet as a mediating space (Silverman, 1995). This provides new opportunities to reinvent and remix the pedagogical and cognitive practices of learning and instruction (Greenhow et al., 2009), affording hybrid or blended learning as well as synchronous or asynchronous occasions to scaffold learners (Dillenbourg, 2002).

Hybrid/Blended Learning

Hybrid or blended learning is a pedagogical approach that combines face-to-face instruction with computer-mediated instruction (Ferdig, Cavanaugh, & Freidhoff, 2012; O'Byrne & Pytash, 2015). In current research, the terms "blended learning," "hybrid learning," and "mixed-mode learning" are often used interchangeably (Martyn, 2003). As a foundation for teaching, it affords opportunities to have students engage with subject matter "outside of, and integrated with, the classroom" (Graham et al., 2014, p. 420).

Consequently, learners and instructors share responsibility in improving the quality of learning and instruction (Bonk & Graham, 2006). The Internet and other educational technologies are used to provide practical opportunities that make learning independent, useful, and sustainable

(Heinze & Procter, 2004), and though continued investigation of hybrid learning and online pedagogy has demonstrated that there is no singularly perfect means of balancing face-to-face and online instruction for every situation and learner (Graham et al., 2014), the hybrid approach serves as a challenging but rewarding means of (a) maximizing student interaction with content and (b) improving real-world application of learned skills.

CONSTRUCTED CASE STUDIES

The limited literature review of trends showcased in this chapter were selected as a means of identifying possible future eventualities for teaching and learning. To make these themes and variations easier to understand, we have developed three illustrative case studies (Datta, 1990; Davey, 1991). This work is qualitative in nature and includes collaborative, creative visions intended to provide opportunities for transformation and empowerment among readers.

Adeline: A Kindergarten Example

Adeline is a girl in a kindergarten classroom in a small village just outside of Paris, France. She is dropped off at school and picked up each day by her parents to help her socialize and play with students in her age group. Once she is dropped off at school, the traditional elementary school experience begins to vanish. Many learning activities are facilitated by students from the local high school who are training to work as educators. The classroom includes many of the toys and exploratory tables found in Montessori schools of the present. In addition to water and sand tables, however, there are stations for gardening and field-testing related to a sustainability experiment Adeline and her peers have been conducting throughout the year. There are also stations set aside for robotics equipped with Arduino boards and simple electronics suitable for children in Adeline's age group. Virtual reality goggles and tablets with augmented reality capabilities are available to help learners engage and explore both real and digital environments.

The students are encouraged to play and learn at their own pace, but collaboration is a key facet of the instructional space. There are ways to call in global experts via an Internet connection to the school's personal learning network. Everyone in the classroom—students, teachers, and teaching assistants—is encouraged to extend and exhaust their creativity as they explore a topic. There is no defined "end time" for learning activities as Adeline plays and learns with friends. She is encouraged to make connections across themes and learning areas, digital and "real-world" tools.

On one occasion, when the class was testing solar cells and their potential implementation throughout the community, most of the necessary tools and networks were already present in the classroom. The class constructed their own solar panels and measured electric power production and other metrics before donning virtual reality goggles to explore the photoelectric effect. Adeline and her peers reached out to an engineer using video conferencing technology, using her as a resource regarding the utility of solar power and other renewable energy sources.

The learning process never ends in Adeline's class. For each learning activity, the teacher collects photos and records video logs of student reflection. That way, they are able to review their work and comment on artifacts long after they have been completed. To reinforce this process, Adeline's teacher has adopted a digital badging system that leverages student-designed work and awarded Adeline's credentials in recognition of behaviors or scholarly work that showcase peer-valued learning dispositions and affective elements (i.e., students identify which skills and practices they cherish as a community and reward individuals who exemplify those skills and practices). Throughout the school year—and Adeline's broader academic career—the students are able to continually review, edit, and audit the portfolios that archive their learning, identity, and growth over time.

Mutindi: A Middle Grades Example

Mutindi is a 6th grader at an international school in Kenya. Importantly, however, she is a sixth grader in name only; her actual grade level varies depending on the content area and its integration within the school's application-oriented programming. Each semester, she joins a community-based project that is supervised by a group of teachers and youth leaders. This year, she is working with an organization responsible for operating and maintaining an urban organic vegetable garden as well as distributing the produce to the surrounding community. This organization has a specialized educational unit that coordinates with the school board. This semester, Mutindi has walked to the organization's facilities and to conduct her project work. The curriculum is inherently transdisciplinary as it revolves around food production, delivery, and public education, and Mutindi is provided numerous opportunities to showcase her exceptional fluency with mathematics and the natural sciences—she is rated at 7th grade level in topics and skills related to chemistry, biology, physics, and mathematics. The program's biology and chemistry units are integrated via instruction centered on natural fertilizers, and students are expected to help analyze the garden's yield using statistical analyses that align with 7th grade mathematical standards (e.g., measures of central tendency, spread, and sampling techniques). Because Mutindi is only at a grade 5 literacy level, she is working to improve her skills through the development of an online adventure game capable of teaching community members best practices for food production and distribution. The game's design construction involves the elements of algorithmic literacy (i.e., coding) and storytelling, both of which help her understand grammatical structures and spelling as well as general reading and writing (Burke, O'Byrne, & Kafai, 2016).

There are many opportunities for Mutindi to collaborate with other students through the program's team-based inquiry projects. Her primary team consists of students ranging from 6th to 9th grade, and while she plays different roles in different teams, this one has her serving as the food production project manager. At the end of the semester, each team will present its results and be evaluated by a combination of team members and the project facilitator. Since each project is aligned with specific content and process standards, Mutindi and her peers are able to monitor their academic progress more closely and consistently than ever before.

Because Mutindi's education is so heavily community- and project-oriented, her schooling is rarely confined to a particular building or location. Rather, the day or week's venue depends on the current project, and the pedagogical model's underlying philosophy is positioned front and center (namely the creation of knowledge for social change). Additionally, assessment consists of three nontraditional tiers: (a) technical disciplinary knowledge relevant to the project, (b) practical application of the relevant knowledge, and (c) the extent to which the project has a potential to influence the social change in question. The layering process is reinforced via web-based technologies like virtual portfolios and digital badges, and the assessment measures themselves are curated by specific licensing bodies (e.g., the Ministry of Education) rather than individual schools or districts.

Javier: A Secondary School Example

Javier is a 10th-grade student attending a science and technology magnet school in New York City. The bulk of instruction is similar to what would be considered traditional in other secondary programs, but as a science- and technology-oriented magnet school, special emphasis is placed on STEM research and initiatives as they relate to other disciplines and postgraduation careers. This involves two substantial deviations from so-called "normal" pedagogy. First, a plurality of instruction occurs via a flipped classroom format where content is made available online, and the students partner with advisors—both academic and professional—to identify and engage in appropriate programs of study. Second, the students rarely attend school as most teens do, instead working from home, telecommuting to meetings, and joining face to face for hands-on activities. This replaces didactic instruction with self-guided, inquiry-driven learning that is deeply personalized both in terms of presentation and assessment.

Each morning, Javier heads to his "real-world" job rather attending class in a school building. The experience is closely aligned with his individualized program of study and functions more like an internship than a traditional 9-to-5 position. It is supported in equal parts by the school district and a global web design firm, and while most of his meetings about yet-to-be-completed company tasks are conducted from the comfort of his living room, he is frequently asked to meet with clients and discuss travel to sign on new clients for the parent web development company. The job pays little more than minimum wage, but it has provided Javier with an opportunity to learn practicable skills and build the resume necessary to break into the workforce as a top applicant. The experience has also earned him credits and credentials from a local community college that partners with the school district. When this young entrepreneur graduates from high school, he will have completed most of his general education requirements and already laid the foundation for becoming a successful computer programmer. The web design company responsible for supporting his internship has expressed an interest in employing him while he focuses on his postsecondary education, and the firm's recruiters have encouraged him to apply for a full-time role once he completes his bachelor's degree.

As his studies continue, Javier has also spent time fine-tuning a digital portfolio capable of demonstrating his skillset. Learning artifacts collected across his educational career have helped Javier reflect on his educational journey and positioned him to continue growing as an adult learner. He is cognizant of how the magnet program has facilitated his learning thus far, and he understands the program's shortfalls—what it is not equipped to teach. To address these shortcomings, Javier and the school's administration have embraced alternative learning experiences (e.g., MOOCs) that can be completed outside of school hours and whose credentials that can be earned by Javier and showcased through social media. This enables Javier to craft a patchwork of scholarly achievements and competencies that will prepare him for the future. The pertinent pathways are continually reviewed and revised by Javier's academic advisor, and the boy's professional advisor works to help him develop an appealing resume and network of capable, reliable professionals.

DISCUSSION

As we consider possible futures for the classroom, we need to remember that this examination is primarily one of future patterns most likely and able to be affected by contemporary understandings of behavioral and ecological psychology. Of course, we cannot account for the whole of human experience or technological advancement (or stagnation) that may come into play, and as such, our compilation is merely a "best guess"—sprinkled with a few of hopes and dreams—that we believe can serve as a well-reasoned blueprint for those in the field of educational gaming as well as educational technology more generally.

We also have to keep in mind that all case studies have the potential to be influenced by the authors' constructions of reality (as driven by individual interactions with the lived-in world). Our cases, for example, have been informed by our conceptions of education, technology, culture, and intersectionality of the three. This is why it is crucial for us to remain vigilant about social milieu, the very stage on which the technological evolution is take place, given how malleable and unstable it can be.

This foundational positioning has led us to a unique and complex academic space, studying human development and awareness as it intersects with ontology and epistemology. When technologies advance, humans are forced to reconcile their existing understandings of the world with the moral and practical implications said technologies can (or should) have in their lives. Post-Patriot Act era—and in light of Edward Snowden's National Security Administration whistleblowing—this also begets a need to understand the role of web literacies as a means of empowering or restricting the livelihood of others. Clashes over privacy, security, and identity can have a chilling impact on individual willingness to share, create, and connect using open, digital tools (Wise & O'Byrne, 2015), and we need to consider how our recommendations for the future are inevitably shaped by worries and celebrations of the moment.

Accordingly, we have done our best to identify a starting point and hypothesized end point (i.e., case studies) for the overarching discussion about technology and its educational role over the next decade, but there is still a way to go. Learning pathways—the series of learning activities that scaffold the development of a learner in a given area—have not yet been defined or optimized. We may need these pathways to be linear or non-linear, *prescriptive* (concerned with guidelines and what must be done to achieve a particular outcome) or *descriptive* (concerned with studying what exists, devising models, and using them to predict future outcomes). Their creation will require substantial legwork—not unlike that of this book's contributing authors—to provide raw materials from which the next great curricula and learning activities can be created.

We must also recognize that imbued through this chapter are elements guided by the literature in learning through making. Learning through making or doing is an approach to education with proponents in the educational literature including Froebel, Dewey, and Papert. By designing learning pathways, learners can participate in activities or build things (digitally or physically) to enhance their own learning. They can demonstrate skills across the web through content they create, demonstrating their newfound abilities. The challenge in this is that this approach of learning through making and doing differs radically from a didactic approach to education. With a learning through making and doing approach, learners generate their own ideas and interact with the web as they learn what it takes to improve their web literacy skills. When learners are engaged to create and produce, we believe that there is greater opportunity to embed fun into inquiry-based literacy activities.

CONCLUDING THOUGHTS

This chapter presents a series of future studies intended to promote discussion and identify possible future options for K–12 and higher education. In this we detail connected research and strive to identify what we believe is the optimal pathway toward a brighter educational future. In this thought experiment, we integrated research from various fields in order to connect opportunities to move learners from simple consumers of digital literacies to curators of content and creators and remixers of digital media (O'Byrne & Pytash, 2017).

As we consider the online and offline literacy practices that our students will need as future events warrant, the one constant is change (Leu et al., 2004). Examining a future in this connected world should provide opportunities for the web to create new, unforeseen learning opportunities. To allow students and mentors to connect, collaborate, and coconstruct new future. Additionally, this should not be viewed as science fiction. Instead this should be viewed as a fundamental human right that allows for learning anywhere and anytime around the globe. With these new technologies, there is a critical responsibility to negotiate this period of profound change from print to digital resources. In adapting and reacting to future evolutions of the Internet and other communication technologies, there are opportunities to change pedagogy and prepare students for the world in which they will interact.

REFERENCES

Atkins, D. E., Brown, J. S., & Hammond, A. L. (2007). *A review of the open educational resources (OER) movement: Achievements, challenges, and new opportunities.* Retrieved from the Hewlett Foundation website: http://www.hewlett.org/uploads/files/ReviewoftheOERMovement.pdf

Barron, B., & Darling-Hammond, L. (2008). *Teaching for meaningful learning: A review of research on inquiry-based and cooperative learning* (Book excerpt). San Francisco, CA: George Lucas Educational Foundation.

Bell, W. (2010) *Foundations of futures studies* (2 vols.). New Brunswick NJ: Transaction Publishers

Bergen, D. (2002). The role of pretend play in children's cognitive development. *Early Childhood Research and Practice, 4*(1), 2–15.

Black, P. J., & Wiliam, D. (1998). *Inside the black box: Raising standards through classroom assessment.* London, England: King's College London School of Education.

Bliss, T., & Patrick, S. (2013). *OER state policy in K–12 education: Benefits, strategies, and recommendations for open access, open sharing.* Retrieved from International Association for K–12 Online Learning website: http://www.inacol.org/wp-content/uploads/2015/02/oer-state-policy.pdf

Bonk, C. J., & Graham, C. R. (Eds.). (2006). *Handbook of blended learning: Global perspectives, local designs.* San Francisco, CA: Pfeiffer.

Bredekamp, S., & Copple, C. (Eds.). (1997). *Developmentally appropriate practices in early childhood programs.* Washington, DC: National Association for the Education of Young Children.

Burke, Q., O'Byrne, W. I., & Kafai, Y. B. (2016). Computational participation. *Journal of adolescent & adult literacy, 59*(4), 371–375.

Coiro, J., Knobel, M., Lankshear, C. & Leu, D. J. (2008). Central issues in new literacies and new literacies research. In J. Coiro, M. Knobel, C. Lankshear, & D. J. Leu (Eds.), *The handbook of research on new literacies* (pp. 1–22). Mahwah, NJ: Erlbaum.

Cremin, T., Burnard, P., & Craft, A. (2006). Pedagogy and possibility thinking in the early years. *Thinking skills and creativity, 1*(2), 108–119.

Dator, J. (2005). Foreword. In R. Slaughter (Ed.), *Knowledge base of futures studies* (vol. 1, pp. xix–xx). Brisbane, Australia: Foresight International.

Datta, L. E. (1990). *Case Study Evaluations.* Washington, DC: U.S. General Accounting Office, Transfer paper 10.1.9.

Davey, L. (1991). *The application of case study evaluations.* ERIC Clearinghouse on Tests, Measurement, and Evaluation.

Dickey, M. D. (2005). Engaging by design: How engagement strategies in popular computer and video games and inform instructional design. *Educational Technology Research and Development, 53*, 67–83

Dillenbourg, P. (2002). Over-scripting CSCL: The risks of blending collaborative learning with instructional design. Three worlds of CSCL. Can we support CSCL?, 61–91.

Ferdig, R. E., Cavanaugh, C., & Freidhoff, J. (2012). *Lessons learned from blended programs: Experiences and recommendations from the field.* Vienna, VA: International Association for K–12 Online Learning.

Friedman, T. L. (2005). *The world is flat: A brief history of the twenty-first century.* New York, NY: Farrar, Straus, and Giroux.

Gamrat, C., Zimmerman, H. T., Dudek, J., & Peck, K. (2014). Personalized workplace learning: An exploratory study on digital badging within a teacher professional development program. *British Journal of Educational Technology, 45*(6), 1136–1148.

Gee, J. P. (2009). Deep learning properties of good digital games: How far can they go? In U. Ritterfeld, M. Cody, & P. Vorderer (Eds.), *Serious games: Mechanisms and effects* (pp. 67–82). New York, NY: Routledge.

Gidley, J. (2004). Futures/foresight in education at primary and secondary levels: A literature review and research task analysis. *Futures in Education: Principles, Practice and Potential. AFI Monograph Series 2004*, (5), 5–72.

Grabinger, R. S., & Dunlap, J. C. (1995). Rich environments for active learning: A definition. *Research in learning Technology, 3*(2).

Graham, L., LaBonte, R., Roberts, V., O'Byrne, I., & Osterhout, C. (2014, January). Open learning in K–12 online and blended learning environments. In *Handbook of Research on K–12 Online and Blended Learning* (pp. 415–445). ETC Press.

Greenhow, C., Robelia, B., & Hughes, J. E. (2009). Learning, teaching, and scholarship in a digital age Web 2.0 and classroom research: What path should we take now?. *Educational Researcher, 38*(4), 246–259.

Groff, J., Howells, C., & Cranmer, S. (2010). *The impact of console games in the classroom: Evidence from schools in Scotland.* Upton Park, England: Futurelab.

Heinze, A., & Procter, C. (2004). *Reflections on the use of blended learning.* Education in a Changing Environment conference, University of Salford, Salford, UK, Education Development Unit. Retrieved from http://www.ece.salford.ac.uk/proceedings/2004.html

Hicks, D. (2006). *Lessons for the Future: The missing dimension in education.* Victoria, BC: Trafford Publishing.

Hicks, D. (2012). Developing a futures perspective in the classroom. In S. Ward (Ed.), *A student's guide to education studies* (3rd ed.). New York, NY: Routledge.

Hilton, J., Wiley, D., Stein, J., & Johnson, A. (2010). The four R's of openness and ALMS analysis: Frameworks for open educational resources. *Open Learning 25*(1), 37–44.

Hmelo-Silver, C. E. (2004). Problem-based learning: What and how do students learn? *Educational Psychology Review, 16*(3), 235–266.

International Reading Association. (2002). *Integrating literacy and technology in the curriculum: A position statement.* Newark, DE: International Reading Association.

Internet Live Stats. (2015). Internet users. Retrieved from http://www.internetlivestats.com/internet-users/

Internet World Stats. (2008, March). *Usage and population statistics.* Retrieved from http://www.internetworldstats.com/stats.htm

Ito, M., Horst, H. A., Bittanti, M., Stephenson, B. H., Lange, P. G., Pascoe, C. J., … & Martínez, K. Z. (2009). *Living and learning with new media: Summary of findings from the Digital Youth Project.* Cambridge, MA: MIT Press.

Ke, F. (2009). A qualitative meta-analysis of computer games as learning tools. In R. E. Furdig (Ed.), *Handbook of research on effective electronic gaming in education* (pp. 1–32). Hershey, PA: IGI Global.

Knight, E., & Casilli, C. (2012). Mozilla Open Badges. Game Changers: Education and Information Technologies. In *EDUCAUSE 2012.* Retrieved from http://www.educause.edu/library/resources/case-study-6-mozilla-open-badges

Koehler, M. J., Mishra, P., Bouck, E. C., DeSchryver, M., Kereluik, K., Shin, T. S., & Wolf, L. G. (2011). Deep-play: Developing TPACK for 21st century teachers. *International Journal of Learning Technology, 6*(2), 146–163.

Lankshear, C., & Knobel, M. (2002). Do we have your attention? New literacies, digital technologies and the education of adolescents. In D. Alvermann (Ed.), *Adolescents and literacies in a digital world* (pp. 19–39). New York, NY: Peter Lang.

Lawson, H. A. (2004). The logic of collaboration in education and the human services. *Journal of interprofessional care, 18*(3), 225–237.

Leu, D. J., Kinzer, C. K., Coiro, J., & Cammack, D. (2004). Toward a theory of new literacies emerging from the Internet and other information and communication technologies. In R. B. Ruddell & N. Unrau (Eds.), *Theoretical models and processes of reading* (5th ed., pp. 1568–1611). Newark, DE: International Reading Association.

Malone, K., & Tranter, P. J. (2003). School grounds as sites for learning: Making the most of environmental opportunities. *Environmental Education Research, 9*(3), 283–303.

McVerry, J. G., Belshaw, D., & O'Byrne, W. I. (2015). Guiding students as they explore, build, and connect online. *Journal of Adolescent & Adult Literacy, 58*(8), 632–635.

Martyn, M. (2003). The hybrid online model: Good practice. *Educause Quarterly, 1*, 18–23.

Mehta, N. B., Hull, A. L., Young, J. B., & Stoller, J. K. (2013). Just imagine: New paradigms for medical education. *Academic Medicine, 88*(10), 1418–1423.

Merchant, G. (2007). Writing the future in the digital age. *Literacy, 41*(3), 118–128.

Miller, E., & Almon, J. (2009). *Crisis in the kindergarten: Why children need to play in school.* College Park, MD: Alliance for Childhood (NJ3a).

New London Group. (1996). A pedagogy of multiliteracies: Designing social futures. *Harvard Educational Review, 66*(1), 60–92.

New London Group. (2000). A pedagogy of multiliteracies: Designing social futures. In B. Cope & M. Kalantzis (Eds.), *Multiliteracies: Literacy learning and the design of social futures* (pp. 9–37). Melbourne, Australia: Macmillan.

O'Byrne, W. I. (2014). Empowering learners in the reader/writer nature of the digital informational space. *Journal of Adolescent & Adult Literacy, 58*(2), 102–104.

O'Byrne, W. I., Schenke, K., Willis III, J. E., & Hickey, D. T. (2015). Digital badges: Recognizing, assessing, and motivating learners in and out of school contexts. *Journal of Adolescent & Adult Literacy, 6*(58), 451–454.

O'Byrne, W. I., & Pytash, K. E. (2015). Hybrid and blended learning. *Journal of Adolescent & Adult Literacy, 59*(2), 137–140.

O'Byrne, W. I., & Pytash, K. E. (2017). Becoming literate digitally in a digitally literate environment of their own. *Journal of Adolescent & Adult Literacy, 60*(5), 499–504. doi: 10.1002/jaal.59

O'Byrne, W. I., Roberts, V., La-Bonte, R., & Graham, L. (2014). Teaching, learning, and sharing openly online. *Journal of Adolescent and Adult Literacy, 58*(4), 277–280.

Oliver, B., & Connors. P. (2013, July). *Development and evidencing achievement of graduate learning outcomes in Deakin University's enhanced MOOC.* Paper presented at the 5th International Conference on Education and New Learning Technologies, Barcelona, Spain.

Paavola, S., Lipponen, L., & Hakkarainen, K. (2004). Models of innovative knowledge communities and three metaphors of learning. *Review of educational research, 74*(4), 557–576.

Partnership for 21st Century Skills. (2004). *Learning for the 21st century.* Retrieved from http://www.p21.org/storage/documents/P21_Report.pdf

Perry, B. D., Hogan, L., & Marlin, S. J. (2000). Curiosity, pleasure and play: A neurodevelopmental perspective. Retrieved from http://thegotomom.blogspot.com/2007/08/curiosity-pleasure-and-play_04.html

Philco-Ford Corporation (Producer), & Madden, L. (Director). (1967). *1999 A.D.* [Motion picture]. United States: Tom Thomas Organization.

Rees, C. (2009). Importance of play for children's development. Retrieved from http://www.ehow.com/about_5245265_importanceplay-children_s-physical-development.html

Salen, K., & Zimmerman, E. (2004). *Rules of play: Game design fundamentals.* Cambridge, MA: The MIT Press.

Silverman, B. G. (1995). Computer supported collaborative learning (CSCL). *Computers & Education, 25*(3), 81–91.

Slaughter, R. (2003). *Integral futures—A new model for futures enquiry and practice.* Melbourne: Australian Foresight Institute.

Slota, S. T., & Young, M. F. (2014). Think games on the fly, not gamify: Issues in game-based learning research. *Journal of Graduate Medical Education, 6*(4), 628–630.

Starko, A. J. (2013). *Creativity in the classroom: Schools of curious delight.* New York, NY: Routledge.

Stover, E. (2009). The role of play in physical development in early childhood. Retrieved from http://www.ehow.com/facts_4926734_play-physical-development-earlychildhood.html

Sternberg, R. J. (2006). The nature of creativity. *Creativity Research Journal, 18*(1), 87–98.

Street, B. V. (1984). *Literacy in theory and practice.* Cambridge, England: Cambridge University Press.

Street, B. V. (1993). Introduction: The new literacy studies. In B. Street (Ed.), *Cross-cultural approaches to literacy* (pp. 1–21). Cambridge, England: Cambridge University Press.

Tharp, R. G., & Gallimore, R. (1991). *Rousing minds to life: Teaching, learning, and schooling in social context.* Cambridge, England: Cambridge University Press.

Toffler, A. (1974). *Learning for tomorrow: The role of the future in education.* New York, NY: Vintage Books.

UNESCO (n.d.). Education. Retrieved from http://www.unesco.org/new/en/education/themes/leading-the-international-agenda/right-to-education/browse/1/

Voros, J. (2008). Integral futures: an approach to futures inquiry. *Futures, 40*(2), 190–201.

Wise, J. B., & O'Byrne, W. I. (2015). Social scholars educators' digital identity construction in open, online learning environments. *Literacy Research: Theory, Method, and Practice, 64*(1), 398–414.

Zigler, E., Singer, D., & Bishop-Josef. (Eds.). (2004). *Child's play: The roots of reading.* Washington, DC: Zero to Three Press.

TEN

TWIST

CHAPTER 9

MEASURING AND SUPPORTING LEARNING IN EDUCATIONAL GAMES

Valerie J. Shute, Seyedahmad Rahimi, and Chen Sun
Florida State University

*"The significant problems of our time cannot be solved
by the same level of thinking that created them."*

–Albert Einstein

We begin this chapter with a general description about current problems in U.S. education, then focus on the unfortunate side effects of standardized testing in K–12 schools. For instance, the increased frequency of administering high-stakes tests tends to (a) narrow the curricula, (b) have dire consequences (for students, teachers, and schools), and (c) exclude support for skills important for success in the 21st century, such as problem solving, critical thinking, creativity, persistence, and collaboration. We also describe specific advances in learning science, psychometrics, and technology that can be leveraged to create more effective and engaging assessments to support the aforementioned new competencies—*educational games*.

Advances in learning science have begun to identify factors affecting learners' growth in knowledge, skills, and other attributes. Additionally, advances in psychometrics allow us to measure complex, multidimensional

Exploding the Castle, pages 201–220

constructs in an ongoing manner and at a refined grain size. That information, then, can be used diagnostically as the basis for targeted and adaptive learning support provided to students and teachers and/or back to the digital learning environment (e.g., educational game) to activate learning, reflection, and self-regulation; provide information for teachers to figure out subsequent instructional support; and appropriately alter the environment or task, respectively.

Technological advances can be leveraged toward education in general (and assessment in particular) to accomplish things that were impossible before, such as gathering and analyzing "big data"—broadly defined as massive quantities of student-related information that can be mined to make inferences about various attributes and outcomes. Big data and associated emerging analysis techniques represent the intersection of computer science, statistics, and ethics or policy (see Dede, 2015). Such accumulated data comprises evidence that can be used to improve students' learning and performance by providing accurate, actionable, and informative assessment information.

STATUS QUO

The United States is one of the world leaders in spending money for education. For example, in 2011–2012, the U.S. spent $621 billion for public elementary and secondary schools (U.S. Department of Education, National Center for Education Statistics, 2015). However, the return on investment is not commensurate with these expenditures. According to the Program for International Student Assessment (PISA; Organization for Economic Co-operation and Development, 2013), U.S. students were outperformed in mathematics literacy proficiency by students in 29 countries, in science literacy by 22 countries, and in problem solving by 18 countries (the average score of these countries was statistically higher than the United States' average score). These results were based on the average scores per test from students in 65 participating countries (i.e., mathematics, science, and problem-solving). Moreover, based on a report from the Economist Intelligence Unit (2012), which combines different international data sets (e.g., PISA, Trends in International Mathematics and Science Study—TIMSS, and Progress in International Reading Literacy Study—PIRLS) together with each country's academic data (e.g., literacy and graduation rates), U.S. education is ranked 14th out of 40 countries. Why is this a problem? We live in a world with complex problems (e.g., climate change, nuclear proliferation, cyber security, racial and religious intolerance, and so on). We need people who are able to think critically, creatively, and systemically and work collaboratively with others to help solve these complex problems (Shute, 2011).

Based on the aforementioned reports, we are falling behind other countries in terms of producing competent individuals, and this can slow down the growth of our country over time (Hanushek & Woessmann, 2012). We need to boost our students' 21st-century competencies (e.g., problem solving, creativity, systems thinking) to effectively compete internationally in the near future (Shute, 2007) and accelerate the growth of our country in the long run.

To improve students' 21st-century competencies, we first need to accurately assess them. We no longer can rely solely on the old types of assessment (e.g., standardized tests with multiple-choice items) to measure these new competencies. However, we can still use standardized assessments when they are appropriate (e.g., when the learning outcome relates to the memorization of facts and equations). Two main reasons for not using the old assessment types to measure the new competencies are: (a) these tests are not capable of measuring the complex new competencies we need in the 21st century (e.g., multidimensional constructs like problem-solving skills cannot easily or accurately be measured using multiple choice questions), and (b) they can have negative, unintended consequences.

Educational researchers have been examining the unintended consequences of standardized testing for years (e.g., Amrein & Berliner, 2002; Jones, 2007; Madaus & Russell, 2010; Smith, 1991). Some salient consequences of increased reliance solely on standardized testing include the adverse impacts on instruction and learning goals such as narrowing of curricula in schools, inciting cheating and corruption on high-stakes tests, and generally increasing students' anxiety (Madaus & Russell, 2010). Additional unintended consequences include the impact on teacher evaluations and the accountability of schools, based mainly on student test performance rather than on what teachers do in classrooms.

Negative Effects on Instruction

Increased emphasis on standardized testing in schools (also known as "teaching to the test") produces a narrowing of curricula (Abrams, Pedulla, & Madaus, 2003; Amrein & Berliner, 2002; Jones, 2007; Madaus & Russell, 2010). And if the tests were all-encompassing, that would be fine, but tests are necessarily limited in scope. Educators (i.e., teachers, administrators, boards of education) note what is being assessed in the standardized tests and then focus instruction towards those subjects, such as reading expository text and writing the five-paragraph essay. As a result, applied work and interdisciplinary problem solving as well as other competencies and subjects (e.g., social science, art, physical education, and even science in the elementary grades) are treated as less important—if not removed altogether from the curriculum (Madaus & Russell, 2010). In short, standardized tests tend to prioritize the subjects taught in school, and instructional goals tend to prepare students to succeed on the standardized tests—not to be creative problem solvers, critical thinkers, and equipped with other 21st-century skills (Shute, Leighton, Jang, & Chu, 2016).

Negative Effects on Learning Goals

Another unintended consequence of standardized testing is that these tests can change students' goal orientation from learning to performance (Jones, 2007; Shute, 2008). For instance, focusing on test performance becomes more important than how much one actually learns. As Jones (2007) observed, high-stakes tests externally motivate students (i.e., supporting a performance goal orientation) rather than internally motivating students (i.e., supporting a learning goal orientation). However, if students develop learning (as opposed to performance) goals, other positive characteristics may be internalized as they spend their time in school (Jones, 2007). Students with learning goals tend to be more persistent when confronting difficult problems and experiencing failure, use more complex learning strategies, and work on challenging tasks voluntarily (Shute, 2008). In short, students with learning goals are better prepared for living in our increasingly complex world.

Cheating and Corruption

Another byproduct of focusing too much on high-stakes tests is that this can influence teachers, students, and other stakeholders to cheat (Madaus & Russell, 2010). That is, when the accountability of teachers, quality of schools, students ranking, and even students' future academic paths depend on the results from standardized tests, the likelihood increases that some schools' personnel, students, and other stakeholders will cheat on tests (Berliner, 2011). For example, test administers in schools may increase the time limits of tests, help students to answer questions, provide the questions to the students before the tests, or even change students' test scores in the system (Amrein & Berliner, 2002). Some students also cheat by impersonation on tests like the GRE or TOEFL. As the *Guardian* reported (Yuhas, 2015), 15 students with fake Chinese passports were charged with impersonating other students to take GRE, TOEFL, and SAT tests.

Student Anxiety

Testing can often create a stressful environment for students (Jones, 2007) that is detrimental to learning. For example, Wheelock, Bebell, and Haney (2000) asked students to draw a picture of themselves when they take a high-stakes test. Not surprisingly, the students illustrated themselves as anxious, frustrated, bored, hopeless, and gloomy. In another study, Culler and Holahan (1980) found that anxiety is negatively related to how well students perform on a test. They pointed out that more anxious students had significantly lower grades than less anxious students, and they had poorer study skills.

These are just a few of the unintended consequences of high-stakes tests in our educational system. However, we are in a position to address many of these problems. In the next section, we present a vision of what education can be like (compared to the status quo). Spoiler alert—this vision involves no tests—at least none of the high-stakes, norm-referenced types of tests that are currently the norm in education today.

VISION

How would you feel—as a student—if you were told that there would be no high-stakes tests throughout the school year? How would you feel—as a teacher—if you did not have to teach to and administer high-stakes tests anymore? How would you feel—as a parent—if you saw your child develop new knowledge and skills and show excitement about learning? The vision presented here is based on the ideas presented by Shute et al. (2016). In a nutshell, next-generation assessments can measure (and in some cases, support) students' growth in important cognitive and noncognitive competencies. High-stakes tests will no longer be the primary means of assessing learning, and thus the time that was used to prepare for and administer tests can be reallocated to substantive student learning activities.

Advances in technology (e.g., ever-increasing computational power, virtual reality, wearable devices, and social networks) have created a world in which we produce many digital footprints, as data. Students can potentially learn a lot through interacting with well-designed digital environments, and the data generated from these interactions can be used for assessing different knowledge and skills. We envision students being assessed unobtrusively while they are learning (i.e., seamlessly within the digital environment). Further, data can be collected almost continuously and across various contexts (i.e., ubiquitously), providing, over time, reliable and valid evidence about students' levels of targeted competencies. This type of unobtrusive and ubiquitous assessment of important knowledge, skills, and other attributes (e.g., dispositions) can provide teachers with rich information to help them guide their students, as well as information to help students develop competencies on their own. In short, we believe that assessment should (a) support the learning process for learners and not undermine it, (b) provide ongoing formative feedback to students during the learning process (with perhaps summative feedback at the end), and (c) reflect current theories about how people learn, both from a general and developmental perspective.

The envisioned unobtrusive and ubiquitous aspects of assessment will require some changes to the current education system. The traditional way of teaching in classrooms today involves providing lectures and giving tests in class, then having students complete homework at home (without guidance when students may become stuck). An alternative pedagogical approach is the "flipped classroom" where students first examine and interact with content on their own (e.g., playing a particular game at home); then, in class, students would apply their new knowledge and skills while instructors and peers are there to support and guide their work (see Bergmann & Sams, 2012). Having a flipped classroom frees up class time for hands-on work and discussion and permits deep dives into the content. Students learn by doing and asking questions, and they can also help each other—a process that benefits a majority of learners (Strayer, 2012).

To accomplish this vision, there are several obstacles that must be surmounted. Following are four issues that need more research.

1. Quality of Assessments

The first hurdle relates to variability in the quality of assessments within current and future educational games and other digital learning environments. Because schools are under local control, students in a given state could engage in sundry games and learning environments during their educational years. Teachers, publishers, researchers, and others will be developing these digital environments, but with no standards in place (or a survival-of-the-fittest mechanism to weed out inadequate products), they will likely differ in curricular coverage, difficulty of the material, scenarios and formats used, and many other ways that will affect the adequacy of the digital environment, tasks, and inferences on knowledge and skill acquisition that can justifiably be made. More research is needed to figure out how to equate educational games or create common measurements (i.e., standardized) from diverse environments. Towards that end, there must be common models employed across different activities, curricula, and contexts. Moreover, it is important to figure out how to interpret evidence where the activities may be the same but the contexts in which students are working differ (e.g., playing alone vs. playing with another student; playing with learning goals vs. playing with trolling goals vs. playing with entertainment goals).

2. Interpreting Different Learning Progressions

The second hurdle involves accurately capturing and making sense of students' learning progressions. That is, while educational games can provide a greater variety of learning situations than traditional face-to-face classroom learning, evidence for assessing and tracking learning progressions becomes heterogeneous and complex rather than general across individual students. Thus there is a great need to model learning progressions in multiple aspects of student growth and experiences that can be applied across different learning activities and contexts (Shavelson & Kurpius, 2012). However, as Shavelson and Kurpius (2012) pointed out, there is no single absolute order of progression as learning in educational games involves multiple interactions between individual students and situations, which may be too complex for most measurement theories in use that assume linearity and independence. Clearly, theories and assessments of learning progressions in educational games need to be actively researched and validated to realize their potential.

3. Expanded Educational Boundaries

The third problem to resolve involves impediments to moving toward the idea of new contexts of learning (e.g., flipped classrooms). One issue concerns the digital divide, where some students may not have access to a home computer. In those cases, students may be allowed to use library resources or a computer lab. Alternatively, online components can be accessed via a cell phone, as many students who do not have computers or Internet at home do have a phone and data plan that can meet the requirements of online activities. In addition, some critics argue that flipped classrooms will invariably lead to teachers becoming outdated. However, teachers become even more important in flipped classrooms, where they educate and support rather than lecture (i.e., "guide on the side" rather than "sage on a stage"). This represents an intriguing way to take back some of the very valuable classroom time and serve as a more efficient and effective teacher. Much more empirical research is needed to determine how this pedagogical approach works relative to traditional pedagogies. Moreover, use of analytics and big data will require the development of new methods and tools beyond traditional empirical research—seamless and context-based.

4. Privacy/Security

The fourth hurdle involves figuring out a way to resolve privacy, security, and ownership issues regarding students' information. The privacy/security issue relates to the accumulation and aggregation of student data from disparate sources. The recent failure of the $100 million in Bloom initiative (see McCambridge, 2014) showcases the problem. That is, the main aim of inBloom was to store, clean, and aggregate a wide range of student information for states and districts, and then make the data available to district-approved third parties to develop tools and dashboards so the data could be easily used by classroom educators. The main issue boils down to this: Information about individual students may be at risk of being shared far more broadly than is justifiable. And because of the often high-stakes consequences associated with tests, many parents and other stakeholders fear that the data collected could later be used against the students.

Despite these hurdles, as well as others not included, constructing the envisioned ubiquitous and unobtrusive assessments across multiple learner dimensions, with data accessible by diverse stakeholders, could yield various educational benefits. First, the time spent administering tests, handling make-up exams, and going over test responses is not very conducive to learning (when the assessment only samples broadly, not deeply from the curriculum). Given the importance of time on task (i.e., engaged time) as a predictor of learning, reallocating those test-preparation activities into ones that are more educationally productive would provide potentially large benefits to almost all students.

Second, by having assessments that are continuous and ubiquitous, students are no longer able to "cram" for an exam. Although cramming can provide good short-term recall, it is a poor route to long-term retention and transfer of learning. Standard assessment practices in school can lead to assessing students in a manner that is in conflict with their long-term success. With a continuous assessment model in place, the best way for students to do well is to do well every day. The third direct benefit is that this shift in assessment mirrors the national shift toward evaluating students on the basis of acquired competencies. With increasing numbers of educators growing wary of pencil-and-paper (and more recently computer-based adaptive) high-stakes tests for students, this shift toward ensuring that students have acquired "essential" skills fits with the envisioned future of assessment.

What would it take to accomplish this vision of the future of educational assessment? The next sections describe a solution to the problem using stealth assessment within well-designed educational games.

STEALTH ASSESSMENT

The Partnership for 21st Century Learning (P21; 2015) has developed a framework providing a blueprint for particular outcomes that students should achieve. In addition to content knowledge like math and science, students need to develop essential skills, as mentioned earlier, such as creativity, problem-solving, and collaboration to succeed in the 21st century. The framework points out the importance of using technology-based assessments to measure and support these skills. Moreover, the Office of Educational Technology (2015) suggested using technology to develop assessment tools to measure the processes of learning, to provide formative feedback, and to systematically gather and analyze information about learning so that teachers and schools can make full use of the data. Technology-based assessments can facilitate learning processes and outcomes by engaging students in learning environments.

Stealth assessment (see Shute, 2011; and for a related idea called situated seamless assessment, see Young, Kulikowich, & Barab, 1997) is such an assessment technology. It involves embedding assessment(s) directly and invisibly into an immersive learning environment (such as a well-designed educational game). This appears to be a viable solution to resolving the rift between learning and testing caused by standardized, traditional tests (Dori, 2003; Hickey & Zuiker, 2012). That is, stealth assessment is intended to be formative, ongoing, and dynamic (Shute & Ventura, 2013). It can also be used to support learning. For example, as a student progresses through an educational game in which the stealth assessment is embedded, the estimates of competency states provided by the stealth assessment can be used as the basis to provide targeted instructional support as well as other types of adjustments to the game which can prepare students for future learning (Schwartz & Martin, 2004). In this way, stealth assessment can comprise an invisible but strong bond linking teaching and learning (Wilson & Sloane, 2000).

Using educational games as a vehicle for assessment and support of learning is justified by the literature (see Van Eck, Shute, & Rieber, in press). For instance, learning is at its best when it is active, goal oriented, contextualized, and interesting (e.g., Bransford, Brown, & Cocking, 2000; Bruner, 1961; Vygotsky, 1978). Instructional environments should thus be interactive, provide ongoing feedback, grab and sustain attention, and have appropriate and adaptive levels of challenge—in other words, the features of well-designed games. So a well-designed game can fulfill the achievement of learning objectives by providing incentives to motivate learners, engaging learners via four types of interaction (i.e., cognitive, affective, behavioral, and sociocultural), encouraging a player to learn from failure, and adapting to players' responses (Plass, Homer & Kinzer, 2015). Plass and his colleagues argued for "accurate and ongoing assessment" for learning in games (2015, p. 266), which is what stealth assessment delivers. In short, stealth assessment is a powerful tool to (a) enhance acquisition of both content knowledge and essential skills required in today's world, (b) integrate learning and assessment in a natural and seamless way, (c) enable valid and reliable inferences of competencies being targeted, and (d) reveal/ visualize learning processes and outcomes—to the student for reflection, to the teacher for support, and to the system for further adjustments and instructional support. The mechanism for ensuring the reliability and validity of a stealth assessment is evidence-centered design (Mislevy, Steinberg, & Almond, 2003).

EVIDENCE-CENTERED DESIGN

Evidence-centered design (ECD) is an assessment framework underpinning the development of assessment tasks. Its strength lies in basing competency estimates on a chain of evidence that is grounded in task performances. That is, ECD directly connects valid claims of competency states to particular performance data, thus ensuring the validity of the assessment (Mislevy & Haertel, 2006; Reese, Tabachnick & Kosko, 2015). There are several main models in ECD that work in concert: (a) competency model (CM), (b) evidence model (EM), and (c) task model (TM).

The competency model (CM) clarifies what needs to be assessed (i.e., knowledge, skills, and other attributes). It delineates the variables that characterize the targeted knowledge and skills and allows for the inference of students' levels on those competencies (see Almond & Mislevy, 1999). ECD is especially powerful in assessing multivariate competencies (although also suited for unidimensional constructs). The instantiation of the CM in an assessment situation creates the *student model*, a term that originated in the intelligent tutoring system literature (see Shute & Psotka, 1996). The student model is like a profile or report card of students' current knowledge and skill states (and trajectories) but can present estimates at a finer grain size than summative types of assessment.

The evidence model (EM) defines particular behaviors (or "indicators") that reveal the targeted competencies as well as the relationship(s) among those behaviors to the competency variables. That is, specific student behaviors (and the scoring thereof) constitute the *evidence rules*, while the statistical connections established between the behaviors and the CM variables constitute the *statistical model*. Evidence rules specify the identification and scoring of particular actions taken within the game, thus comprising weighted evidence. Statistical models set values to the specified evidence, accumulate the evidence (i.e., observable variables), then statistically link the observables to the competency variables (i.e., unobservables). The statistical model can employ simple dichotomous models (e.g., correct/incorrect; present/absent) but also graded models (e.g., low, medium, high) used in Bayesian networks (see Shute & Ventura, 2013). The EM entails ongoing accumulation of evidence and continuous updating of the CM variables across tasks.

The task model (TM) specifies the features of tasks (e.g., difficulty level and format) that can elicit particular behaviors to be used as evidence. That is, the goal of the TM is to produce assessment tasks that are constructed explicitly to elicit evidence that is aligned with targeted competency variables. Overall, a TM contains a wide collection of tasks and task types (see Almond, Kim, Velasquez & Shute, 2014). The EM serves as the glue between the TM and CM. Together, the CM, EM, and TM form a dynamic system that is the backbone of stealth assessment's functionality.

HOW DOES STEALTH ASSESSMENT WORK?

Stealth assessment, using ECD for its assessment design, aligns the embedded assessment tasks with targeted competencies. The main purpose of stealth assessment is to make valid inferences about competency levels based squarely on collected evidence. Using stealth assessment in educational games enables one to directly link actions/behaviors in the game to the targeted competencies without interrupting students' learning (Shute, 2011). Players interact with the tasks/levels in a game (the TM), and behaviors are captured in a log file and analyzed according to the scoring rules in the EM. Results of the scored observables are processed statistically in the EM then entered into the student model (i.e., the player's CM). As the interaction continues, the student model keeps receiving data and updating claims about competency levels in the form of probabilities reflecting real-time estimates of learners' competencies. The estimations can be used to adapt tasks to meet learners' current level (e.g., choosing suitable difficulty level, or providing prompts/hints). Such support during gameplay is important to engage learners (Shute & Wang, 2017; Walkington, 2013) and to facilitate learning. A recent meta-analysis by Wouters and van Oostendorp (2013) has shown that games using adaptivity show an effect size of .34.

In the next section, we illustrate the implementation of stealth assessment in a digital game to assess a particular competency—problem-solving skill.

APPLICATION OF STEALTH ASSESSMENT

In a recent study in our lab, we embedded a stealth assessment of problem-solving skills in a popular game called Plants vs. Zombies 2 (PvZ2, Electronic Arts). PvZ2 presents players with situations where they must select plants (with different characteristics) to protect their home base from being over-run by zombies (which also differ in terms of their characteristics). A player chooses appropriate plants to form both a defense as well as offense in the lawn, set up in a grid like a chess board. To guard against zombies making it through to the home base, players need to engage their problem-solving skills and come up with different strategies to deal with different situations. Problem-solving skill was thus the targeted competency (see Shute, Moore, & Wang, 2015; Wang, Shute, & Moore, 2015).

Establishing the competency model of problem-solving skills began with an extensive literature review. This resulted in the identification of four main facets: (a) analyze givens and constraints, (b) plan a solution pathway, (c) use tools effectively and efficiently, and (d) monitor and evaluate progress. To align the game levels with the targeted competency variables, we specified particular indicators (observables) to be used as evidence for problem-solving skills. Next, we iteratively evaluated each indicator in terms of its relevance to the CM as well as its feasibility of automatic collection and scoring from gameplay (Shute et al., 2015). This yielded a total of 32 indicators aligned to the four facets (see Table 9.1 for some examples). The first and second facets have seven indicators each. The third contains 14 and the last includes 4.

After identifying indicators and creating scoring rules, we assigned statistical relationships between indicators and competency variables. Next, we categorized each indicator into discrete levels (e.g., poor, OK, good, very good). Bayes nets (BN) processed the data when an indicator was demonstrated, calculating the probability per level (e.g., low, medium, high) and per facet of problem-solving skill. We constructed a BN for each level in the game to ensure that each level had its own specific indicators and rubrics (not all indicators were applicable in each level).

TABLE 9.1 Competency Model and Examples of Indicators

Facet	Example Indicators
Analyzing Givens & Constraints	• Plants > 3 Sunflowers before the second wave of zombies arrives • Selects plants off the conveyor belt before it becomes full
Planning a Solution Pathway	• Places sun producers in the back, offensive plants in the middle, and defensive plants up front • Plants Twin Sunflowers or uses plant food on (Twin) Sunflowers in levels that require the production of X sun
Using Tools and Resources Effectively	• Uses plant food when there are > 5 zombies in the yard or zombies are getting close to the house (within 2 squares) • Damages > 3 zombies when firing a Coconut Cannon
Monitoring and Evaluating Progress	• Shovels Sunflowers in the back and replaces them with offensive plants when the ratio of zombies to plants exceeds 2:1

Source: Shute et al., 2015

For example, in PvZ2, iceberg lettuce is a defensive plant that can slow down the zombies by freezing them, while a snapdragon is an offensive plant that breathes fire to burn/kill zombies. When these two plants are placed next to each other, their powers cancel each other out (e.g., if an iceberg lettuce freezes a zombie, and a proximal snapdragon breathes fire on the zombie, it will reanimate the zombie). Placing these two types of plants close to one another (e.g., within two spaces) comprises evidence of ineffective tool use. For the scoring rule, we set the ratio as the number of iceberg lettuces planted in the range of a snapdragon, divided by the total number of iceberg lettuces planted (see indicator #37 in Figure 9.1). Smaller ratios are better in this case.

During gameplay, actions that players take are scored in real time relative to specific indicators. The BNs are continuously updated regarding the current estimates of problem solving skill, overall and at the level of the facets. As seen in Figure 9.1, there is a probability of .61 that the player is currently estimated to be "low" on the "tool use" facet. Moreover, other variables change as well. Overall, BNs graphically portray the relationships between the main competency, its facets, and the associated indicators. BNs are used to ensure dynamic communication between the data and the beliefs of certain competencies (Reese et al., 2015).

To validate the stealth assessment in PvZ2, we selected two external measures of problem-solving skills: Raven's Progressive Matrices (RPM; Raven, 1941) and MicroDYN (Wüstenberg, Greiff, & Funke, 2012). The former tests learners' inductive ability (i.e., rule identification), while the latter requires the application of existing information to solve problems (rule

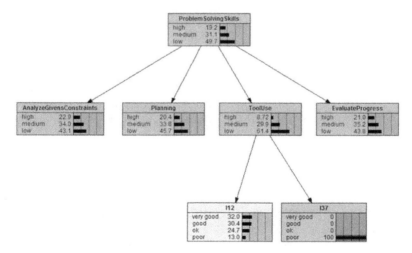

Figure 9.1 An example of a BN with data for indicator #37 entered (poor use of iceberg lettuces).

application). The scores from the two external tests significantly correlated with the estimates from the stealth assessment ($p < .01$) (Shute et al., 2015). Thus, the stealth assessment embedded in the game shows both internal and external validity (convergent validity).

After the stealth assessment is embedded into the game and the states of players' competencies are assessed and validated, the next logical step is to use this information to provide adaptive learning support (Shute, Ke, & Wang, in press) to the player. In this case, adaptive support can refer to personalized feedback (regarding the competency or game level), increasing the difficulty level based on estimates of the player's abilities, and so on.

DEFINING ADAPTIVITY

Csikszentmihalyi (1997) claimed that learners learn best when they are fully engaged in some process, or in the state of flow. Inducing a state of flow involves the provision of clear and unambiguous goals, challenging yet achievable levels of difficulty, and immediate feedback (Cowley, Charles, Black, & Hickey, 2008; Csikszentmihalyi, 1997). Based on flow theory, a task that is too difficult can be frustrating while a task that is too easy may be boring; thus, the optimal state (of flow) resides between the two. Similarly, Vygotsky's zone of proximal development (ZPD; 1978) suggests that learning is at its best when the learning materials are just beyond students' existing level of understanding and ability (Vygotsky, 1978). Considering these two aspects of deep learning—facilitating the state of flow and providing materials compatible with learners' ZPDs—adaptive learning environments can be used to facilitate both via adapting to learners' current competency state(s).

Adaptivity generally refers to the ability of a person or device to alter its behavior according to changes in the environment (Shute & Zapata-Rivera, 2012). Some common examples of adaptive devices include thermostats and cruise control in many cars. In the context of instructional environments, adaptivity can help to provide personalized instruction for different learners with varying ZPDs and facilitate the state of flow throughout the learning process. An adaptive learning environment should monitor various (and often evolving) characteristics of learners and then balance challenges and ability levels to improve learning (Shute & Zapata-Rivera, 2012).

ADAPTIVITY IN EDUCATIONAL GAMES

When people play well-designed games, they often lose track of time (i.e., experience the state of flow). Teachers try to engage students with learning materials, but the engagement is usually not comparable to that experienced with good video games (Gee, 2003, 2005; Prensky, 2001). Over the past couple of decades, there has been growing interest in designing and developing educational games as a way to fully engage students in learning and also add learning opportunities into games (Kickmeier-Rust & Albert, 2010). Again, adaptive educational games can help maintain players' state of flow (Csikszentmihalyi, 1997; Vygotsky, 1978) and ultimately improve their learning (Andersen, 2012) by keeping players within their ZPD.

One way to include adaptivity in educational games is to use *micro-adaptation* (Kickmeier-Rust & Albert, 2010; Shute, Graf, & Hansen, 2005). This approach entails monitoring and interpreting the learner's particular behaviors, as with stealth assessment. Micro-adaptivity then may provide the learner with appropriate educational supports and/or adjust various aspects of the game (e.g., level difficulty) based on the student model estimates without disrupting the state of flow (Kickmeier-Rust & Albert, 2010). Adaptive games can adapt challenges to the current estimated levels of player's knowledge and skills (Csikszentmihalyi, 1997; Vygotsky, 1978) and provide formative feedback (Shute, 2008) and other types of support in unobtrusive ways (Peirce, Conlan, & Wade, 2008).

PUTTING IT ALL TOGETHER

Currently, while the U.S. educational system is doing a good job producing test-takers, we really need to refocus our attention to producing creative and critical problem solvers. Towards this end, we need to consider using (a) new approaches (e.g., stealth assessment) for measuring 21st-century competencies, as well as (b) adaptive technologies within learning environments (e.g., educational games) to promote these competencies.

To effectively adapt to students' current competency states, one needs to first accurately estimate their current state. Shute, Ke, and Wang (in press) describe nine steps towards designing and developing stealth assessment in interactive environments (e.g., educational games). They suggested that the next logical step is to use the information from the stealth assessment to adapt to the learners' ability to maintain their ZDP and the state of flow (Csikszentmihalyi, 1997; Vygotsky, 1978). With learning environments that can accurately measure students' skills and competencies and then adapt to their skill level, we can help students improve their learning processes and outcomes, which will better prepare them for future learning.

CONCLUSION AND FUTURE DIRECTIONS

In this chapter, we illustrated some of the problems we have in our educational system relative to 21st-century needs, described a future with few if any high-stakes tests and with better teaching approaches than now exist, provided an example of embedding stealth assessment into a video game, and elaborated on how the information gained from stealth assessments can help to create learning environments such as educational games that can effectively adapt to students' abilities and other attributes.

This chapter is intended to ignite ideas and research streams that can help to move the vison towards reality. To achieve this goal, we suggest that researchers may want to tackle some of these problems: (a) focus on research questions that can address any of the four hurdles we face to accomplish the presented vision; (b) explore ways to make the output of stealth assessment more user friendly (e.g., a dashboard of students' states by which teachers can make relevant instructional support decisions); (c) examine the when, what, and how to adapt without disrupting the flow in educational games to achieve the outcomes we are looking for; and (d) investigate the questions of how to make the components of stealth assessment (i.e., CMs and EMs) recycled into other games in a plug-and-play manner.

REFERENCES

Abrams, L. M., Pedulla, J. J., & Madaus, G. F. (2003). Views from the classroom: Teachers' opinions of statewide testing programs. *Theory Into Practice, 42*(1), 18–29.

Amrein, A. L., & Berliner, D. C. (2002). High-stakes testing and student learning. *Education Policy Analysis Archives, 10* (18), 1–74.

Almond, R. G., Kim, Y. J., Velasquez, G., & Shute, V. J. (2014). How task features impact evidence from assessments embedded in simulations and games. *Measurement: Interdisciplinary Research and Perspectives, 12*(1–2), 1–33.

Almond, R. G., & Mislevy, R. J. (1999). Graphical models and computerized adaptive testing. *Applied Psychological Measurement, 23*(3), 223–237.

Andersen, E. (2012). Optimizing adaptivity in educational games. In W. Ryan (Ed.), *Proceedings of the International Conference on the Foundations of Digital Games*, (pp. 279–281). Raleigh, NC, USA.

Bergmann, J., & Sams, A. (2012). *Flip your classroom: Reach every student in every class every day.* Arlington, VA: International Society for Technology in Education.

Berliner, D. (2011). Rational responses to high stakes testing: The case of curriculum narrowing and the harm that follows. *Cambridge Journal of Education, 41*(3), 287–302.

Bransford, J., Brown, L. L., & Cocking, R. R. (2000). *How people learn: Brain, mind, experience, and school* (expanded ed.). Washington, DC: National Academies Press.

Bruner, J. S. (1961). The act of discovery. *Harvard Educational Review, 31*(1), 21–32.

Culler, R. E., & Holahan, C. J. (1980). Test anxiety and academic performance: The effects of study-related behaviors. *Journal of Educational Psychology, 72*(1), 16.

Cowley, B., Charles, D., Black, M., & Hickey, R. (2008). Toward an understanding of flow in video games. *Computers in Entertainment (CIE), 6*(2), 20.

Csikszentmihalyi, M. (1997). *Finding flow: The psychology of engagement with everyday life.* New York, NY: Basic Books.

Dede, C. (Ed.). (2015). *Data-intensive research in education: current work and next steps.* Washington, DC: Computing Research Association. Retrieved from http://cra.org/wp-content/uploads/2015/10/CRAEducationReport2015.pdf

Dori, Y. J. (2003). From nationwide standardized testing to school-based alternative embedded assessment in Israel: Students' performance in the matriculation 2000 project. *Journal of Research in Science Teaching, 40*(1), 34–52. doi:10.1002/tea.10059

Economist Intelligence Unit. (2012). *The learning curve. Lessons in country performance in education.* London: Pearson. Retrieved from http://thelearning-curve.pearson.com/the-report

Gee, J. P. (2003). What video games have to teach us about learning and literacy. *Computers in Entertainment (CIE), 1*(1), 20–23.

Gee, J. P. (2005). *Why video games are good for your soul: Pleasure and learning.* Melbourne, Australia: Common Ground Publishing.

Hanushek, E. A., & Woessmann, L. (2012). Do better schools lead to more growth? Cognitive skills, economic outcomes. *Journal of Economic Growth, 17*(4), 267–321. doi:10.1007/s10887-012-9081-x

Hickey, D., & Zuiker, S. (2012). Multilevel assessment for discourse, understanding, and achievement. *Journal of the Learning Sciences, 21*(4), 522–582. doi:10.1080/10508406.2011.652320

Jones, B. D. (2007). The unintended outcomes of high-stakes testing. *Journal of Applied School Psychology, 23*(2), 65–86. doi: 10.1300/J370v23n02_05

Kickmeier-Rust, M. D., & Albert, D. (2010). Micro-adaptivity: Protecting immersion in didactically adaptive digital educational games. *Journal of Computer Assisted Learning, 26*(2), 95–105.

Madaus, G., & Russell, M. (2010). Paradoxes of high-stakes testing. *The Journal of Education, 190*(1/2), 21–30.

McCambridge, R. (2014). Legacy of a failed foundation initiative: inBloom, Gates and Carnegie. *Nonprofit Quarterly.* Retrieved from https://nonprofitquarterly.org/2014/07/02/legacy-of-a-failed-foundation-initiative-inbloom-gates-and-carnegie/

Mislevy, R. J., & Haertel, G. D. (2006). Implications of evidence-centered design for educational testing. *Educational Measurement: Issues and Practice, 25*(4), 6–20.

Mislevy, R. J., Steinberg, L. S., & Almond, R. G. (2003). On the structure of educational assessments. *Measurement: Interdisciplinary research and perspectives, 1*(1), 3–62.

Office of Educational Technology. (2015). *Assessment: Measure what matters.* Washington, DC: U.S. Department of Education. Retrieved from http://tech.ed.gov/netp/assessment-measure-what matters/

Organization for Economic Co-operation and Development. (2013). *PISA 2012 results in focus: What 15-year-olds know and what they can do with what they know.* Retrieved from http://www.oecd.org/pisa/keyfindings/pisa-2012-results-overview.pdf

Partnership for 21st Century Learning. (2015). *Framework for 21st-century learning*. Retrieved from http://www.p21.org/storage/documents/P21_framework_0515.pdf

Peirce, N., Conlan, O., & Wade, V. (2008). Adaptive educational games: Providing non-invasive personalised learning experiences. In *Second IEEE International Conference on Digital Games and Intelligent Toys Based Education* (pp. 28–35). Banff, Canada: IEEE.

Plass, J. L., Homer, B. D., & Kinzer, C. K. (2015). Foundations of game-based learning. *Educational Psychologist, 50*(4), 258–283. doi:10.1080/00461520.2015.1122533

Prensky, M. (2001). Digital natives, digital immigrants, part 1. *On the Horizon, 9*(5), 1–6.

Raven, J. C. (1941). Standardization of progressive matrices, 1938. *British Journal of Medical Psychology, 19*(1), 137–150.

Reese, D. D., Tabachnick, B. G., & Kosko, R. E. (2015). Video game learning dynamics: Actionable measures of multidimensional learning trajectories. *British Journal of Educational Technology, 46*(1), 98–122. doi:10.1111/bjet.12128

Reigeluth, C. M., & Karnopp, J. R. (2013). *Reinventing schools: It's time to break the mold.* Lanham, MD: Rowman &Littlefield Education.

Schwartz, D. L., & Martin, T. (2004). Inventing to prepare for future learning: The hidden efficiency of encouraging original student production in statistics instruction. *Cognition and Instruction, 22*(2), 129.

Shavelson, R. J., & Kurpius, A. (2012). Reflections on learning progressions. *Learning progressions in science* (pp. 13–26) Springer.

Shute, V. J. (2007). Tensions, trends, tools, and technologies: Time for an educational sea change. In C. A. Dwyer (Ed.), *The future of assessment: Shaping teaching and learning* (pp. 139–187). New York, NY: Lawrence Erlbaum Associates, Taylor & Francis Group.

Shute, V. J. (2008). Focus on formative feedback. *Review of educational research, 78*(1), 153–189.

Shute, V. J. (2011). Stealth assessment in computer-based games to support learning. In S. Tobias & J. D. Fletcher (Eds.), *Computer games and instruction* (pp. 503–524). Charlotte, NC: Information Age.

Shute, V. J., Ke, F., & Wang, L. (2017). Assessment and adaptation in games. In P. Wouters, & H. van Oostendorp (Eds.), *Instructional techniques to facilitate learning and motivation of serious games* (pp. 59–78). New York, NY: Springer.

Shute, V. J., Leighton, J. P., Jang, E. E., & Chu, M. (2016). Advances in the science of assessment. *Educational Assessment, 21*(1), 1–27.

Shute, V. J., & Ventura, M. (2013). *Measuring and supporting learning in games: Stealth assessment.* Cambridge, MA: The MIT Press. Retrieved from Cambridge, MA: The MIT Press.

Shute, V. J., Ventura, M., Small, M., & Goldberg, B. (2013). Modeling student competencies in video games using stealth assessment. In R. Sottilare, X. Hu, A. Graesser, & H. Holden (Eds.), *Design recommendations for adaptive intelligent tutoring systems: Learning modeling* (pp. 141–152). Washington, DC: Army Research Laboratory.

Shute, V. J., Graf, E. A., & Hansen, E. (2005). Designing adaptive, diagnostic math assessments for sighted and visually-disabled students. In L. PytlikZillig, R. Bruning, & M. Bodvarsson (Eds.), *Technology-based education: Bringing researchers and practitioners together* (pp. 169–202). Greenwich, CT: Information Age.

Shute, V. J., Ke, F., & Wang, L. (in press). Assessment and adaptation in games. In P. Wouters & H. van Oostendorp (Eds.), *Techniques to facilitate learning and motivation of serious games*. New York, NY: Springer.

Shute, V. J., Moore, G. R., & Wang, L. (2015). Measuring problem solving skills in Plants vs. Zombies 2. *Proceedings of the 8th International Conference on Educational Data Mining (EDM 2015)*. Madrid, Spain.

Shute, V. J., & Psotka, J. (1996). Intelligent tutoring systems: Past, present, and future. In D. Jonassen (Ed.), *Handbook of research for educational communications and technology* (pp. 570–600). New York, NY: Macmillan.

Shute, V. J., & Ventura, M. (2013). *Stealth assessment: Measuring and supporting learning in video games*. Cambridge, MA: The MIT Press.

Shute, V. J., & Wang, L. (in press). Assessing and supporting hard-to-measure constructs. In A. Rupp, & J. Leighton (Eds.), *Handbook of cognition and assessment*. New York, NY: Springer.

Shute, V. J., & Zapata-Rivera, D. (2012). Adaptive educational systems. In P. J. Durlach & A. M. Lesgold (Eds.), *Adaptive technologies for training and education* (pp. 7–27). New York, NY: Cambridge University Press.

Shute, V. J., & Ventura, M. (2013). *Measuring and supporting learning in games: Stealth assessment*. Cambridge, MA: The MIT Press. Retrieved from Cambridge, MA: The MIT Press

Smith, M. L. (1991). Put to the test: The effects of external testing on teachers. *Educational Researcher, 20*(5), 8–11.

Strayer, J. F. (2012). How learning in an inverted classroom influences cooperation, innovation and task orientation. *Learning Environments Research, 15*(2), 171–193.

U.S. Department of Education, National Center for Education Statistics. (2015). *Fast facts: Expenditure*. Retrieved from http://www.ed.gov/about/overview/fed/10facts/index.html

Van Eck, R. N., Shute, V. J., & Rieber, L. P. (in press). Leveling up: Game design research and practice for instructional designers. In R. Reiser & J. Dempsey (Eds.), *Trends and issues in instructional design and technology* (4th ed.). Upper Saddle River, NJ: Pearson Education.

Vygotsky, L. (1978). Interaction between learning and development. *Readings on the Development of Children, 23*(3), 34–41.

Walkington, C. A. (2013). Using adaptive learning technologies to personalize instruction to student interests: The impact of relevant contexts on performance and learning outcomes. *Journal of Educational Psychology, 105*(4), 932–945. doi:10.1037/a0031882

Wang, L., Shute, V., & Moore, G. R. (2015). Lessons learned and best practices of stealth assessment. *International Journal of Gaming and Computer-Mediated Simulations, 7*(4), 66–87. doi:10.4018/IJGCMS.2015100104

Wheelock, A., Bebell, D., & Haney, W. (2000). What can student drawings tell us about high stakes testing in Massachusetts? *Teachers College Record*, November 2.

Wilson, M., & Sloane, K. (2000). From principles to practice: An embedded assessment system. *Applied Measurement in Education, 13*(2), 181–208. doi:10.1207/S15324818AME1302_4

Wouters, P., & van Oostendorp, H. (2013). A meta-analytic review of the role of instructional support in game-based learning. *Computers & Education, 60*(1), 412–425. doi:10.1016/j.compedu.2012.07.018

Wüstenberg, S., Greiff, S., & Funke, J. (2012). Complex problem solving—more than reasoning? *Intelligence. 40*(1), 1–14.

Young, M. F., Kulikowich, J. M., & Barab, S. A. (1997). The unit of analysis for situated assessment. *Instructional Science, 25*, 133–150.

Yuhas, A. (2015). Chinese nationals charged with cheating by impersonation on US college tests. *The Guardian*. Retrieved from http://www.theguardian.com/us-news/2015/may/28/china-nationals-cheating-college-tests

CHAPTER 10

SITUATING BIG DATA

Jennifer Dalsen
University of Wisconsin–Madison

Craig G. Anderson, Kurt Squire,
and Constance Steinkuehler
University of California–Irvine

In Washington, DC, contemporary educational reform is increasingly defined in terms of shifting education from a "data poor" activity to a "data rich" activity (T. Kalil, White House Office of Science and Technology Policy, personal communication, September 1, 2013). Over the previous decade, we have seen not only a rise in shared national and state (common core) standards and frameworks that articulate what we, as a country, believe young people and adults should be able to think, know, and do, but also a concomitant rise in large-scale, data-rich strategies for assessing such knowledge, skills, and dispositions. While inroads into so-called "big data" techniques (the capture, curation, storage, and analysis of massive, complex quantitative data sets) have been made on some fronts, particularly in relation to game-based technologies for learning, they have not yet caught up to our more sophisticated and inclusive frameworks for learning goals.

Take for example the National Academy of Science's (Bell & Lewenstein, 2009) "six strands of science learning" framework that unifies goals across

Exploding the Castle, pages 221–249
Copyright © 2017 by Information Age Publishing
221

both formal and informal science learning environments to include not only content knowledge (strand 2) and inquiry practice (strand 3) but also interest (strand 1), epistemological disposition (strand 4), identity development within the domain (strand 6), and longer-term participation in the field (strand 5). Big data techniques applied to learning have made some progress in areas such as content knowledge (Hien & Haddawy, 2007; Nebot, Castro, Vellido, & Mugica, 2006; Pardos, Heffernan, Anderson, & Heffernan, 2007) and, to a lesser extent, inquiry practice (Quellmalz et al., 2013; Wasson, Hanson, & Mor, 2016). Both are areas in which more traditional techniques already fare well, but big data has not yet made progress in the more challenging assessment areas that link interest, identity, participation, and epistemology. Putting such constructs in conversation with one another would create a more coherent and convincing data ecology for making strong inferences about learning. If we want to catalyze progress toward more expanded frameworks for learning goals that include tricky variables, such as identity and dispositions, then we must make traction on their empirical measure in ways that are commensurate with contemporary data-rich corpora and techniques—and we must do so in ways that are theory-driven and comprehensive, and not simply a list of strands or themes.

Theories of situated cognition restore coherence to the study of learning as knowledge, skill, disposition, interest, participation, and identity by focusing on learning as shifting (inter)action with the social and material world. This body of work includes activity theory (e.g., Engestrom, Miettinen, & Punamaki, 1999), d/Discourse theory (Gee, 2010), distributed cognition (Hutchins, 1995), ecological psychology (Gibson, 1986), ethnomethodology (Garfinkel, 1967), mediated action (Wertsch, 1998), situated learning (Lave & Wenger, 1991), sociocultural theory (Vygotsky, 1978), and situativity theory (Greeno & Moore, 1993). Despite differences among these traditions, each shares a common emphasis on social and material interaction as not just the vehicle for the development of domain knowledge and practices (from social practices such as argumentation to material practices such as bench lab procedures for growing cells), but also as identity within community (Gee, 2010), interest and engagement, and epistemological understanding (Holland & Quinn, 1987). Human understanding is a process that involves not just individuals but also tools, representations, artifacts, and social interaction. Educational interventions should be designed to produce deepening participation in complex, authentic social practices (Lave & Wenger, 1991) and increase competence in the use of complex, authentic tools and resources (Pea, 1993). Individuals learn to use tools and resources through regular interactions, which are themselves shaped by membership in communities that give meaning to these tools and resources (Derry & Steinkuehler, 2003). Thus, it is through a series of social and material interactions that individuals develop new identities as capable learners and members within a given community (Gee, 2010; Greeno, 1997).

Nowhere are such situated accounts of cognition more empirically tractable than in online, technology-mediated environments—foremost, games that offer an interactive media environment, the capacity for joint activity within and beyond the game, a normative following of active online communities of practice, and increasing integration into formal and informal educational environments as a means for learning. Games are both *technologies* and *communities*, and their potential for learning can be understood in terms of both. As a technology, games are simulated worlds that offer players "designed experiences" (Squire, 2006) of the world from new points of view or from points of view wholly inaccessible in regular life. In terms of community, games function as new "third places" (Oldenburg, 1999) for informal sociability (Steinkuehler & Williams, 2006). Every game, no matter how obscure, develops its own "affinity space" (Gee, 2004) where mastery is collective (Jenkins, 2006; Levy, 1999; Steinkuehler & Duncan, 2009) and reciprocally apprenticed (Steinkuehler, 2004).

Like any other learning technology, however, games are still only sociotechnical artifacts (Bijker, 1995) whose potential for learning, like that of any instructional tool, is highly influenced by its context of use. Whether it's a textbook, calculator, or high-end 3-D graphical data display, a tool is only as good as the activities and practices in which it is embedded. The online communities around games are one important part of that ecosystem; the in-room formal and informal environments of implementation are another. Meta-analyses of games for learning confirm that the context of the game and not just the technology in isolation are key factors in their effectiveness (Clark, 2013; Sitzmann, 2011; Vogel, Vogel, Cannon-Bowers, Bowers, Muse, & Wright, 2006; Wouters, van Nimwegen, van Oostendorp, & van der Spek, 2013; Young et al, 2012). However, to date we have no models for how we might connect the forms of contextual data that theories of situated cognition emphasize as most important with the forms of "big data" produced from the technology in isolation and increasingly the sole focus of assessment.

In this chapter, we describe an ongoing project that seeks to marry theories of situated cognition to the big data movement by connecting clickstream data from technologies in isolation to key forms of multimodal data available from their contexts of use in a theoretically principled and empirically validated manner. Our goal is to connect the broader forms of data considered central from the theory of situated cognition—data including individual and group discourse (online and in-room), artifact analysis, classroom assessments, and school performance data (grades and test scores)—to data exhaust from educational games in order to create a more authentic account of learning. In this chapter, we begin by reviewing the current research on big data analyses of game data exhaust and on game-based social interactions. We then describe the game-based curriculum we used to generate and capture both forms of game-related data (telemetry and talk) in order to create a heterogeneous data corpus for mixed method analysis. We then discuss two key issues that confront us in such an analysis, detailing how abstract theoretical concerns materialize in our methodological and practical work, in the everyday mundane activity of obtaining, organizing, and analyzing data such as these. We conclude with general reflections on the implications of this effort and concerns it raises about our recent national obsession to convert teaching and learning into a data-rich enterprise.

BIG DATA ANALYSES OF GAME DATA EXHAUST

Digital games enable embedded assessments of learning through evaluation of how authentic activity changes, a fruitful contrast to more traditional task-extrinsic measures of learning such as post hoc tests or pre/post measures that can mark endpoints of the learning process or aggregated change over time but cannot trace its full trajectory. Data exhaust from games provides a massive volume of automatically transmitted clickstream or "telemetry" data of trackable actions and choices generated as a byproduct of gameplay by the user. Their analysis holds the promise of allowing us to continuously assess, refine, and even personalize learning.

The majority of successful efforts to use game data exhaust to date lie within the commercial games industry. Within game development companies, such analyses typically focus on maximizing replayability and profits through repeated iteration of A/B tested design features (Kohavi, Longbotham, Sommerfeld, & Henne, 2009). For example, the online social game company Zynga, makers of *Farmville* and *Words with Friend*s, collects over 15 terabytes of gameplay exhaust data daily for analysis of play patterns in order to constantly iterate and improve their game content and monetized offerings (Asthana, 2011). Game data exhaust has also been analyzed by game studies scholars in order to examine the nuances of play behaviors within various commercial game titles. Thurau and Bauckhage (2010) examined social interactions in the game *World of Warcraft* to detail the patterns of group formation and interaction. Weber and Mateas (2009) used data mining techniques and machine learning to model and predict opponent strategy use. Drachen and Canossa (2011) used telemetry data to examine spatial patterns of game level exploration, showing patterns in how players navigate a virtual space. Drachen, Canossa, and Yannakakis (2009) used such data to introduce methods of determining qualitative "play styles" or groupings based on different ways that people play. In another study,

Bauckhage, Kersting, Sifa, Thurau, Drachen, and Canossa (2012) analyzed telemetry data for traces of interest, predicting how long players will persist in a game. Gagné, El-Nasr, and Shaw (2011) use data mining techniques to investigate how players deviate from the designed game paths.

More moderate progress has been made in the analysis of game data exhaust towards pedagogical ends. Big data efforts in educational research fall under the general rubric of educational data mining (EDM) or learning analytics (LA), where EDM typically describes broad analysis of a large number of learners (>1K) and LA describes a deeper analysis of a smaller set of learners. Using such techniques, Baker, D'Mello, Rodrigo, and Graesser (2010) examined how in-game behavior relates to cognitive affect and performance metrics to find that boredom was more detrimental to learning than frustration. Clark and Martinez-Garza (2012) assessed intuitive and formal understanding of specific physics content and found that playing a physics-based game developed players' general understanding of physics but had no direct impact on formal physics questions. Berland, Martin, Benton, Petrick Smith, and Davis (2013) demonstrated student learning of programming through strategic game mechanics, highlighting the importance of tinkering in novice programmer skill development. Lewis, Trinh, and Kirsh (2011) studied distributed attention among champion competitive real-time strategy game players to discover a new model for task management training. Such research illustrates the promise of big data analyses for education, although to date no research has integrated contextual "paradata" from implementation that might account for social interaction.

ANALYSES OF GAME-BASED SOCIAL INTERACTIONS

With this rise of quantitative analyses of game-based big data sets over the last several years, we see a similar rise of qualitative analyses of game-related social context and interaction, although the two bodies of research have heretofore remained largely disconnected. Much of this latter body of research has focused on game-based affinity spaces, social spaces in which individuals who share a common interest in a given game or gather online asynchronously (or, more rarely, synchronously in person) to share and discuss information about the game (Gee, 2004; Gee & Hayes, 2010). Over time, this loose, distributed network of individuals with a common interest in the game becomes a sort of "community of common interest" with its own structures of membership (Gee, 2007; Gee & Hayes, 2010), discursive and virtual practices (Steinkuehler, 2006), peer mentoring (Squire, 2011), and apprenticeship (Steinkuehler & Oh, 2012).Through such structures, participants share not just knowledge and skills but also dispositions or values—loosely shared orientations toward what "counts" as valuable about a given game or accomplishment (Steinkuehler & Oh, 2012).

The body of research on game-related social interaction and affinity spaces documents the formative role of social context and interaction in learning through games. Studying the game of dominoes, Nasir (2005) observed the intertwining relationship between individual and social processes during play. A player's prior knowledge of gameplay, balanced by teamwork, conversation, and negotiation, afforded the discovery of alternate play goals. Simultaneously, players built competency through seeking help and offering unsolicited advice to those around them. Steinkuehler (2004) evaluated the structure of apprenticeship in the massively multiplayer online game *Lineage I* to find that newcomers gained genuine expertise through apprenticeship and joint activity with more advanced players. A study of peer interaction around *Civilization III* by Squire and Giovanetto (2008) found high engagement in player pairs as each group shared strategies and struggles. More experienced players used sophisticated language as a means to communicate their advanced knowledge to less experienced players. Nardi's (2010) ethnography of *World of Warcraft* described a learning environment comprised of social organizations, ranging from online communities to friends and family members, in which learning resulted not simply from individual exploration but from social participation and conversation. Here, cognition in games was seen as a socially distributed process. In a later study of the same game, Martin (2012) found WoW players as active producers of their community's knowledge base through the production of transmedia materials including YouTube videos, blogs, forums, and personal websites. Even among players who did not actively seek advice from other players still leveraged the collective intelligence of their community through these materials, thereby engaging in an indirect form of learner-directed mentorship. Similarly, Ducheneaut, Yee, Nickell, and Moore (2006) found that such indirect mentorship can also be identified via in-game chat channels: While not every player is obligated to participate in discussion, typed information on general advice or background chatter nevertheless creates a shared feeling of social presence and community shared information. A study by Seay, Jerome, Lee, and Kraut (2004) on Project Massive, a website designed to study how online game subscribers played, organized, and communicated information with each other, demonstrated significant variation in community talk. The majority of players surveyed (77%) shared advice and offered support to each other. In contrast, few players actively shared information about themselves or their personal experiences to other people. Educational multiplayer online games such as *Quest Atlantis* (Barab, Thomas, Dodge, Carteaux, & Tuzun, 2005) or *River City* (Dede, Ketelhut, Nelson, Clarke, & Bowman, 2004) offer hybrids of online and offline learning wherein players can adopt new roles and actively participate through the game's educationally oriented narrative and content. Such multimodal approaches to learning, in combination with community engagement, are the basis for the design for the *Virulent* project detailed herein.

CONTEXT OF INVESTIGATION

The goal of this project was to connect qualitative analyses of game-related talk and interaction to quantitative analyses of big data sets from in-game activity. Toward this end, we first needed to create a rich context for investigation that would generate sufficiently rich data of both types. Given our situated, sociocultural perspective, we wanted to create an activity that would engage students in authentic social practices (Lave & Wenger, 1991) using complex tools and resources (Pea, 1993) representative of a given domain while yet remaining playful, in keeping with the overall intention and spirit of a games-based approach. It needed to be structured in such a way as to elicit significant game play (i.e., time on task) as well as substantive conversation around and about gameplay (i.e., paradata) with some element of group affiliation and identity. Toward these ends, we developed a week-long workshop for middle school students over spring break entitled "Game-A-Palooza." Over the course of five days, participants worked in collaborative groups to decipher viral function and human cellular response as a means for stopping the fictional "Raven Virus" from reaching global pandemic and, thus, triggering a worldwide apocalypse.

Curriculum Context

Participants in our week-long Game-A-Palooza (GaP) event role-played as scientists recruited by the Center for Disease Control (CDC) to stop the "Raven Virus" from spreading across the world. To enhance roleplay, students received a lab coat, field notes journal, and "digiscope" device, which was an iPad loaded with the game *Virulent* whose game levels were called dynamic "microscopic slides" (Figure 10.1). Throughout the week, students played through the "microscopic slides" of the game to figure out how the Raven virus functioned and how the human immune system reacted. Toward these ends, participants created shared paper models of cell and viral systems, debated within and between small groups to decide which model and possible solution was most viable, wrote persuasive letters to the CDC, and recorded science presentation videos for final group solutions to the threatening apocalypse.

Throughout the week, participants were encouraged to play through the science of virus and cell structure and function. Each day began with a

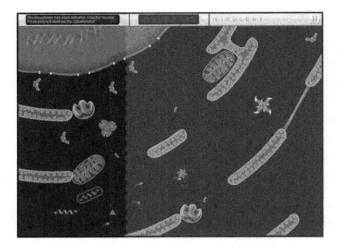

Figure 10.1 The "digiscope" or GLS tablet game *Virulent* on the Apple iPad.

(prerecorded) Skype call from mock scientists at the CDC that included updated information about the Raven Virus and its ongoing spread (Figure 10.2). A map illustrating the increasing infection rate of the Raven Virus was displayed each day, with more countries infected by this unknown microorganism each day. The curriculum was designed with structured questions (e.g., How do viruses spread?) and activities (e.g., small group model construction) guiding each day's activities, with students divided into small groups of three to four students and assigned a facilitator (who also served

Figure 10.2 Game-A-Palooza daily mock CDC Skype call with unfolding information about the Raven Virus.

as a researcher gathering field notes and monitoring other forms of data collection, described below). Each small group worked collaboratively to compete with one another to construct a predictive model for how the virus worked inside the body and to make a persuasive argument for a group proposal for stopping its spread. Through joint activity, conversation and facilitator mentoring, participants advanced toward their assigned challenge: to stop the Raven Virus in its tracks.

In order to accomplish this, each small group or "research team" (Figure 10.3) met daily over five days to work collaboratively and competitively through the problem. On day one, participants met their teammates, completed pre-assessments, investigated the Raven Virus, and wrote a preliminary letter to the CDC. On day two, they conducted initial investigations on "microscopic slides" (game levels) and constructed a preliminary model of how the Raven Virus was infecting the body. On day three, students conducted more "digiscope" research and revised their model based on what they discovered, then produced a short video presentation to explain their model to other scientists (other student groups and the mock CDC scientists). On day four, each small group presented their model to the cohort and deliberated collectively on ways to improve or change it based on the accumulated shared knowledge. At the end of day four, players were informed that the CDC scientists themselves were now infected and thus the race to produce a solution based on an accurate model began. On day five, since the CDC was infected and could no

Figure 10.3 A research team works collaboratively to determine the structure and function of the virus and the cell.

longer assist in researching ways to stop the spread, students were told that they were now on their own to collectively, as a cohort, find a solution to stop the Raven Virus from taking over the world. They were given background materials (fictionalized but scientifically based literature including a journal article, a news article, and a book excerpt) on three choices available—create a vaccine, use an RNA inhibitor, or use a drug to inhibit the cell's mitochondria—and had to decide, based on their collective model, which avenue to pursue. Thus, on the final day, groups came together to hold a final cohort debate with each group presenting their argument and then individual students placing final votes to decide which option they pursue as the new stand-in scientists for the CDC.

Throughout the week, all participants were given 24/7 access to their "digiscopes" and were encouraged to take them home and work on the problem on their own time. To drive out-of-session engagement beyond the daily curricula, participants received "coin rewards" for completing optional tasks—for example, finishing a specific challenge level or completing every level of the game, which are both activities outside of the formal curriculum. At the end of the program, students could then exchange these points for various prizes such as pocket microscopes, video game character plushies, and raffle tickets to win an iPad.

The Game Virulent

Virulent (see Figure 10.1) is a real-time strategy game designed to introduce players to viral replication and how the body reacts to infection. Players control the Raven Virus, moving level by level to infect host cells and attack the immune system with viral proteins. Each level takes players deeper into the microscopic world with the support of audio and visual directions. Specific actions that players may accomplish during gameplay include "hijacking" different cellular parts (e.g., mitochondria), evading free antibodies, and ridding the body of slicer enzymes. A graphic almanac serves as reference to different virus and immune system components encountered during gameplay. A series of "challenge" levels also accompanies the game, whereupon players can engage in timed tasks or other "test your mettle" type events.

DATA COLLECTION

Participants

Data were collected across three separate events: As part of a GLS spring break camp called Game-a-Palooza ($n = 43$), within a local private school's extended day program ($n = 11$), and within a larger summer camp run by the Boys & Girls Club ($n = 27$). Participants were separated into research teams, each of which comprised 3–4 students supported by a Games + Learning + Society facilitator. Thus, there were 21 student research teams across three cohorts. Teams were assembled randomly based on age and served as the primary context for interaction during the 90-minute session.

Recruitment for each cohort varied. For the spring break event, participants were recruited via flyers around the local community and schools. For the extended day program, we worked with administrative staff to fold existing activities, like coding and other computational interests, into our curriculum structure. For the Boys & Girls Club event, we worked with directors to advertise our event to children already attending their summer program. Across all three groups, participant time was compensated.

The average participant age was 11.5 years old (range from 9 to 14 years). The majority of participants identified as Caucasian ($n = 27$), African American ($n = 13$), and Hispanic ($n = 8$). One participant identified as multiple race and other students chose not to answer this question. Of the students who listed gender, 35 identified as male and 22 as female.

A total of 22 participants attended all five days of the spring break session, with eight participants four days, six attending only three, and seven attending two or fewer (and thus considered a dropout). No participants dropped from the private school extended day program; two participants dropped from the Boys & Girls Club session. Across all three sites then, our total retention rate was 89%. Our final n-size for analysis was 72. To capture group dynamics and effects, participants who dropped out of the event were still included in discourse analyses and any other analysis tied into it.

To ensure player data were tracked across each day (both in and out of formal event sessions), developers at GLS created a QR code login system. QR codes were carried by each participant on paper and scanned using the iPad camera. Each QR code was attached to a particular anonymized, randomly generated ADAGE ID (e.g., "Fluffy Sandals") in order to track player action. This system ensured that the clickstream data remained organized and tied to a particular player no matter when or where they played. This also simplified the login process, resolving likely problems with students forgetting or losing their unique login details. Gameplay data collected from daily program sessions were structured by the curriculum and therefore considered "formal gameplay"; gameplay occurring outside of sessions was considered "informal play." Informal play included game activity during break time between sessions, lunchtime, and home activity. Partitioning the data in this way was straightforward using ADAGE generated timestamps.

Data Corpus

A rich, diverse stream of data was collected across these contexts during the five-day events as detailed in Figure 10.4. Here, individual—nested in student research team (small group), which in turn is nested in cohort (each of three locations)—is the primary unit of analysis. Game data exhaust from each participant's iPad was recorded via ADAGE (described above), with both formal and informal gameplay recorded and stored in the same data corpus. Group artifacts were collected, photographed, and uploaded to a secure server, with original materials transferred to a secure office in a university building and stored in locked cabinets. To allow remote teams access to the data for analysis, IRB-approved channels were set up to transfer and collaborate on data. Once stored on secure servers, the data were cleaned and anonymized. Anonymized data were shared with collaborating university sites and housed on a secure online account. All procedures were IRB approved.

Pretest/Posttest Assessments

Each participant was administered a pre/post assessment on (a) general science content knowledge and attitudes and (b) content knowledge specific to virology. The general science assessment was paper-based, whereas the virology assessment was completed on a tablet. The first was designed to gauge the participants' understanding of and attitudes towards science and included items designed to elicit their understanding of what scientists do and what models are for (Figure 10.5). The second was designed to assess the participants' content knowledge relate to virology specifically as well as their confidence in their ability to learn similar or more advanced content related to it. Both were framed as assessments of our materials and for

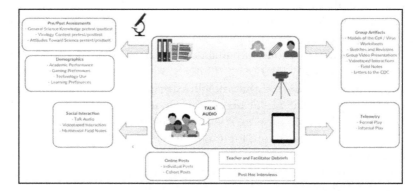

Figure 10.4 Diagram of the context of investigation, data streams, and main variables of interest per data stream.

In the space below, draw a scientist at work.

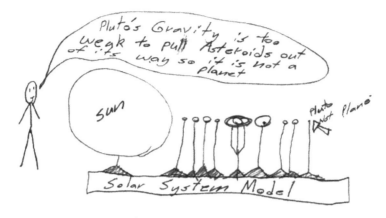

Why do scientists use models (like the model of the solar system)?

To explain theories and to understand or show something.

Figure 10.5 Example data from a posttest general science assessment.

feedback on our research agenda and game/material design, not formal assessments of their individual performance.

Demographic Data

A survey of demographic data was administered prior to all activities. Here, we collected standard information related to gender, age, and ethnicity, as well as participants' prior experience with technology, game genre preferences, motivations in gameplay (e.g., collecting items, winning the endgame), interest in science, favorite school subject, and average grades received. All information was self-reported.

Social Interaction Data

Interactional (verbal) data were captured via small recorders worn around their neck on a lavalier name tag to avoid obstructing movement or conversation. Because some participants are naturally more soft-spoken, individual recorders helped ensure a more reliable data stream. Facilitators helped verify that recorders were functioning before small or large group activities, but each participant was in control of his or her own recorder and its use.

Conversation was recorded for all research team (small group) conversations throughout the curriculum and all cohort (large group) activities and debates. Small group research team conversations included general discussion of the game and game strategies, identification of virus or immune system parts, questions raised, discussion around model making, and social banter. Cohort (large group) conversations included model presentations and cohort debates. Model presentations included small group explanations of virus and immune system functioning, with discussion and feedback about each model. Cohort debates consisted of three stages: (a) small group persuasive presentations of proposals for how to stop the Raven Virus based on their model and collected evidence, (b) collaborative interrogation among fellow cohort members of the proposals, and (c) a final synthetic conversation on what proposal was best. Each cohort was also video recorded, with cameras placed in the back of each classroom and left there throughout the duration of events.

Group Artifacts

Student artifacts including virus models, structured worksheets, research team video presentations, and letters to the CDC were collected from each participant following each session. All artifacts were digitized, labeled by participant ID and group number, and stored on secure servers at the end of each day less each research team's model, which was photographed but kept on the premises for subsequent daily activity.

Virus Models

Each research team created and revised a model of the virus and its impact on the immune system (Figure 10.6). Models were paper-based. No specific template existed for this model-making task. Models were based on a collective decision from group members on how they chose to represent the virus and immune system relationship. Available material for model making included: markers, tape, colored pencils, glue, paper, post-it notes, arrow stickers, and pipe cleaners.

Structured Worksheets

Participants were given structured worksheets on Day 1 to help them identify virus and immune system components and on Day 5 to present three possible ways to stop the Raven Virus from spreading. Participants wrote evidence to support or refute each solution.

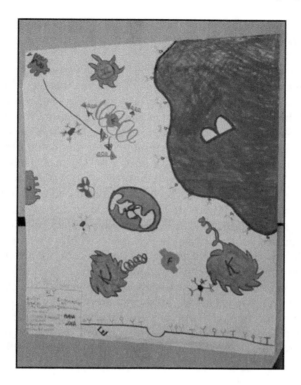

Figure 10.6   Example group model of the Raven Virus.

Letters to the CDC

Each research team wrote a letter to the mock CDC to present their initial proposal (on Day 1) for how to how to stop the Raven Virus from spreading across the world and to justify that claim based on observations made through their digiscope (i.e., from gameplay).

Research Team Video Presentations

Each research team produced a 5-minute video presentation of their model and a possible intervention for the Raven Virus (on Day 3) based on it for the mock CDC. All team videos, both practice drafts and final versions, were collected for analysis.

Online Portal Postings

An online portal allowed students to write and post messages to each other within and outside of structured activities each day. Each cohort had password-protected access to a group message board and was encouraged to pose questions, offer advice, or challenge other peers in gameplay. All posts were monitored and collected throughout activities.

Telemetry Data

Like other games from the Games + Learning + Society Center (GLS), *Virulent* is integrated into a cross-platform and cross-game-title data framework called the Assessment Data Aggregator for Gaming Environments (ADAGE). ADAGE guides game developers to articulate the content model of their games through a metadata tagging process that facilitates data mining of play patterns and key events in game play (Owen & Halverson, 2013). In effect, ADAGE scrapes all game actions from players' gameplay and then stores it digitally on GLS servers. Such data can then be pushed to a JSON or CSV file for analysis. As Figure 10.7 illustrates, each line of data constitutes a game action and is tagged with multiple attributes to identify what the action is, who performed it, when it happened, and any other identifying features that are relevant. Such clickstream data can then be manipulated to show patterns in individual or aggregated gameplay—from level attempts made to almanac usage to broader playstyles. Example telemetry variables we culled from *Virulent* data exhaust for this study included starting a session, spawning a unit, unit paths, unit collisions, and unit deaths. Each of the variables were tagged with player ID, timestamp, session token, and other relevant event details. The result is a dense numeric data corpus over two million lines.

Teacher and Facilitator Debriefs

Each day, following completion of activities, we conducted a debrief interview with the cohort teacher and led a group debriefing session among all facilitators, providing us an opportunity to identify and address any issues or problems as they arose. Facilitators also recorded their observations about their assigned small groups as field notes immediately following each session. Field note observations focused on issues of individual player engagement, group social dynamics, the model development process, and any

1		player	epoch time	_id	application_n	application_v	timestamp	session_toke	game_id	ada_base_ty	key	deviceinfo	adage_versio	user_id	updated_at	created_at	level_id	name	parent_name	success	group
2	1033970	elegant_cow	1.4344E+12	557f12da8bf	Virulent	ipad_1a7cb6	1.4344E+12	5EB3F0C5-ADFF-4413-84F8		["ADAGEDate	ADAGEStartS	{"device_mo	electric_eel	57949	2015-06-15 1	2015-06-15 18:00:58 UTC					
3	1033971	elegant_cow	1.4344E+12	557f12da8bf	Virulent	ipad_1a7cb6	1.4344E+12	5EB3F0C5-ADFF-4413-84F8		["ADAGECont	LevelStart		electric_eel	57949	2015-06-15 1	2015-06-15 1	1	Level 0		FALSE	
4	1033972	elegant_cow	1.4344E+12	557f12da8bf	Virulent	ipad_1a7cb6	1.4344E+12	5EB3F0C5-ADFF-4413-84F8		["ADAGEPlay	UnitSpawnEvent		electric_eel	57949	2015-06-15 1	2015-06-15 18:00:58 UTC					Capsid
5	1033973	elegant_cow	1.4344E+12	557f12da8bf	Virulent	ipad_1a7cb6	1.4344E+12	5EB3F0C5-ADFF-4413-84F8		["ADAGECont	MainMenuStart		electric_eel	57949	2015-06-15 1	2015-06-15 18:00:58 UTC		MainMenu		FALSE	
6	1033974	elegant_cow	1.4344E+12	557f12da8bf	Virulent	ipad_1a7cb6	1.4344E+12	5EB3F0C5-ADFF-4413-84F8		["ADAGEPlay	UnitSpawnEvent		electric_eel	57949	2015-06-15 1	2015-06-15 18:00:58 UTC					Capsid
7	1033975	elegant_cow	1.4344E+12	557f12da8bf	Virulent	ipad_1a7cb6	1.4344E+12	5EB3F0C5-ADFF-4413-84F8		["ADAGECont	PreLevelEnd		electric_eel	57949	2015-06-15 1	2015-06-15 1	1	Level 0		FALSE	
8	1033976	elegant_cow	1.4344E+12	557f12da8bf	Virulent	ipad_1a7cb6	1.4344E+12	5EB3F0C5-ADFF-4413-84F8		["ADAGECont	PreLevelStart		electric_eel	57949	2015-06-15 1	2015-06-15 1	1	Level 0		FALSE	
9	1033977	elegant_cow	1.4344E+12	557f12dd8bf	Virulent	ipad_1a7cb6	1.4344E+12	5EB3F0C5-ADFF-4413-84F8		["ADAGEData	ADAGEMouseEvent		electric_eel	57949	2015-06-15 1	2015-06-15 18:01:01 UTC					
10	1033978	elegant_cow	1.4344E+12	557f12dd8bf	Virulent	ipad_1a7cb6	1.4344E+12	5EB3F0C5-ADFF-4413-84F8		["ADAGEPlay	PathChangeEvent		electric_eel	57949	2015-06-15 1	2015-06-15 18:01:01 UTC					Capsid
11	1033979	elegant_cow	1.4344E+12	557f12e28bf	Virulent	ipad_1a7cb6	1.4344E+12	5EB3F0C5-ADFF-4413-84F8		["ADAGECont	MainMenuEnd		electric_eel	57949	2015-06-15 1	2015-06-15 18:01:06 UTC		MainMenu		FALSE	
12	1033980	elegant_cow	1.4344E+12	557f12e28bf	Virulent	ipad_1a7cb6	1.4344E+12	5EB3F0C5-ADFF-4413-84F8		["ADAGEPlay	UnitDeathEvent		electric_eel	57949	2015-06-15 1	2015-06-15 18:01:06 UTC					Capsid
13	1033981	elegant_cow	1.4344E+12	557f12e28bf	Virulent	ipad_1a7cb6	1.4344E+12	5EB3F0C5-ADFF-4413-84F8		["ADAGEPlay	UnitDeathEvent		electric_eel	57949	2015-06-15 1	2015-06-15 18:01:06 UTC					Capsid
14	1033982	elegant_cow	1.4344E+12	557f12e28bf	Virulent	ipad_1a7cb6	1.4344E+12	5EB3F0C5-ADFF-4413-84F8		["ADAGECont	LevelEnd		electric_eel	57949	2015-06-15 1	2015-06-15 1	1	Level 0		FALSE	
15	1033983	elegant_cow	1.4344E+12	557f12e28bf	Virulent	ipad_1a7cb6	1.4344E+12	5EB3F0C5-ADFF-4413-84F8		["ADAGECont	LevelStart		electric_eel	57949	2015-06-15 1	2015-06-15 1	2	Level 1		FALSE	
16	1033984	elegant_cow	1.4344E+12	557f12e28bf	Virulent	ipad_1a7cb6	1.4344E+12	5EB3F0C5-ADFF-4413-84F8		["ADAGEPlay	UnitSpawnEvent		electric_eel	57949	2015-06-15 1	2015-06-15 18:01:06 UTC					Monomer
17	1033985	elegant_cow	1.4344E+12	557f12e28bf	Virulent	ipad_1a7cb6	1.4344E+12	5EB3F0C5-ADFF-4413-84F8		["ADAGEPlay	UnitSpawnEvent		electric_eel	57949	2015-06-15 1	2015-06-15 18:01:06 UTC					Monomer
18	1033986	elegant_cow	1.4344E+12	557f12e28bf	Virulent	ipad_1a7cb6	1.4344E+12	5EB3F0C5-ADFF-4413-84F8		["ADAGEPlay	UnitSpawnEvent		electric_eel	57949	2015-06-15 1	2015-06-15 18:01:06 UTC					Monomer
19	1033987	elegant_cow	1.4344E+12	557f12e28bf	Virulent	ipad_1a7cb6	1.4344E+12	5EB3F0C5-ADFF-4413-84F8		["ADAGEPlay	UnitSpawnEvent		electric_eel	57949	2015-06-15 1	2015-06-15 18:01:06 UTC					Monomer
20	1033988	elegant_cow	1.4344E+12	557f12e28bf	Virulent	ipad_1a7cb6	1.4344E+12	5EB3F0C5-ADFF-4413-84F8		["ADAGEPlay	UnitSpawnEvent		electric_eel	57949	2015-06-15 1	2015-06-15 18:01:06 UTC					Monomer
21	1033989	elegant_cow	1.4344E+12	557f12e28bf	Virulent	ipad_1a7cb6	1.4344E+12	5EB3F0C5-ADFF-4413-84F8		["ADAGEPlay	UnitSpawnEvent		electric_eel	57949	2015-06-15 1	2015-06-15 18:01:06 UTC					Monomer
22	1033990	elegant_cow	1.4344E+12	557f12e28bf	Virulent	ipad_1a7cb6	1.4344E+12	5EB3F0C5-ADFF-4413-84F8		["ADAGEPlay	UnitSpawnEvent		electric_eel	57949	2015-06-15 1	2015-06-15 18:01:06 UTC					Monomer
23	1033991	elegant_cow	1.4344E+12	557f12e28bf	Virulent	ipad_1a7cb6	1.4344E+12	5EB3F0C5-ADFF-4413-84F8		["ADAGEPlay	UnitSpawnEvent		electric_eel	57949	2015-06-15 1	2015-06-15 18:01:05 UTC					Monomer
24	1033992	elegant_cow	1.4344E+12	557f12e28bf	Virulent	ipad_1a7cb6	1.4344E+12	5EB3F0C5-ADFF-4413-84F8		["ADAGEPlay	UnitSpawnEvent		electric_eel	57949	2015-06-15 1	2015-06-15 18:01:06 UTC					Monomer
25	1033993	elegant_cow	1.4344E+12	557f12e28bf	Virulent	ipad_1a7cb6	1.4344E+12	5EB3F0C5-ADFF-4413-84F8		["ADAGEPlay	UnitSpawnEvent		electric_eel	57949	2015-06-15 1	2015-06-15 18:01:06 UTC					Monomer
26	1033994	elegant_cow	1.4344E+12	557f12e28bf	Virulent	ipad_1a7cb6	1.4344E+12	5EB3F0C5-ADFF-4413-84F8		["ADAGEPlay	UnitSpawnEvent		electric_eel	57949	2015-06-15 1	2015-06-15 18:01:06 UTC					Monomer
27	1033995	elegant_cow	1.4344E+12	557f12e28bf	Virulent	ipad_1a7cb6	1.4344E+12	5EB3F0C5-ADFF-4413-84F8		["ADAGEPlay	UnitSpawnEvent		electric_eel	57949	2015-06-15 1	2015-06-15 18:01:06 UTC					Monomer
28	1033996	elegant_cow	1.4344E+12	557f12e28bf	Virulent	ipad_1a7cb6	1.4344E+12	5EB3F0C5-ADFF-4413-84F8		["ADAGEPlay	UnitSpawnEvent		electric_eel	57949	2015-06-15 1	2015-06-15 18:01:06 UTC					Monomer
29	1033997	elegant_cow	1.4344E+12	557f12e28bf	Virulent	ipad_1a7cb6	1.4344E+12	5EB3F0C5-ADFF-4413-84F8		["ADAGEPlay	UnitSpawnEvent		electric_eel	57949	2015-06-15 1	2015-06-15 18:01:06 UTC					Monomer
30	1033998	elegant_cow	1.4344E+12	557f12e28bf	Virulent	ipad_1a7cb6	1.4344E+12	5EB3F0C5-ADFF-4413-84F8		["ADAGEPlay	UnitSpawnEvent		electric_eel	57949	2015-06-15 1	2015-06-15 18:01:06 UTC					Monomer

Figure 10.7 Example telemetry data (not all variables included) from *Virulent*.

idiosyncratic group synonyms or metaphors used for virus and immune system components or other content covered.

Post Hoc Interviews

Finally, a month after all events were over, we conducted follow-up interviews with a subset of participants to test the durability of changes in science understanding and attitudes targeted by the intervention. Interviews were conducted face to face on campus and lasted roughly 30 minutes.

Data Analysis

Obviously, the first question we must ask is, was the intervention useful? The answer is yes. Pre-post assessments show an increase in participants' content knowledge related to virology and biology (a two grade increase or 22.1%, $t(61) = 7.5$, $p < 0.0001$), increases in positive orientation and attitudes toward science ($t(68) = 2.5$, $p < 0.05$), and confidence in their ability to complete science-related tasks ($t(49) = 3.5$, $p < 0.001$). Thus, the program as a whole was demonstrably a success.

For this project, however, demonstrating the merit of the game and its curriculum is merely a preliminary condition that must be met to justify the subsequent in-depth analysis. The main research questions of interest for our project are methodological: Which data streams from the contexts surrounding the game can be meaningfully and practically combined with telemetry data from the game itself? Specifically, of the contextual data theoretically suggested by a situation cognition approach, which data streams are:

1. feasible to collect in a standard research or classroom setting?
2. quantifiable for integration into a single "big data" set?
3. productive for building algorithms and predictive models of student learning and performance?

In order to answer these questions, we treat the game-based curricular intervention across all three sites as a single instrumental case (Stake, 1995). Within the case, we can then explore what is or is not methodologically feasible, useful, and generative in making sense of the dynamics of individual and group learning. Toward these ends, we ask questions of the data about the nature of learning within this specific case, use mixed-method techniques on the heterogeneous data corpus in order to answer them, and then reflect on the feasibility, usefulness, and generalizability of our methodological approaches for a broader set of cases.

Given the goals of the game and curriculum, we define *learning* in this case context in terms of biology content, argument, and modeling. We also assess student *interest* as a fourth and final construct in keeping with prior work on science learning in informal environments (Bell & Lewenstein, 2009) and given our overarching commitment to pedagogies that increase not only conceptual knowledge and skills but also productive dispositions toward the domain. Table 10.1 shows the data streams to which each learning construct is applied.

Biology Content

In order to trace biology content, we developed an inclusive coding scheme based on all terms that appeared in the game, the in-game almanac, and curriculum materials related to viruses (e.g., virion, antigenome, mRNA) and cells (e.g., nucleus, mitochondria, cytoskeleton site). We coded explicit use of each term as well as synonyms, metaphors, and misstatements (such as mispronunciations). For each instance of use, we coded for correct use of the concept used.

Argumentation

In order to trace students' argumentation, we developed a coding scheme based on the work of Berland and Reiser (2011) to capture both individual and group work with claims and their justifications:

- *Construct a Claim*: State a declarative fact (e.g., "We can destroy the virus with a vaccine.")
- *Defend a Claim*: Provide an example or reason for why the claim is true. (e.g., "No, it's because there are more virions and that's why the body is attacking them more.")
- *Question a Claim*: Request for clarification or justification for a claim. (e.g., "How could it start at the budding site?")
- *Evaluate a Claim*: Confirm or deny that a claim is true without providing reason as to why (e.g., "I don't think so.")
- *Revise a Claim*: Revise a claim that has already been made due to new information gathered. (e.g., "Well, maybe a virus is alive but it's not like . . . really intelligent, at least not here.'")

Modeling

In order to trace students' development and use of models, we constructed a coding scheme based on the work of Russ et al. (2008) that captures relationships among components within the students' model and connections to outside knowledge and understanding:

- Relationships
  - *Chaining*: Reasons backwards or forwards in time (e.g., "If we remove the protein receptors, then the cell won't be able to get any proteins, and it will die.").

TABLE 10.1 Analytic Constructs and the Data Streams to Which They Are Applied

	Pre/Post Assessments	Demographics	Social Interaction	Group Artifacts	Telemetry	Online Posts	Teacher & Facilitator Debriefs	Post Hoc Interviews
Biology Content	X		X	X	X	X		X
Argument	X		X			X		X
Modeling	X		X	X				X
Interest	X		X		X	X		X

- *Modification:* Changes, adds, refines, or removes parts of the model (e.g., "We're missing the RNA. We need to draw them here.").
- Connection to Other Knowledge

  - *Phenomena:* Compares what the model tells them about viruses to their own experiences in the world in order to evaluate the model (e.g., "I have to get a flu vaccine every year, so that means vaccines aren't always effective forever. The virus must change in some way.").
  - *Analogies:* Compares the virus or cell to some other system (e.g., "The mRNAs are like the running backs on the virus team. They're fast and they can avoid the slicers.").

Interest

Finally, in order to trace student interest in science, we constructed a coding scheme based on the work of Hidi and Renninger's (2006) four-phase model of interest development that captures participants' value statements about the ongoing activities and their difficulty, overt displays of participation and curiosity, and identity statements related to their role in the activity or material:

- *Value Statements* (Positive, Negative, Other): Expression of positive or negative feelings towards the game, event, or content matter, including statements about the merit of activities or their appeal (e.g., "This music is really cool.").
- *Difficulty Evaluations* (Easy, Hard, Unknown): Statements about the level of difficulty or challenge of the content.
- *Participation Displays* (Volunteering, Persistence, Withdrawing): Overt displays of participation in the form of unprompted volunteering for tasks (e.g., "I want to do it!"), persistence, especially in the face of failure (e.g., "I want to play just a bit longer."), or withdrawing (e.g., "I'm not doing that.").
- *Curiosity* (Exploratory, Extension Questions): Extension questions about the content covered in the activity (e.g., "I wonder if . . . ").
- *Identity Statements:* Statements about their own attributes or aspirations related to the game, curriculum, or content matter (e.g., "I want to be a . . . ").

In order to calculate interrater reliability, we randomly sampled 10-minute segments from the data corpus and had two to three individual research team members analyze the data using one of the four analytic constructs (biology content, argumentation, modeling, interest). Each coder independently coded roughly 1,600 turns of talk. Interrater reliability was calculated using Fleiss's kappa between coders. Constructs with a kappa less than .60 required meeting to discuss and resolve discrepancies before recoding and recalculating interrater reliability. This process was repeated until sufficient reliability was achieved.

Together, these four constructs for learning (biology content, argumentation, modeling, and interest) are applied across the qualitative data corpus using MAXQDA (Gibbs, 2008), quantified, and combined with telemetry data that have been analyzed using the same broad constructs detailed above but here operationalized in terms of behaviors traceable via user clickstream data. Specifically, biology content can be linked to interactions with game units (virion, mitochondria, etc.), along with the player's use of the in-game almanac. The amount of exposure to given game elements can be linked to scientific arguments made with those elements. Information complexity increases with each new level played, incrementally providing additional information on the cell to cell cycle of the virus, which can then be linked back to model development. The amount of time engaging in informal gameplay completed by players can be used to gauge interest. Demographic data collected as part of pretest assessments are used to group participants by age, gender, and gaming experience to investigate differences based on these key variables and to control for science knowledge and interest at time one. Group membership data (small research team group membership, facilitator assignment, cohort membership) are used to examine individual and group dynamics as well as effects of facilitator assignments. Time stamp data are used to explore patterns in the ways that players engage with *Virulent* while in and out of structured activity sessions. Teacher and facilitator daily debriefs are used to triangulate individual and group patterns and to generate potential hypotheses to explain differences between and within student teams (for example, in the basis of varying social dynamics within or across groups).

EARLY CHALLENGES

The goal of collecting such copious and mixed data and analyzing them using single constructs operationalized in multiple ways is to resituate "big data" analyses of technology data exhaust with equally rich streams of data from their context of use. In terms of individual analytic strategies, there is nothing new here: Pretest/posttest comparisons, quantified coding of qualitative data (Chi, 1997) from group interaction and interviews, analysis of scientific models generated by a group and revised over time are hardly methodologically risky or innovative. Attempting to reframe such analyses as an important and currently missing component of so-called "big data" approaches is. In truth, this attempt to collect and analyze qualitative data with the goal of not only quantifying it (for inclusion in big data sets) but even (partially) automating the process is a bit audacious. As such, it faces multiple challenges. Here, we describe two.

The Lamest Bottleneck Is the Greatest Bottleneck: Transcription

Exploratory talk, or thinking critically about proposed ideas among group members (Mercer, Wegerif, & Dawes, 1999), is beneficial to establishing stronger scientific arguments (Rojas-Drummond & Zapata, 2004). As such, we explicitly created a curriculum to promote exploratory talk within small groups and across cohorts. Such dialogues, especially in the most engaged and fully involved moments throughout the study, were energetic and frequently impassioned, with overlapped speech and more than one student initiating, elaborating, evolving, and even contradicting an idea. These conversations in the data corpus represented some of the more substantively dense moments in the corpus—and also the most difficult to disentangle and simply transcribe.

Given our aim of testing the feasibility of automating such data collection, our strategy for recording and representing social interaction was lavalier mics placed on each child and a transcription service that relied on voice recognition software. The mics were durable, portable, and inexpensive ($8), fitting easily into children's name badges and successfully picking up the audio stream of the wearer quite well. Ambient noise, however, was a continual problem for automated transcription of the data. Transcripts were returned with lexical and syntactic errors and misrepresentations, particularly for the specific terms we were most interested in related to biology and virology content. Even worse, the documents contained few or no speaker designations from the audio given the nature of overlapping speech and an inability to discern one child's voice from another, even within a small group of three or four. In some transcripts, there were lengthy omissions of entire conversations—especially when multiple individuals were speaking at once in close enough proximity for a mic to capture audio on more than one speaker: in other words, right when exploratory talk emerged and conversations became the most animated and engaged.

To remedy the issue, research team members who had attended the event in person had to review each transcript while listening to the audio files and correct documents line by line, clarifying specialized biology and game-related terms, disentangling attributions of the utterances, and filling in large gaps that often represented critical moments of engagement in the curriculum. Such shoring up of the transcripts was expensive, time-consuming, and tedious work that set the project back by several months before any real analysis could begin. Even then, speech pattern and intonation were still not always enough to distinguish one participant from another. As a result, we resigned ourselves to attributing talk to individuals where possible but designating unrecognizable utterances as "speaker unknown." Of the entire corpus of social interaction data, approximately 5% was lost for analysis of individual learning by the sheer fact that group talk data are onerous to transcribe by hand and simply impossible to transcribe automatically by voice recognition software at this time. Automated services are good enough for single-speaker data, especially when calibrated to one person's voice, but are not yet at a point where they can be applied to small group talk, let alone classroom interaction.

The Problem of Deixis

In research, we naturally carve the world into "text" and "context," foregrounding a portion of the phenomenon (here, the game and talk transcript) as central and backgrounding the remainder as material that can be used to disambiguate or pin down the meaning of the text we are most interested in. There is no sharp dividing line along which text and context are easily separated, however. Context is implicated on all talk through deixis, or "the ways in which languages encode or grammaticalize features of the context of utterance or speech events" (Levinson, 1983, p. 54). From the overt use of indexical expressions (e.g., pronouns such as "we" or "I" or pointing words such as "here" or "that") to the covert use of allusions to conceptual and materials, worlds presumed or implied by the speaker in their talk, a given utterance always depends on an analysis of the context of that utterance. And thus, we use context to disambiguate such elements of interaction. And when contextual information is lacking or falls short, we bemoan the inadequacy of our contextual data, believing that if we simply had more data or the "right" data, we could resolve and disambiguate meaning in interaction itself. Rarely, however, is this task complete. And yet, what context is the right context? How much context is enough? These issues can be addressed but only provisionally; each new utterance holds the promise of a new and shifted context made relevant to ongoing interlocution.

Talking through new concepts and ideas helps solidify understanding and challenge misconceptions (Dove, Everett, & Preece, 1999; Rennie & Jarvis, 1995), yet such talk necessarily ranges in expression, precision, and quality. In our intervention, like most, science content was not served up as keywords and vocabulary exercises for participants to use in controlled ways. Rather, new science concepts were situated in their day-to-day conversation and activity: game exploration, small group discussion, model making, and cohort debate. Over time, ideas take shape and precision, come to be used accurately and consistently, and stabilize as new tools for "cheating the game" (Squire, 2004). "Squiggly hot dogs" and "ninja stars," early metaphors that scaffold understanding (Jakobson & Wickman, 2007) at the early stage when it is most fragile, evolve into virions and slicer enzymes because the task requirements demand understanding and precision and group discourse demands increasingly precise language in order to make models and claims and defend them. Tracing such evolution is crucial in the analysis, yet disambiguating imprecise terms and their connection to other concepts is tricky and time-consuming work. No amount of contextual data will necessarily get you out of the problem of deixis. No computer code or algorithm readily exists for a given speech act to apply off the shelf in order to catch in its net all terms and synonyms and metaphors and creative monikers and their relation to one another. Such work therefore cannot be easily automated and instead requires old-fashioned reading and interpretation of lengthy transcripts.

SUMMARY

The recent proliferation of big data analytics marks a transformation in the way we collect, interpret, and use information (Mayer-Schönberger & Cukier, 2013) by exponentially increasing scale. Such large corpora provide tremendous analytic power for the detection and comparison of patterns of technology use that, ostensibly, can be used to infer user understanding and learning. But these data are limited by the very fact that contextual data, especially talk and interaction data around the device, are largely absent. From a situated and sociocultural point of view, talk and interaction are an important—perhaps *the* important—vehicle for learning. As such, their inclusion into large scale data analysis is crucial if we are to not fall prey to the streetlight effect (Freedman, 2010) and find ourselves, like the old drunkard in the story, searching for keys under the street light simply because that's where the light is best.

And yet, including contextual data into larger sets used for research and assessment also raises some real concerns. Is it ethical and wise to record social interaction in classrooms, even if we intend to mine them only for those variables directly related to ongoing learning? Do we, as educators and citizens, really want students to wear to data-recording wearable devices in school settings? More broadly, what role might more inclusive "big data" efforts inadvertently play in our recent national obsession for assessments and accountability? There are significant issues of consequential validity (Messick, 1988) this work necessarily raises; our current project seeks to understand better what's possible, but it cannot easily answer what's advisable. For this, broader deliberation and discussion is required.

REFERENCES

Asthana, P. (2011, October). Big data and little data. *Forbes*. Retrieved from http://www.forbes.com/sites/dell/2011/10/31/big-data-and-little-data

Baker, R .S. J. d., D'Mello, S. K., Rodrigo, M. M. T., & Graesser, A. C. (2010). Better to be frustrated than bored: The incidence, persistence, and impact of learners' cognitive-affective states during interactions with three different computer-based learning environments. *International Journal of Human-Computer Studies, 68*(4), 223–241.

Barab, S., Thomas, M., Dodge, T., Carteaux, R., & Tuzun, H. (2005). Making learning fun: Quest Atlantis, a game without guns. *Educational Technology Research and Development, 53*(1), 86–107.

Bauckhage, C., Kersting, K., Sifa, R., Thurau, C., Drachen, A., & Canossa, A. (2012). How players lose interest in playing a game: An empirical study based on distributions of total playing times. In Preuss, M. (Eds.) *Computational Intelligence and Games (CIG 2012)* (pp. 139–146). IEEE, New York, New York.

Bell, P., & Lewenstein, B. (2009). *Learning science in informal environments*. Washington, DC: National Academies Press.

Berland, M., Martin, T., Benton, T., Petrick Smith, C., & Davis, D. (2013). Using learning analytics to understand the learning pathways of novice programmers. *Journal of the Learning Sciences, 22*(4), 564–599.

Berland, L. K., & Reiser, B. J. (2011). Classroom communities' adaptations of the practice of scientific argumentation. *Science Education, 95*(2), 191–216.

Bijker, W. E. (1995). *Of bicycles, bakelites, and bulbs: Toward a theory of sociotechnical change*. Cambridge, MA: MIT Press.

Chi, M. T. H. (1997). Quantifying qualitative analysis of verbal data: A practical guide. *Journal of Learning Sciences, 6*(3), 271–315.

Clark, D. (2013, June). *Meta-analysis of digital games and learning in terms of the NRC's Education for Life and Work outcomes*. Paper presented at the Games+Learning+Society Conference 9.0, Madison WI.

Clark, D. B., & Martinez-Garza, M. (2012). Prediction and explanation as design mechanics in conceptually-integrated digital games to help players articulate the tacit understandings they build through gameplay. In C. Steinkuehler, K. Squire, & S. Barab (Eds.), *Games, learning, and society: Learning and meaning in the digital age* (pp. 279–305). Cambridge, England: Cambridge University Press.

Ducheneaut, N., Yee, N., Nickell, E., & Moore, R. J. (2006, April). Alone together?: Exploring the social dynamics of massively multiplayer online games. In R. Grinter, T. Rodden, P. Aoki, E. Cutrell, R. Jeffries, & G. Olsen (Eds.), *Proceedings of the SIGCHI conference on Human Factors in computing systems* (pp. 407–416). ACM Press, New York, NY.

Dede, C., Ketelhut, D., Nelson, B., Clarke, J., & Bowman, C. (2004). Design-based research strategies for studying situated learning in a multi-user Virtual environment. In Y. B. Kafai, W. A. Sandoval, & N. Enyedy (Eds.), Proceedings of the International Conference on Learning Sciences (pp. 158–165). Mahwah NJ: Lawrence Erlbaum and Associates.

Derry, S. J., & Steinkuehler, C. A. (2003). Cognitive and situative theories of learning and instruction. In L. Nadel (Ed.), *Encyclopedia of Cognitive Science* (pp. 800–805). London, England: Nature Publishing Group.

Dove, J., Everett, L. A., & Preece, P. F. W. (1999). Exploring a hydrological concept through children's drawings. *International Journal of Science Education, 21*(5), 485–497.

Drachen, A., & Canossa, A. (2011). Evaluating motion: Spatial user behaviour in virtual environments. *International Journal of Arts and Technology, 4*(3), 294–314.

Drachen, A., Canossa, A., & Yannakakis, G. N. (2009). Player modeling using self organization in Tomb Raider: Underworld. In Hingston, P. (Eds.), *Computational Intelligence and Games (CIG 2009)* (pp. 1–8). IEEE, Milano, Italy.

Engestrom, Y., Miettinen, R., & Punamaki, R.-L. (1999). *Perspectives on activity theory.* Cambridge, England: Cambridge University Press.

Freedman, D. H. (2010). Why scientists are so often wrong: The streetlight effect. *Discover Magazine.* Retrieved from http://discovermagazine.com/2010/jul-aug/29-why-scientific-studies-often-wrong-streetlight-effect

Gagné, A. R., El-Nasr, M. S., & Shaw, C. D. (2011). A deeper look at the use of telemetry for analysis of player behavior in RTS games. In J. Anacieto, S. Fels, M. Graham, B. Kapralos, M. Seif El-Nasr, & K. Stanley (Eds.), *Entertainment Computing (ICEC 2011)* (pp. 247–257). Springer, Heidelberg, Germany.

Garfinkel, H. (1967). *Studies in ethnomethodology.* Englewood Cliffs NJ: Prentice-Hall.

Gee, J. P. (2004). *Situated language and learning: A critique of traditional schooling.* New York, NY: Routledge.

Gee, J. P. (2007). *Good video games and good learning: Collected essays on video games, learning and literacy.* New York, NY: Peter Lang.

Gee, J. P. (2010). *An introduction to discourse analysis: Theory and method* (3rd ed.). London, England: Routledge.

Gee, J. P., & Hayes, E. R. (2010). *Women and gaming: The Sims and 21st century learning.* London, England: Palgrave Macmillan.

Gibbs, G. R. (2008). *Analysing qualitative data.* London, England: SAGE.

Gibson, J. J. (1986). *The ecological approach to visual perception.* Hillsdale NJ: Erlbaum.

Greeno, J. G. (1997). On claims that answer the wrong question. *Educational Researcher,* 5–17.

Greeno, J. G., & Moore, J. L. (1993). Situativity and symbols: Response to Vera and Simon. *Cognitive Science, 17,* 49–59.

Hidi, S., & Renninger, K. A. (2006). The four-phase model of interest development. *Educational Psychologist, 41*(2), 111–127.

Hien, N. T. N., & Haddawy, P. (2007, October). A decision support system for evaluating international student applications. In Meier, R. (Eds.), *Frontiers in Education Conference-Global Engineering: Knowledge Without Borders, Opportunities Without Passports, 2007. FIE'07. 37th Annual* (pp. F2A-1). IEEE.

Holland, D., & Quinn, N. (Eds.). (1987). *Cultural models in language and thought.* Cambridge, England: Cambridge University Press.

Hutchins, E. (1995). *Cognition in the wild.* Cambridge, MA: MIT Press.

Jakobson, B., & Wickman, P. O. (2007) Transformation through language use: Children's spontaneous metaphors in elementary school science. *Science & Education, 16,* 267–289.

Jenkins, H., III. (2006) *Convergence culture.* New York, NY: New York University Press.

Kohavi, R., Longbotham, R., Sommerfield, D., & Henne, R. M. (2009). Controlled experiments on the web: Survey and practical guide. *Data mining and knowledge discovery, 18*(1), 140–181.

Lave, J., & Wenger, E. (1991). *Situated learning: Legitimate peripheral participation.* Cambridge, England: Cambridge University Press.

Levinson, S. C. (1983). *Pragmatics.* Cambridge, England: Cambridge University Press.

Levy, P. (1999). *Collective intelligence: Mankind's emerging world in cyberspace* (R. Bononno, Trans.). Cambridge, MA: Perseus Books.

Lewis, J. M., Trinh, P., & Kirsh, D. (2011). A corpus analysis of strategy video game play in starcraft: Brood war. In L. Carlson (Ed.), *Proceedings of the 33rd annual conference of the Cognitive Science Society* (pp. 687–692). Cognitive Science Society, Boston, Massachusetts.

Martin, C. (2012). Video games, identity, and the constellation of information. *Bulletin of Science, Technology, & Society, 32*(5), 384–392.

Mayer-Schönberger, V., & Cukier, K. (2013). *Big data: A revolution that will transform how we live, work, and think.* Boston, MA: Houghton Mifflin.

Mercer, N., Wegerif, R., & Dawes, L. (1999). Children's talk and the development of reasoning in the classroom. *British Educational Research Journal, 25*(1), 95–111.

Messick, S. (1988). The once and future issues of validity: Assessing the meaning and consequences of measurement. In H. Wainer & H. I. Braun (Eds.), *Test validity* (pp. 33–45). Hillsdale, NJ: Lawrence Erlbaum Associates.

Nardi, B. (2010). *My life as a night elf priest: An anthropological account of World of Warcraft.* Ann Arbor, MI: University of Michigan Press.

Nasir, N. I. S. (2005). Individual cognitive structuring and the sociocultural context: Strategy shifts in the game of dominoes. *The Journal of the Learning Sciences, 14*(1), 5–34.

Nebot, A., Castro, F., Vellido, A., & Mugica, F. (2006, January). Identification of fuzzy models to predict students' performance in an e-learning environment. In V. Uskov (Eds), *The Fifth IASTED international conference on web-based education, WBE* (pp. 74–79). ACTA Press, Anaheim, CA.

Oldenburg, R. (1999). *The great good place: Cafés, coffee shops, community centers, beauty parlors, general stores, bars, hangouts, and how they get you through the day.* New York, NY: Marlowe.

Owen, V. E., & Halverson, R. (2013). ADAGE (Assessment Data Aggregator for Game Environments): A click-stream data framework for assessment of learning in play. In C. Williams, A. Ochsner, J. Dietmeier, & C. Steinkuehler (Eds.), *Proceedings of the 9th Annual Games+ Learning+ Society Conference, ETC Press.* Pittsburgh, PA, USA.

Pardos Z. A., Heffernan N. T., Anderson B., & Heffernan C. L. (2007) The effect of model granularity on student performance prediction using Bayesian networks. In C. Conati, K. McCoy, & G. Paliouras (Eds.), *User Modeling 2007. UM 2007. Lecture Notes in Computer Science, vol 4511.* Springer, Berlin, Heidelberg

Pea, R. D. (1993). Practices of distributed intelligences and design for education. In G. Solomon (Ed.), *Distributed cognitions: Psychological and educational considerations* (pp. 47–87). Cambridge, England: Cambridge University Press.

Quellmalz, E. S., Davenport, J. L., Timms, M. J., DeBoer, G. E., Jordan, K. A., Huang, C. W., & Buckley, B. C. (2013). Next-generation environments for assessing and promoting complex science learning. *Journal of Educational Psychology, 105*(4), 1100.

Rennie, L. J., & Jarvis, T. (1995). Children's choice of drawings to communicate their ideas about technology. *Research in Science Education, 25*(3), 239–252.

Rojas-Drummond, S., & Zapata, M. P. (2004). Exploratory talk, argumentation and reasoning in Mexican primary school children. *Language and Education, 18*(6), 539–557.

Russ, R. S., Scherr, R. E., Hammer, D., & Mikeska, J. (2008). Recognizing mechanistic reasoning in student scientific inquiry: A framework for discourse analysis developed from philosophy of science. *Science Education, 92*(3), 499–525. doi:10.1002/sce.20264

Seay, A. F., Jerome, W. J., Lee, K. S., & Kraut, R. E. (2004, April). Project massive: A study of online gaming communities. In E. Dykstra-Erikson & M. Tscheligi (Eds.), *CHI '04 extended abstracts on Human factors in computing systems* (pp. 1421–1424). ACM, New York, NY.

Sitzmann, T. (2011). A meta-analytic examination of the instructional effectiveness of computer-based simulation games. *Personnel Psychology, 64*, 489–528. doi:10.1111/j.1744-6570.2011.01190.x

Squire, K. (2004). *Replaying history: Learning world history through playing Civilization III* (Unpublished doctoral dissertation). Indiana University, Indianapolis, IN.

Squire, K. (2006). From content to context: Videogames as designed experience. *Educational Researcher, 35*(8), 19–29.

Squire, K. D., & Giovanetto, L. (2008). The higher education of gaming. *E-Learning and Digital Media, 5*(1), 2–28.

Squire, K. (2011). *Teaching and participatory culture in the digital age.* New York, NY: Teachers College Press.

Stake, R. E. (1995). *The art of case study research.* Thousand Oaks, CA: SAGE.

Steinkuehler, C. A. (2004). Learning in massively multiplayer online games. In Y. B. Kafai, W. A. Sandoval, N. Enyedy, A. S. Nixon, & F. Herrera (Eds.), *Proceedings of the Sixth International Conference of the Learning Sciences* (pp. 521–528). Mahwah, NJ: Erlbaum.

Steinkuehler, C. A. (2006). Massively multiplayer online videogaming as participation in a Discourse. *Mind, Culture & Activity, 13*(1), 38–52.

Steinkuehler, C., & Duncan, S. (2008). Scientific habits of mind in virtual worlds. *Journal of Science Education and Technology, 17*(6), 530–543.

Steinkuehler, C. & Oh, Y. (2012). Apprenticeship in massively multiplayer online games. In C. Steinkuehler, K. Squire, & S. Barab (Eds.), *Games, learning, and society: Learning and meaning in the digital age* (pp. 154–184). Cambridge, England: Cambridge University Press.

Steinkuehler, C., & Williams, D. (2006). Where everybody knows your (screen) name: Online games as "third places." *Journal of Computer-Mediated Communication, 11*(4), 885–909.

Thurau, C., & Bauckhage, C. (2010, August). Analyzing the evolution of social groups in World of Warcraft®. In G. Yannakakis & J. Togelius (Eds.), *Computational*

Intelligence and Games (CIG), 2010 IEEE Symposium on (pp. 170–177). IEEE, Copenhagen, Denmark.

Vogel, J. J., Vogel, D. S., Cannon-Bowers, J., Bowers, C. A., Muse, K., & Wright, M. (2006). Computer gaming and interactive simulations for learning: A meta-analysis. *Journal of Educational Computing Research, 34*, 229–243. doi:10.2190/FLHV-K4WA-WPVQ-H0YM

Vygotsky L. S. (1978). *Mind in society: The development of higher psychological processes.* Cambridge MA: Harvard University Press.

Wasson, B., Hanson, C., & Mor, Y. (2016). Grand challenge problem 11: Empowering teachers with student data. In J. Eberle & K. Lund (Eds.), *Grand challenge problems in technology-enhanced learning II: MOOCs and beyond* (pp. 55–58). New York, NY: Springer International Publishing.

Weber, B. G., & Mateas, M. (2009). A data mining approach to strategy prediction. In P. Hingston (Eds.), *Computational Intelligence and Games (CIG) IEEE Symposium* (pp. 140–147). IEEE, Milano, Italy.

Wertsch, J. V. (1998). *Mind as action.* New York, NY: Oxford University Press.

Wouters, P., van Nimwegen, C., van Oostendorp, H., & van der Spek, E. D. (2013, February 4). A Meta-Analysis of the Cognitive and Motivational Effects of Serious Games. *Journal of Educational Psychology.* Advance online publication. doi: 10.1037/a0031311

Young, M. F., Slota, S., Cutter, A. B., Jalette, G., Mullin, G., Lai, B., Simeoni, Z., Tran, M., & Yukhymenko, M. (2012). Our princess is in another castle: A review of trends in serious gaming for education. *Review of Educational Research, 82*(1), 61–89.

KETSU

CONCLUSION

CHAPTER 11

DISTRIBUTED TEACHING AND LEARNING SYSTEMS IN THE WILD

Jeffrey B. Holmes, Kelly M. Tran, and Elisabeth R. Gee
Arizona State University

This chapter develops a theory of *distributed teaching and learning systems* (DTALS), in which teaching and learning happen across a range of sites within and around video games. We are particularly interested in these as teaching sites and how the relationships between these sites can be intentionally designed as well as emerge from the participation of a particular learner (Holmes, 2015). Indeed, over the last decade and a half, the significant growth in interest in game-based learning has led to tremendous insights into how and why games might be good models for learning (see Whitton, 2014, for a concise summary; see also Tobias & Fletcher, 2011, for a meta-analysis of the field, and Perotta, Featherstone, Aston, & Houghton, 2013, for a brief but illuminating literature review). At the same time, a great deal of research into out-of-school or informal settings has stressed the kinds of deep and meaningful learning that happens across digital and physical spaces (see, for instance, Ito et al., 2013), and how learning

Exploding the Castle, pages 253–269
Copyright © 2017 by Information Age Publishing
All rights of reproduction in any form reserved.

happens between various sites in "media ecologies" (Jenkins, 2006) and in various "affinity spaces" (Gee & Hayes, 2010; Hayes & Duncan, 2012).

The role of teaching has been given much less attention in this work, however, and discussions of teaching are often only implied or absent altogether. One core goal of this chapter is to explicitly address how games are designed to teach and how games and the extra-game sites that often accompany them can be organized—by game designers, gaming communities, and the players themselves—to customize specific teaching and learning pathways. We argue that a DTALS model addresses both the designed and emergent organization of these sites and the way that teaching and learning can be spread across many different events, spaces, people, and tools. To do so, we will outline several important features of DTALS and look at examples from the commercial game Dota 2 as well as the game development tool Twine in order to see how these systems are used in specific situations "in the wild" (Hutchins, 1995) and what that might tell us about designing and studying these kinds of systems in games, in schools, and beyond.

DEFINING DTLS

Young and Slota (this volume) argue that researchers interested in the potential of games to support learning should attend not only to player–game interactions, but also to the "game ecosystem," which they describe as interactions that emerge from game play but take place beyond the boundaries of the game. A game ecosystem has the potential to be quite vast, however, and here we propose the concept of "distributed teaching and learning system" as a means of directing attention more closely to the elements of this larger ecosystem that are organized around the purpose of teaching and learning. A larger game ecosystem (or system; we'll define our terms below) can include many elements or interactions that do not *intentionally* teach, such as fan art or fan fiction, rants over glitches in a game, contests or competitions, stores or sites that sell games, and so forth. While participants might learn something from these things (i.e., reading a great work of fan fiction might teach me something about writing), we wish to focus in particular on understanding *teaching* as it is manifested and distributed across a wide range of spaces, resources, practices, and people. Furthermore, we are interested in understanding the relationships among all of these spaces, resources, practices, and people. Rather than viewing them as a somewhat haphazard collection of game-related teaching events or tools, we argue for understanding them as comprising a distributed teaching and learning *system*.

To demonstrate the value of adopting a systems perspective to understand teaching and learning around game play, we first need to define some terms and concepts. Defining "systems" and more specifically, what kind of systems we are discussing, is key, of course.

At the most basic level, a system consists of interconnected and interdependent elements and processes that form a whole, with properties and behaviors that are different from those of its parts. Individual video games are good examples of systems; the interaction of game elements in even the most simple game—rules, player behaviors, game mechanics—creates an experience could not result from individual elements in isolation. Similarly, a DTLS provides teaching and learning opportunities that go beyond what individual teachers or resources could provide. As we will describe, a DTLS can support what we call "learning pathways" that give players the opportunity to pursue deeper and richer learning experiences than what might be possible in isolation.

One challenge in adopting a systems perspective is setting boundaries on the system of interest. All phenomena can be studied through a systems lens (Wilensky & Jacobson, 2014); systems exist within larger systems and can take many different forms. Typical approaches to defining a system involve identifying the system's *purpose*; in our case, we have identified teaching as the central purpose of DTALS. Systems can be either natural or designed by humans to achieve a particular purpose. However, the actual purpose of a system might not be what it was intended to do, if designed, or even what it is perceived to do. Thus, for example, our educational system might be overtly designed to educate all children in an equitable manner, but in reality its elements may combine to serve the purpose of reinforcing social class differences.

As we will discuss, DTALS can vary in the extent to which the entire system is intentionally designed to support teaching and learning. DTALS "in the wild" (Hutchins, 1995)—that is, DTALS that were not designed at a systems level—include elements that were designed to teach, such as fan sites, tutorials, and other tools, but they become interconnected as players move across them, link them, direct other players to them, and otherwise build a system "from the bottom up." In other words, such DTALS have *emergent* properties, arising out of the interactions of originally disparate elements.

Other attributes of DTALS, as we define them, are that they are *complex* (there are diverse, multidirectional relationships among elements), *dynamic* (the elements in a DTALS and the relationships among elements are constantly changing), and *adaptive* (DTALS respond to changes in the larger environment; for example, an update to a game might make some teaching resources irrelevant and lead to the creation of new ones). Accordingly, DTALS can be described only approximately and at one particular time. New people, resources, tools, and affinity spaces are continually entering the system, and elements within the system are constantly changing. To complicate matters further, any one person typically interacts with only one portion of the system, and thus individuals will have different conceptions of the system and its parts.

Lastly, what does it mean that these teaching and learning systems are *distributed*, and why is that important? First, and most obviously, the teaching that takes place through DTALS is distributed across space and place, both real and virtual. Second, teaching is distributed across human and technical agents. To master a particularly challenging task in a game, for example, I might consult a video walkthrough, post a question on a forum and receive replies from multiple people, and get in-game tips from an automated guide. Thirdly, teaching is distributed temporally, across time. There is always some kind of teaching available to the potential learner, often "just-in-time" or on-demand, when the learner needs it.

EXAMPLE SYSTEMS

We briefly describe two somewhat different systems below which will help us to illustrate features of DTALS. One of them, *Dota 2*, is a game proper with a robust player base and competitive esports communities; the other, Twine, is a text-based game development tool supported by many users across different websites and forums. We chose these examples because they cut across several important dimensions of DTALS (how they can be organized and designed, what people do with them, and so on) and hopefully demonstrate the variety and breadth of such systems in the wild. Our purpose here is to quickly highlight important specific parts of each of these systems before attempting to develop some common features of each in the next section.

Dota 2

Dota 2 is a multiplayer online battle arena (MOBA) game in which two teams attempt to destroy the opposing team's base while protecting their own. Players can choose from over 100 characters, each with multiple abilities and items. They work together in teams of five, and these teams can utilize many different strategies depending on the makeup of the characters selected. Players can play with and against the computer, but in large part the game is played with other people. Indeed, *Dota 2* is one of the largest in the burgeoning esports scene, with multimillion dollar tournaments held regularly. *Dota 2* is also one of the most popular games played on Twitch, an online game streaming service where viewers watch and comment on live games as they happen.

Dota 2 is a complex game. Beyond learning the "basics" of the game (mechanical ones, like moving the characters and using the interface, and gameplay ones, like what various kinds of attacks do and how they work), players must also learn many nuanced things within the game (the best ways to use abilities, when to purchase items, and other strategic choices) and beyond it (how to work and communicate with teammates, how to strategically build teams and how various combinations of characters function best, even things like common jargon and "insider" ways of talking). Further, like many modern games, *Dota 2* is constantly evolving with the addition of new characters and features, balance tweaks, and other changes patched into the game. So players need to learn, relearn, and unlearn things as they continue to play.

Part of what makes *Dota 2* so interesting—and so illustrative of DTALS—is the many interrelated ways players can learn these things, and how various sites are designed to teach them. As we have described elsewhere (Holmes, 2015), the game's designer, Valve, included resources like a tutorial, an in-game "library" of information, and online guides to help teach players about the game (what we have called *designed* teaching elements). Valve also created somewhat unique features within the game client where players themselves carry out the teaching through a special coach mode, interactive player-created guides, and in-game streaming tools that utilize the interactive nature of the client so players watching can control the game camera and get access to other players' screens (we have called these *designed-for-emergent teaching* elements). Like many other games, *Dota 2* has spawned many "big G" (Gee, 2003) sites such as forums, FAQs, YouTube videos, Twitch streams, cosplay, fan art, and more. These are sites created by players to teach others and where new players can go to learn about the game as well as about the communities of players around it (what we have called *emergent* teaching elements). Together, these various elements make up the system, which players can organize and navigate to learn how to play the game, some of which are designed specifically as teaching sites, and some of which must be strategically used by learners as part of their own learning.

Twine

Twine is a platform for authoring games and hypertext stories. This platform illustrates DTALS in several important ways that both compliment as well as contrast with *Dota 2*. First, the official materials offered for learning the platform are socially mediated, open for editing, and not the product of a single author. This stands in contrast to traditional teaching materials such as manuals and textbooks, but it also stands in contrast the top-down, designed systems around *Dota 2*. Second, Twine is a versatile platform that is used by different people for many different reasons. Differing communities with various Discourses (Gee, 2004) use Twine, and as a result the DTALS involves a diverse set of sites. For examples, seasoned game designers, novices who are using Twine as their first game design tool, and writers of interactive fiction all might use Twine and be part of the DTALS around it. Third, although the tool itself is rather easy to learn given the right materials, finding those materials and distinguishing relevant information from outdated information is no small task. The path of a learner through the teaching materials is a particularly interesting example of how a DTALS can be complex, requiring him or her to be self-directed in finding resources. Unlike with *DOTA 2*, there is not a clear barrier between the designed and designed-for-emergent teaching systems.

In order to start using Twine, a potential learner must first visit Twinery. org, where they can either download the program or use it online. This "official" website is an essential site and is a necessary place for a learner to start. This serves as the "on-ramp" for the Twine DTALS. There is no manual offered with Twine, however. When a visitor uses the tool for the first time, there is a brief introduction, which directs users to two different resources: the forums and the wiki. The links to the forums and wiki are on the front page of the site as well. Together, these two resources comprise all of the "official" help, or designed teaching materials. Unlike a traditional manual, both of these are dynamic, socially mediated resources.

Rather, they both contain links to many outside sources, tutorials, and other materials. In order to start learning to use Twine, even from official materials, a learner must still explore different spaces of the DTALS around Twine. In this way, the learner must be able to navigate the various Discourses of the sites around Twine, and understand how to distinguish what information is relevant from the plethora of information out there.

In this way, Twine also affords unique opportunities for teaching. Most of the available information on how to use Twine has been written by individuals and posted on personal blogs or websites. As such, becoming a teacher of Twine once an individual is proficient with the tool has a low barrier to entry. Such a teacher, however, must possess a different set of literacy skills. He or she must know what types of information people are looking for regarding Twine. It might also be necessary for a teacher to post about a tutorial that he or she has written elsewhere, such as by responding to a post on the forum or linking to it in the comments of a blog post.

FEATURES OF DISTRIBUTED TEACHING
AND LEARNING SYSTEMS

Using both *Dota 2* and Twine as illustrative cases, below we outline important features of DTALS. This list of features is not meant to be exhaustive but instead is meant to highlight *some* of the specific and essential affordances of DTALS that differentiate it from other ways of thinking about teaching and learning. Different DTALS may demonstrate different configurations of the various features and may vary in the degree to which they demonstrate any given feature. Furthermore, these features are intimately related (for instance, the way the system is centered on a "deep" problem is a key reason why it is distributed across different sites), so the particular configuration of the features in a given system might be quite complex but illuminating.

Our approach is inspired by Gee's (2004) description of affinity spaces and summarized succinctly by Hayes and Duncan (2012):

> While explicitly not a set of criteria that are either necessary or sufficient for defining the affinity space, the list [developed by Gee] represents a set of potential attributes that can be used to describe the features of a given affinity space and in particular, affinity spaces that seem to be most supportive of learning. That is, they serve as a set of *features* [emphasis in original] that can describe an affinity space but are not necessary for one—Gee's intent seems to have been to broadly describe the potential of affinity spaces to give rise to a number of interesting learning opportunities and literacy practices, but not to firmly demarcate what 'counts' as an affinity space just yet. (p. 7)

What we are doing here, in such a spirit, is to begin to outline features that broadly describe the potential of DTALS to give rise to interesting learning opportunities—but also as ways these can be designed as teaching opportunities as well. Our hope is that these features will serve as analytical language for studying these kinds of systems as well as inspiration for designing them.

1. Centered on "Deep" Problem(s)

One important feature of a DTALS which requires it to be distributed across many sites is that the system must be centered on a deep problem that does not offer a simple answer. These deep problems are ones that learners can gain a passion for, passion that my drive their continued participation and work towards mastery. Few people become truly passionate about how to replace a lightbulb; far more people become deeply passionate about politics or NFL football or goat farming. For these kinds of deep problems, there may not be a single site or single source of learning about the topic or the varied ways to participate, and no one teaching event can cover the complexity of such deep problems; a distributed system of many sites that focus on various features becomes the way that people learn about and build a passion for the problem.

Video games, by their nature, are generally centered on these kinds of deep problems to varying degrees. "Simple" games may not require much to learn, and so may not need a DTALS for players. *Flappy Bird* is relatively rudimentary and has only one mechanic to learn and master (keep the bird avatar from falling or hitting an obstacle by tapping the screen). Learning to play the game is also relatively simple and doesn't require much instruction at all, instead the rules are gleaned mostly by actively playing the game—there is only the simplest of instructions when starting the game (an icon of a finger with the word "tap" next to it and the bird in "flight"), and few resources on websites about how to play (though there are a fair amount of "high score" videos where players have performed extremely well). *Flappy Bird* doesn't really require an entire system in order to teach how to play the game, only a site or two.

More complex games, like *Dota 2*, involve far more variables to learn (many more mechanics, hundreds of different characters, multiple play styles and strategies, and so on). Covering all of this information in any single instructional setting would be quite unwieldy. Valve breaks it up into multiple different elements: a multipart interactive tutorial covering the fundamentals of gameplay, in-game and online guides, an in-game library, and so on. Other sites emerge—some "sponsored" by Valve but created by other players (such as user-generated guides or within the coach mode), some on outside websites like theory-crafting forums or YouTube walkthroughs.

Learning to use Twine, as well, can be surprisingly complex. While learning to link screens of a game together—the most basic function in Twine—can be learned through the official or "sponsored" Twine materials, learning to do anything more complex with this requires users to seek outside help. If a designer wants to add images, keep track of variables (if a player has found a key, let her open this door), or change the way the game looks, all of this requires exploration of other sites in Twine.

2. Distributed Across Many Different Sites

Another important feature of DTALS is that teaching and learning are distributed across many different sites. A complex problem likely requires many different sources of teaching since no single intervention can adequately cover all the things necessary to master complex problems. By distributing teaching and learning across different sites, different types of problems with different types of information and different ways of teaching can exist and be given to or accessed by a learner when they need it (just-in-time, on-demand, or just-in-case). These sites can be physical or conceptual (and probably both), "official" sites and user-controlled spaces, people or tools, and even complementary or contradictory.

In *Dota 2*, for instance, Valve designed a series of highly scaffolded tutorial levels, each introducing new concepts and letting players learn by reading about them and then putting the ideas into practice. They also included those other sites (guides, the library). But Valve never teaches players about common tactics used in the community, such as "ganking" or the "Deathball" strategy, despite the importance of these concepts (often referred to as the metagame). Plenty of other sites teach these kinds of things, from YouTube guides and tutorials to theory crafting websites to community podcast discussions and more. A novice player doesn't need to know about Deathballing, and so won't likely expend his or her limited resources to develop teaching materials for this kind of knowledge, but a distributed system of teaching and learning sites—with the power of many thousands of players and many kinds of tools at their disposal—can. It's more than just an economy of scale, however; such a distribution of people and teaching and learning resources can cover things that the designer may not intend or even want (say, how to cheat or exploit the game). A distributed system removes some control from the designer, and its effects can be both beneficial (teaching the ever-changing metagame) and harmful (teaching how to cheat).

Twine demonstrates this distributive feature even more. In order to begin using Twine, a potential learner must first visit Twinery.org. It is here that the program can be either downloaded or used online, and it is necessary for a learner to start here. This serves as the "on-ramp" for the Twine DTALS. There is no manual offered with Twine, however. When a visitor uses the tool for the first time, there is a brief introduction, which directs users to two different resources: the forums and the wiki. The forums and wiki are linked to from the front page of the site, as well. Together, these two resources comprise all of the "official" help. However, unlike a traditional manual, both of these are dynamic, socially mediated resources.

The two main sources for Twine, which a user is directed to from the front page, are the wiki and the forums. Unlike a printed (or digital) manual, both of these sources are dynamic, changing as users add to and modify it. They are also not bounded sources, like a traditional manual. Rather, they both contain links to many outside sources, tutorials, and other materials. In order to start learning to use Twine, even from official materials, a learner must still explore different spaces of the DTALS around Twine.

3. Pathways Emerge From the Interaction of the Learner and System

Because DTALS are distributed across many different sites—some sanctioned and some not—learners can (at least partially) customize which sites they activate at any given time. Learners engage with the system and become part of the system; they affect it just by engaging with it. The open nature of a DTALS (where learners can enter and traverse the system from many different points) also means that how a learner engages with the system, and what elements they engage with, are up to the learner. Some sites may be requisite (for instance, an unskippable tutorial mission often found in many video games). Others may only be available after accessing and mastering previous sites (unlocking new abilities after leveling up, for example). Different systems may handle these with different strategies with different results (say, allowing players to skip a tutorial or only including on demand or just-in-case instructional material like a game manual). But players may have already encountered other sites where they learned much of the same information: watching a friend or Twitch streamer play the game, reading websites, watching structured YouTube walkthroughs, and so on. Because these players have already learned at least some of the content of the officially designed sites, these sites may simply reinforce what the player has learned, add nothing new to their learning, or even undermine what they were taught elsewhere (if they learned how to cheat or to play "wrong," for example). Furthermore, players can often choose where to go next based on their interests (perhaps they want to know more specific information about a play style, or get background stories about the characters, or know more about the development of the game itself and so on). They can then seek out and activate sites within the system based on these interests, some of which may be officially supported within the game or by the game developer, but others will emerge from fans of the game on the distributed user-controlled sites.

Dota 2 offers great insight into the variety of designed and player-determined trajectories. Certainly the multipart tutorial is designed to teach learners within the game client, and Valve's inclusion of the "designed-for-emergent" sites allows for other players to do a great deal of teaching with the support of the tools (while keeping players within the sanctioned space of the game client itself). But the tutorial is optional; players can go straight to playing matches without ever accessing that site. Perhaps they have watched friends or streams, they are familiar with other MOBAs, or they have read about the game and learned the same kinds of core concepts covered by the tutorial. They configured their own pathway through the various sites around the game in such a way as to not need the officially designed teaching sites at all. A DTALS like this supports multiple pathways into the game and lets learners choose how and where to learn. This is not without some risk, to be sure; players may learn from the wrong kinds of teachers or the wrong kinds of things and feel frustrated by their lack of success with the game, while very novice players may have great difficulty sorting out what sites to access and how to arrange them at all. A well-designed DTALS like *Dota 2* mitigates some of these problems by including a strong top-down set of sites prominently displayed to new players and easily accessible while still allowing players some choice on whether they access those sites or not.

Twine faces a different set of problems because there is little scaffolding across sites. A learner must figure out which information is relevant and which is not for any given task, and there is no specific order of resources or learning materials which are suggested to users. Additionally, the DTALS of Twine encompasses resources for other topics as well. For example, in order to really change the look of a game, players need to use CSS (cascading style sheets). CSS is a computer language generally used for the design of web pages, and learning to use CSS is in itself a very complex problem.

In order for a Twine designer to visually change his or her game, then, this designer must (a) figure out that this is accomplished by using CSS, (b) find resources for learning CSS, and (c) figure out how to apply this knowledge of CSS to a Twine game. All of this is tangential to actually learning how to use the features that are built into Twine, which is a separate learning path. Thus, a learner of Twine must decide which sites are relevant and therefore determine which ones to access and learn from.

4. Supports Multiple Discourses

Players come to a video game (or other kinds of tools or practices) for a variety of reasons: for entertainment, to socialize, to research, or to critique, among many others. As Gee and others have pointed out through the concept of "affinity spaces," these players can find others who share their same interests and passions for a particular facet of a game (theory crafters can share and argue about statistical elements of the game; cosplayers can learn how to make different costumes or accessories and share their designs; artists can showcase their work and critique that of others; players focused on cutting-edge dungeon raiding in an MMO can form guilds). Learners can engage these affinity spaces to interact with expert peers or to access tremendous amounts of information about the game; Gee (2004) argues that affinity spaces can be very effective learning spaces (and, by extension, good teaching spaces too). Often these spaces form outside of the game within the "big 'G' game" like forums and through social media, though (as in the case of a guild) they can cross into the game itself.

Affinity spaces were never explicitly defined as bounded spaces or single sites (like a forum or an after-school club), though this is often how the concept has been taken up and commonly understood. Whereas much of the research into affinity spaces has primarily focused on one type of player and affinity space, a DTALS model can help account for the many different types of players and different kinds of teaching and learning around the game, the relationships between these various sites, and the specific pathways designers build and learners use. In other words, a DTALS model includes all of the various places learners can go (both within the game and around the Game) for whatever purpose; because learners can customize their pathways through these various sites, they can create their own set of teaching and learning resources to meet their particular needs, but the DTALS also includes sites they may never access. Put yet another way, a DTALS includes everything around the game that the player can access, though they may only choose a few sites. The DTALS nevertheless supports many different kinds of learners. DTALS are, in a sense, a kind of network of many affinity spaces, all focused on the game but each with a particular focus or emphasis and with a specific kind of thing to teach.

Twine highlights this feature particularly well. Some users may use Twine simply to mock-up larger game ideas that they will execute in another program; for them, they use Twine to test the logic of a particular system or get an idea of a sequence of if-then statements. These users likely don't need to know about the ways of including art assets or how to publish a game, so the kinds of sites they might access are particularly focused on a specific way of using the tool, while those other resources still exist and are accessible (but never activated by the user). Other users may use Twine in very different ways (as a game publishing engine, for instance). These users access different sites than the user who is simply mocking-up ideas; they may need those resources which teach them how to include pictures or other media and so access those sites within the DTALS. They customize their pathway based on their interests and needs, only using parts of the entire DTALS, but the DTALS still supports those other kinds of learners too.

Players of *Dota 2* follow similar pathways based on their interests. Some may only play socially, learning from their friends over voice chat or in coach mode; some might be interested in competitive play and watch streamers (in-game or on external sites like Twitch) to learn popular meta-play techniques; still others may read about the game in order to write about it in academic papers and learn how to talk about the game. Like the Twine example, the *Dota 2* DTALS supports all of these different learning pathways, though players customize which parts they use. Both examples also demonstrate that players may have many "ins" to the game/tool; how they get introduced to it and apprenticed into it, for instance, helps shape what pathway they follow and how they customize it (a player introduced to the game by friends likely gets a lot of teaching from those same friends, through discussion or watching them play, while another player who watches Twitch tournaments and so gets into the competitive scene may have very different pathways). These pathways will likely lead to the central site (the game of *Dota 2* or the Twine program itself) though these may not be the primary sites of either learning or participation (a player might really like fan fiction and so spend most of their time in these sites, learning about the lore and character background and sharing with other writers; the game may be tangential to their primary learning goals). While the shape of each particular learner may be unique, the system itself supports all of these different trajectories.

5. Relationships Between Resources Are Socially Mediated and Shape the System

One challenge to a distributed system of teaching and learning sites is that accessing various sites and customizing their path through the various sites requires some real savvy on the part of the learner when judging the reliability, usefulness, and connections between various sites, savvy that novice learners may lack. By novices we mean novices to learning or media strategies in general (say a young learner) or novices to the particular game/object in particular (a new player, for instance). These novices may not understand what is and is not important and how to manage what they should pay attention to, focusing on the minutiae of game mechanics before understanding the general concepts of the game. They may not be able to understand the tone and conventions of insiders and not know whom or what to trust; *Dota 2* players, for example, are often quite sarcastic and find humor in subverting or "trolling" other players, and often write humorous guides or tutorials that appear genuine but that an insider knows is completely wrong—something a novice may completely miss and learn the "wrong" way to play the game.

Navigating a DTALS is very much like any other literacy practice in that the learner must understand both the discourse (the types of "languages" used) and the Discourse (the identities and roles that make sense of the discourse), filter through information to determine its salience and validity within the various D/discourses, and traverse deeply social practices to which they may be outside of. A risk in a DTALS is that there are many competing D/discourses and a learner (who comes to the game/tool from one of many potential sources, as described in the feature above) must judge for themselves how to navigate those D/discourses, possibly without much strong guidance. They are, in a sense, responsible for developing their own "literacy," which may be beyond novices.

One solution is to have a relatively strong authority with some sense of acceptance by the many D/discourses around it. For example, *Dota 2* has Valve, the game's designers; they understand the game and speak from a place of authority (what they say is likely true since they made the game). They have included the various teaching sites (the tutorial, the guides, and the "designed-for-emergent" sites), which can more or less be trusted to be truthful, accurate, or correct. The game itself is also a source of authority, as it's easy to test out an idea and get direct feedback on that idea (a theory crafter's formula can be tested within the game, for instance, and be relatively proven or disproven). This is not unlike something like a traditional classroom, with an authority (a teacher, a text) that learners assume is correct and can reasonably rely on their teaching as valid.

This kind of authority may work best for conditions that are concrete or disprovable (a claim, say, that one ability does more damage than another can be tested and shown to work or not). It may not be as effective in abstract problems or more diffuse areas (the best way to link objects and story elements in Twine, for example, is debatable and there may not be a discernable "best"). In these situations, "authority" is somewhat negotiable and relies on the various Discourses to grant it to people or objects they deem correct. A Twine designer may be well respected in a given community, and her advice or techniques may be promoted and referenced by others and thus gain authority. In these cases, information is socially mediated, and the kinds of connections between sites can be strengthened or weakened based on the actions of members of the Discourse. In turn, this shapes how a learner moves and customizes his or her own learning pathway. Someone interested in cosplay might enter the DTALS from one of many different sites (a Tumblr profile, talking to other cosplayers at a convention, a site found on Google, an article in a magazine). Many of these entry sites may point to the same person or resource as an authority and direct the learner to that site. The learner gets socialized into the D/discourse and gets the benefit of social apprenticing into the "right" information by the social mediation of that information (by culling and promoting various sites). Thus, in some ways, the risk of learners going "off the rails" is lessened by the social forces that shape the DTALS, either through highly authoritative positions (such as a game's designer) or through the social mediation that determines "right" and "wrong" ways to learn and participate.

IMPLICATIONS

A DTALS model provides several tantalizing implications for rethinking our current understanding of both game-based learning and more traditional school-centered teaching designs. We have already broadly pointed out some potential implications associated with a DTALS model above, including both benefits to learners (they can customize their learning pathways based on their interests, for example) as well as risks and challenges (such as the need for literacy knowledge and apprenticing for learners or the possibility that they may access and activate the "wrong" kinds of sites). Some of the features of DTALS are meant to overcome these inherent risks (the way socially mediated information helps to guide novice learners to the "right" sites, or the way learners can access different sites at the right time and benefit from the work of many teachers, not just a select few). We wish here to turn our attention to more specific implications for analyzing and designing these kinds of systems and to consider what a DTALS model might mean in a place like school.

Video games are not the only starting point for DTALS, of course; DTALS can be identified around all kinds of activities, from auto repair to sewing to farm-to-table cooking to computer hacking and many, many others. Our focus on video games stems primarily from our access to many compelling examples from different games; since most modern games are deeply enmeshed in larger digital media ecologies, they can provide a rich domain for potential research into the melding of virtual and material teaching and learning experiences and resources. However, we argue that a DTALS framework can be useful for both understanding and designing teaching and learning in other domains, and in particular, for rethinking formal education.

The open nature of a DTALS means that learners can encounter teaching elements and "on-ramps" to learning from many different directions and in different sequences; each learning pathway may be unique to each learner. For researchers, tracing these potential and actual entryways and pathways may provide insight into how learners learn, how the system is designed, and how connections are made between various sites. The potentially large variety of these sites, however, may be challenging to map, so researchers will need new tools to identify elements of a system and capture the dynamics of the system, as well as new methods of analyzing learners' varied pathways.

Designers (of games and of teaching events) must also account for the various ways into the learning and so create and leverage different kinds of teaching designs at different points. They must also work to build connections between sites (to "sanction" or "promote" some particular site that they believe is valuable) as well as accommodate the sites learners may use that they have not intended (or even desire, such as a site on how to exploit some feature of the game). Because DTALS can support many different ways of using the system and different purposes for learning (such as the various Discourses that might use Twine), designers, learners, and researchers must contend with potential conflicts between these different agendas as well as leverage the opportunity to potentially cross different interests in order to grow shared interest, passions, and knowledge. Designers can organize teaching resources beyond their ability to produce, and so help build richer opportunities for learning, but they also must recognize that some learning is out of their control.

Indeed, perhaps most importantly, a distributed system implies that no single entity, institution, or individual has a monopoly on creating, disseminating, or controlling when and how teaching and learning happens. More than 30 years of informal learning research, and more than 15 years of game-based research, have shown that formal institutions like school are not the only sources of teaching and learning, and their authority is not uncontested; instead, they are one of many sources that learners can navigate, place next to each other and compare, and create their own set of meaningful teaching and learning resources. DTALS may serve as a bridge between schools and informal teaching and learning sites. Indeed, we see DTALS as a potential way to augment, if not outright challenge, the inherent (just or otherwise) authority of schools by collecting and considering as valid many sources of teaching and learning beyond formal school.

Practically, DTALS show that there is some benefit (especially to novice learners) for a strong, authoritative source of teaching; just as players of *Dota 2* can trust the teaching Valve provides through the designed teaching channels (and can then test it out directly in the game), schools that are part of distributed teaching and learning systems can be relatively trustworthy by connecting many different sites that feed back into the formal spaces of learning and evaluation. Further, DTALS shows that outside or distributed teaching sites can cover a far greater range of information, teaching styles and objects, and ways of learning than any single central site, so a model of school that includes many other outside teaching sites as valid means learners get both a reliable source of teaching as well as the opportunity to customize very deep learning beyond school. Schools benefit both from retaining a central role in teaching and learning but also by validating resources that go far beyond what they can develop and offer, and learners benefit both from being apprenticed into a reliable way of learning as well as the opportunity to make meaningful choices about where, what, and how they learn that is still treated as valid within the larger construct of formal education.

A great deal of work remains in terms of defining the various features of DTALS and for tracing specific examples and particular learners as they traverse these systems. This chapter is meant to begin to outline these features as a starting point and to promote future refinement and evidence for (and against) this model. A DTALS model suggests that teaching and learning are all around us, and we should pay attention to who makes and uses all of the various teaching and learning sites in order to both design new and emerging learning opportunities as well as develop critiques and adjustments of existing models.

REFERENCES

Gee, J. P. (2003). *What video games have to teach us about learning and literacy.* New York, NY: Palgrave Macmillan.

Gee, J. P. (2004). *Situated language and learning.* New York, NY: Routledge.

Gee, J. P., & Hayes, E. (2010). *Women and gaming: The Sims and 21st century learning.* New York, NY: Palgrave Macmillan.

Hayes, E., & Duncan, S. (Eds.). (2012). *Learning in video game affinity spaces.* New York, NY: Peter Lang.

Holmes, J. (2015). Distributed teaching and learning systems in *Dota 2. Well Played,* *4*(2), 92–111.

Hutchins, E. (1995). *Cognition in the wild.* Cambridge, MA: MIT Press.

Ito, M., Gutierrez, K., Livingstone, S., Penuel, B., Rhodes, J., Salen, K.,... Shresthova, S. (2013). *Connected learning: An agenda for research and design.* Irvine, CA: Digital Media and Learning Hub.

Jenkins, H. (2006). *Convergence culture: Where old and new media collide.* New York, NY: New York University Press.

Perrotta, C., Featherstone, G., Aston, H., & Houghton, E. (2013). *Game-based learning: Latest evidence and future directions.* NFER Research Programme: Innovation in Education. Slough: NFER.

Tobias, S., & Fletcher, J. D. (2011). *Computer games and instruction.* Albany: State University of New York Press.

Whitton, N. (2014). *Digital games and learning: Research and theory.* New York, NY: Routledge.

Wilensky, U., & Jacobson, M. J. (2014). Complex systems and the learning sciences. In R. K. Sawyer (Ed.), *The Cambridge handbook of the learning sciences* (pp. 319–338). Cambridge, England: Cambridge University Press.

CHAPTER 12

THE INEVITABILITY
OF EPIC FAIL

Exploding the Castle
With Situated Learning

Stephen T. Slota and Michael F. Young
University of Connecticut

Deconstruction of previous large-scale efforts to leverage innovative technology toward school improvement reveals a developmental trend of initial excitement followed by careful research, promising results, and—tragically—some mutation that leads to an eventual loss of impact. This applies to all major educational technology endeavors over the last half-century and is observable in any situation where designers and innovators have close and direct involvement with teacher training but the innovation's core theoretical foundations and key concepts are gradually (or abruptly) shed during and post-implementation. For those of us who study and design playful learning environments, this emphasizes a critical need to ask: Why do technology-rich research innovations always seem to fail once they grow beyond the control of the design team?

Exploding the Castle, pages 271–284

In this closing chapter, we describe the three pillars of a concept we refer to as Epic Fail. Doing so will help us identify applicable, overarching concerns with contemporary instructional design and provide suggestions that can help address difficulties with dissemination, local customization, and modding beyond the scope of an original designer's control. Additionally, it will help us tie suggestions to nongame innovations in order to highlight how such issues exist across educational subfields and how we—educators, designers, and researchers—might be able to make inevitable epic failures a bit less inevitable.

A BASIS IN SITUATED COGNITION

As noted throughout this book, ecological psychology research suggests that students play games and participate in online communities based on goals and intentions that arise in the moment through social interactions with other players, in-game objects, and nonplayer characters (NPCs)—in other words, interactions that emerge on the fly and in the context of a narrative of play (see Chapter 1, "Castle Upon a Hill"). Yet nearly all standard empirical studies of instructional game development and implementation to date (i.e., horse-race, t-test comparisons of playful learning vs. traditional classroom learning) have presumed that game design and playful learning behave like pharmaceutical medications that are chemically identical and organized in premeasured dosages for all learners. Educational researchers have hyperfocused on game effects (measured via high-stakes or other exams) by controlling for course content, learner characteristics, and value-added features (e.g., core mechanics, visuals, narrative structure, etc.) under the assumption that fiddling with a particular independent variable will yield a particular, predictable result.

But consider the logic underpinning this approach. Generally speaking, if one assumption is true (i.e., individual prior experiences inherently shape individual future experiences), the other (i.e., games can be a magic "pill" to treat learning), necessarily, cannot be. Are players individual learners who experience gameplay on a personal level that cannot be replicated, even across the same player playing the same game multiple times? Or are individuality, pre-existing experience, and environmental context irrelevant with respect to solving macroscopic instructional challenges? The paradoxical nature of these questions is the primary reason we see current educational game research as fundamentally flawed (and believe it's a blind spot for practicing teachers, technology innovators, and others seeking to add educational games to their respective instructional toolkits).

We base our argument on the notion that game players play with slightly different goals in mind each time they enter a given world or universe.

Irrespective of whether or not a player has previously played the same game with the same individual objective(s), microdifferences in player attitudes, knowledge, and movements through the game environment will always yield new emergent goals and experiences (even if a new play session might superficially appear indistinguishable from an earlier one). The phenomenon becomes more pronounced as we consider the wide variation of game interactions across players and across content/update patches of a particular game. This is why, returning to our earlier analogy, the highly individual and continually evolving nature of play renders game-based instruction (in and of itself) a mostly useless treatment for instructional maladies: individual games prescribed as "pills" would need dynamic content capable of self-modification to produce positive outcomes for any individual patient, and patients would need personalized dosages (or different medications altogether) to treat the same underlying illness.

Thus far, the messy, inconclusive uninterpretability of player experiences across games, players, and time (studied via meta-analytical techniques) has yielded little actionable data (see Clark, Tanner-Smith, & Killingsworth, 2016; Vogel, Vogel, Cannon-Bowers, Bowers, Muse, & Wright, 2006; Wouters, van Nimwegen, van Oostendorp, & van der Spek, 2013; Young et al., 2012) and underscored our suggestion that data reduction by way of averaging across studies, game players, games, and curricular content stands in opposition to the fundamental tenets of situated cognition and ecological psychology. Instead, analyses should be targeting the dynamic interactions between players and game affordances (given that distillation of player–game–environment interactions into a one-size-fits-all result obscures important learning outcomes at the individual difference level). To drive this point home, we need only examine real-world cases where traditional empirical research—specifically in the realm of educational technology design—fell apart during or after implementation.

THE INEVITABILITY OF EPIC FAIL

Looking back on a number of high-profile, technology-driven projects aimed at creating new approaches to instruction, there is a decades-long pattern of learning science, instructional design, and cognitive theory coalescing into some spectacular innovation that eventually disintegrates as quickly as it came into being—a phenomenon we refer to as Epic Fail.

In general, Epic Fail begins with early data collection revealing one or more important findings for a given instructional variable (e.g., student-side variables like test achievement, self-regulation, course completion, motivation, and engagement OR teacher-side variables like advanced content knowledge, wait time, inquiry-based pedagogy use, and collaboration among teams of teachers). Once the results are published, widespread excitement and adoption begins to spread (e.g., interdistrict collaboration, statewide or national implementation). However, follow-up research conducted weeks, months, or years later ultimately reveals that the project's purported benefits were not sustained: They arise when project originators are closely involved with teacher training and classroom implementation but disappear when project originators pull back to let the innovation thrive on its own. Notable victims of this cycle include Logo (Papert, 1980), *The Adventures of Jasper Woodbury* (Cognition and Technology Group at Vanderbilt [CTGV], 1992), Apple's Hypercard, inquiry-based simulations like Model-It (Fretz, Wu, Zhang, Davis, Krajcik, & Soloway, 2002), and—perhaps unsurprisingly—game-based instruction, with positive short-term and negative long-term outcomes befalling a variety of educational video games (Honey & Hilton, 2011; Young et al., 2012), games for nonacademic instruction (e.g., Aronowsky, Sanzenbacher, Thompson, Villanosa, & Drew, 2012; Sylvan, Larsen, Asbell-Clark, & Edwards, 2012), and scholastic tabletop roleplaying games (e.g., Slota, Travis, & Ballestrini, 2012).

With such limited long-term success and sustained impact on classroom learning, we can't help but wonder: Why do technology-rich research innovations always seem to fail once core designers are no longer directly involved? In the following subsections, we'll explore our question using a few of the high-profile examples cited above. We'll also propose three possible (if not probable) reasons for the inevitability of Epic Fail: (a) fatal mutation due to assimilation, (b) loss of fidelity, and (c) failure to thrive.

LEARNING FROM THE PAST

There is still debate over the extent to which even simple technologies like calculators and word processors have meaningfully affected school classrooms, never mind more advanced tools like geospatial mapping software, programming languages, 3D avatar-based virtual worlds, scientific modeling environments, and online video series used to flip classrooms (Bergmann & Sams, 2012). The rise and subsequent fall of said technologies demonstrates how no amount of time, effort, and money can guarantee sustained, long-term change. As it turns out, the inherent complexity of novel, tech-driven instruction can undermine both good ideas and intentions.

Logo

Based on Papert's exploration of constructionism-based learning environments, Logo was developed in 1967 as a programming language that made

LISP-like artificial intelligence programming accessible to elementary education students through the graphical representations of a small, robotic half-sphere resembling a plastic turtle. It received widespread research and acclaim by teachers at the time of its implementation, but rather than acknowledging a new paradigm for student learning, schools tended to assimilate Logo into their tried-and-true method of education: direct instruction. Once the developers and researchers left the school environment, classroom teachers defaulted to teaching *about* Logo in place of teaching *with* Logo. As a result, students were led to memorize Logo programming commands (e.g., FD 50 RT 90) from teacher-generated worksheets. After peaking in the mid-1980s (largely due to the development of the Apple II computer), most of Logo's 197 compilers/interpreters fell out of educational use despite numerous research studies demonstrating Logo's instructional effectiveness when implemented as Papert originally envisioned. Not long after, Papert (1993) concluded that large-scale school reform was likely impossible and chose to focus on smaller-scale projects (Papert, 1997).

The Adventures of Jasper Woodbury

Vanderbilt University's Jasper Woodbury videodisc series was a professionally filmed video production designed to support middle school mathematics and problem solving. Drawing on contemporary learning theories (i.e., situated cognition, anchored instruction), these videos were meant to provide a meaningfully authentic learning context prior to and in conjunction with other instructional activities. Unfortunately, fearing that students were unprepared to handle the series' outward complexity, many teachers chose to educate their classes using the stories as post-instruction word problems rather than a context for inquiry-driven learning. Once the program's researchers ceased their direct interaction with participating educators, the videos became mainly capstone activities, relieving them of any potential they once had for grounding abstract learning in the real world. The migration of videodisc to DVD coupled with rapid antiquation of the series' content (e.g., the price of gas as part of the calculations) further sealed the program's fate. By the late 1990s, Jasper had been shelved.

HyperCard

HyperCard was an Apple, Inc. invention similar to a programmable PowerPoint slide presentation that served as a framework for several other learning technology innovations in the late 1990s and early 2000s. It was most widely used by teachers and subject matter experts hoping to create focused classroom tutorials, collect dribble file data for assessments, and interactively control videodisc players. However, rapid technological advancement during the 1990s rendered HyperCard obsolete and sidelined all related instructional materials. Once Apple stopped supporting the system in favor of HTML and Java (the last update was made in 1998 even though services were supported until March 2004), work derived from thousands of HyperCard programming hours was lost or abandoned. With no simple migration path, HyperCard vanished from the classrooms its creators hoped it would revolutionize. Like other instructional innovations, the project's failed implementation highlights how Information Age technologies come and go so quickly that tech-specific innovative pedagogy may be doomed to fail (or at least fade) even if project originators remain available for widespread training and implementation.

Inquiry-Based Science Simulations

Acknowledging that the advanced sciences were increasingly reliant upon algorithm-driven theoretical models of phenomena rather than direct observational data, cognitive scientists in the early 2000s began providing middle and high school students with tools that would enable inquiry-based exploration of dynamic environmental systems. Tools like Model-It (Fretz et al., 2002) and the Virtual Solar System (Barab et al., 2000) were designed to help students identify central variables and catalog complex variable interrelationships by developing theoretical models that could be tested via animated simulation (Tsurusaki, Amiel, & Hay, 2003).

These and similar projects were meant to transform American education by encouraging science teachers to adopt inquiry-based pedagogy when teaching about complex systems, to model a particular theory-driven approach to instruction rather than assume the role of a be-all end-all instructional silver bullet, and to usher a wholesale re-envisioning of our educational institutions. As with other high-profile projects, work proceeding from small-scale laboratory studies to school-based trials suggested that students were fully capable of using instincts about environmental phenomena to construct workable theoretical models. But the broad pool of educators who signed on via publishing companies and other distribution networks lacked direct access to the research literature and frameworks of inquiry necessary for understanding program development and implementation. Not every student in the class easily understood the modeling software. Students working in groups met with widely variable success depending on difficult-to-predict group dynamics. Funding from public and private stakeholders evaporated among reports of lost instructional time and teachers teaching how to navigate the tool rather than the course content. Eventually, user interest in patches, updates, user-created mods, and online discussion hubs flagged.

After just a few short years, Model-It and the Virtual Solar System had been relegated to the educational innovation graveyard.

UNDERSTANDING TRAJECTORIES OF FAILURE

Given the number and scale of investments made to support endeavors like those described above, it initially struck us as odd that Epic Failure could be so frequent (both inside and outside the realm of educational technology: e.g., instructional design, adult education, creativity, learning science, special education, multicultural education, etc.). Naturally, we would not be so naive as to think all educational technology projects could or should take only a trajectory to success, but no single project—that we know of—has ever spurred large-scale educational reform, regardless of project originator, institution, or technology. Likewise, all major projects that we know of—regardless of those same elements—have fallen apart before reaching successful large-scale implementation. That leaves us asking: What gives?

After thoughtful analysis and discussion with our contemporaries, we have come to believe that there are three major counter forces common to technology-rich educational research innovations that move developers and researchers onto a trajectory of failure. Each counterforce, while bearing some similarity to the others, is a unique challenge that must be controlled pre-, during-, and post-implementation—a difficult (if not impossible) prospect.

Below, we explore how and why they occur *in situ* as a consequence of project implementation.

1. Fatal Mutation Due to Assimilation

Fatal mutation due to assimilation refers to teacher-generated changes that are fundamentally in opposition to a project's theoretical foundations and goals. Our word choice here is intentional: like certain genetic mutations in biological life, a single or small number of mutations to the theoretical DNA of a large-scale project can bring about a swift, painful death. In the case of Logo, constructivist theory dictated that students would *discover* the programming language in context, including having younger students possess and share information that older students had not yet learned. Once schools started rejecting this approach (arguing that older students should learn more advanced content than younger ones), teachers began having their classes memorize decontextualized commands before allowing any interaction with the cybernetic turtle. While some teacher-directed modifications might have been less damaging than others, vulnerabilities emergent through the project's wide implementation made it possible— likely, even—for minor problems to erode Logo's viability and sustainability. For Papert (1980), this amounted to a kind of Piagetian assimilation, with new ideas being forced into existing schemata (i.e., direct, teacher-led instruction) rather than leveraged toward the reformation of schools as learning ecologies.

2. Loss of Fidelity

For the purposes of this discussion, we characterize loss of fidelity as participants doing what the designers and researchers intended but failing to focus on core content, adding materials that are antithetical to project objectives, and/or watering down required activities to the point that they are no longer effective. This can be thought of, in part, as personal teacher preference running up against designer recommendations, but the problem is actually a bit more complex, occurring whenever there is a schism between individual teacher intentions, classroom constraints, and school reality. Dusenbury, Brannigan, Falco, and Hansen (2003) explored this precise issue in the context of drug abuse prevention programs, identifying five major measures of fidelity: dosage, adherence, program differentiation, participant responsiveness, and quality of program delivery. We believe their framework applies directly to the technology-based classroom interventions in our chosen examples.

Dosage includes agreed participation in a daily intervention program but—rather than implementing the set treatment each day—only following through with that program once per week or less. In the case of a schoolteacher, intervention might be interrupted by legitimate competing events (e.g., fire drills, required testing, schedule changes), or it may manifest as a timing issue wherein dosage is miscalculated or deliberately modified to fit some preconceived schedule (e.g., teaching *about* the tool instead of *with* it to ensure students can complete all of their learning stations before the bell rings). Returning to one of our real-world cases, teachers who sought to utilize *The Adventures of Jasper Woodbury* but were concerned about the instructional time commitment would often present the first episode (i.e., "Journey to Cedar Creek") following direct instruction about distance, rate, and time, thus "covering" the content in fewer than three days. Even if instruction took place during the appropriate content unit, any teacher who modified the implementation timeline (regardless of reasoning) inherently altered dosage as well (i.e., showing the videos *after* instruction instead of using them as a macro-context for the coming week's activities).

Adherence and *program differentiation* refer to the addition of instructional practices or pedagogies that make a unique program more like a particular pre-existing program. While the researcher may wish to implement a purely constructivist program, for instance, a participating classroom teacher might choose to add *Classdojo*™ or a similar behaviorism-based tool to reinforce certain learning behaviors (i.e., adhering to Behaviorist pedagogy). This eclectic approach *can* enhance an intervention, but it can also make novel innovations less distinguishable from existing programs (thus preventing the researcher from assessing any uniquely added benefit or even measuring the innovation's general effectiveness).

Quality of delivery refers to how well instructors understand the theoretical foundations of a given innovation and dynamically interact with learners in a manner consistent with the underlying design principles, especially when their guides and prepared curriculum don't work out exactly as planned. Teaching "in the cracks" (i.e., in a live classroom where interactions cannot be scripted) requires implementers to "fill" nonprogram activities and discussion with information and responses that are consistent with the designer's theoretical framework. This bears a direct relationship to *participant responsiveness*, the way instructional interventions are received by the target audience (i.e., both teachers and students). Because instruction is intended to induce particular learning experiences and interactions, miscommunication or ineffectual implementation may lead the audience to miss the intervention's situated value. When elements like dosage (e.g., how much Jasper or Logo instruction is needed before measurable changes in math achievement can be expected) conflict with school scheduling or administrative initiatives, quality of delivery and participant responsiveness tend to suffer dramatic setbacks.

3. Failure to Thrive

The third counter force, failure to thrive, represents a pattern wherein lack of researcher oversight or sustained grant funding causes instructors to gradually shift away from program goals, theories, and procedures present at the time of initial implementation. In part, this appears to involve situations where participating educators "do it for the researcher(s)" as a personal favor, or for the status of being part of the research team, or to obtain resources/benefits for participating in a grant-funded project. Once the project originators leave, the teachers simply move on or revert to prior instructional practices.

In describing a situated view of naval quartermasters, Hutchins (1995) addressed how success arises from interaction among people and artifacts in the world. From this perspective, failure can occur when any one of these potential interactions is interrupted: teacher–tool, researcher/designer–tool, and teacher–researcher. Each interaction must be functioning and ongoing in some form to provide the feedback necessary for sustaining technology-rich programs over time. While teachers often crave interactions with talented adults and welcome the opportunity to share their insights, debate with researchers, reflect on and explain their own pedagogy, and receive critiques of their teaching from academic peers, the social and cognitive factors arising from broken interaction can obscure progress toward a common objective. Barron (2003) explained this as smart groups capable of generating workable solutions ignoring those solutions as a result of structural social dynamics. Following this line of logic, any interruption of teacher–researcher interaction, intended or not, may allow misunderstanding, lack of personal buy-in or time investment, social conflict, or other social dynamics to overshadow the project's original goals. These issues eventually consume program implementation and push participating teachers back into their respective comfort zones.

AVOIDING THE PRECIPICE OF EPIC FAILURE

With the advent of major government efforts to improve schools (e.g., No Child Left Behind, Race to the Top, Common Core State Standards, Every Student Succeeds), sweeping instructional change is even more complicated to achieve than it was during the late 20th century. Devotion to improved performance (as tracked via traditional quantitative measures) has come largely at the expense of innovation, and direct instruction in the form of test preparation has served almost exclusively as the means to contend with the ever-growing clamor for accountability and data-driven decision making. This has forced designers to meet parent, teacher, district, and researcher needs while simultaneously avoiding pitfalls that transformed Logo, Jasper, HyperCard, and inquiry-based modeling into mutant forms of their former selves.

Of course, because no two school environments are identical, some customization *should* be expected at each implementation site. We believe such customization must be proactive, carefully planned, and organized such that program fidelity is maintained and project originators are able to recognize the Epic Fail trajectory before falling victim to it. This requires a clear articulation of program elements that can be altered for convenience, changed within a set margin, or not changed at all (including content and implementation methods). Additionally, it means anticipating which program elements might challenge traditional school instruction and, accordingly, planning ahead to minimize disruption of the innovation's theoretical integrity. At times, we have referred to this as a "fixin's bar" approach where designers propose an array of potential modifications (e.g., adding or removing particular activities, procedures, etc.) that (a) will not dramatically deviate from the program's core mission/foundation and (b) can be used to locally customize the program without ruining its "flavor."

Fatal mutation due to assimilation can be avoided with planned customization and clear designation of critical components. Project originators know that new sites will seek to customize the intervention to meet unique characteristics of their context. For game-based learning designers and researchers in particular, this necessitates various options for play and a clear list of innovation-specific recommendations that can help instructors fit games into pre-existing core curricula. A 1:1 learning and game objective relationship can ensure overlap between state and national standards (e.g., Young et al., 2012) and decrease the likelihood that participating teachers will simply assimilate games into existing practices like direct instruction or timed "stations."

Similarly, researchers and designers can pre-empt loss of fidelity by making the parameters, theoretical frameworks, and logic models that drive their designs as transparent as possible. Assumptions made during tool or program development must be aligned with how the tool or program is intended to operate *in situ*. Teacher support through regular follow-up (including audio/video, ongoing training, face-to-face focus groups, surveying, student feedback, and other qualitative tools) should target teacher understanding of learning theory in addition to technical operating procedures and troubleshooting techniques. Above all, users must be invited to join as many development discussions as possible, ensuring the innovation's on-the-ground implementation can and will actually support student learning outcomes.

Failure to thrive can be combatted through the creation of a self-sustaining, dynamic communities of practice (e.g., Lave & Wenger, 1991) that exist alongside the original innovation. Any such (metagame) community must be able to evolve over time under standard innovation parameters and within the innovation's underlying theoretical framework. While this might include the creation of a webpage, forum, YouTube channel, wiki, and/or series of regular face-to-face meetings, continued success will only come from ongoing facilitation by leading experts (i.e., project originators and trained practitioner-specialists). All teachers hoping to become community practitioner-specialists should be capable of describing the program's underlying theory and show evidence of their ability to adapt the theory to fit within the scope of a living classroom environment. When possible, original practitioners and other expert researchers should return to the community for two-way dialogue concerning information regarding progress in the field, modifications to the theory, and related research projects. The application of cost-sharing user fees may increase school buy-in, providing impetus to remain involved with the innovation and assist with the burden of community development. Though teacher–tool and researcher/designer–tool interactions will likely continue regardless of community formation, teacher–researcher communication is the only element that will sustain program fidelity beyond the original scope of the project.

To us, it seems clear that innovation implementation should be planned with early consideration of learning effects, customizability within design parameters, and purity of theory-based interaction goals. For that to happen, player goals and solution trajectories must align with socially constructed knowledge (i.e., core curricula) at a 1:1 ratio, made easier when developers create implementation boundary constraints in anticipation of Epic Failure. Of course, averaging across user behavior may seem like a simple way to separate outcome chaff from wheat (it requires fewer resources, reduces development time, and makes statistical analysis rather straightforward), but doing so also comes with risks, not least of all discarding valuable data as chaff even if it isn't. This is why we've argued that a situated cognition worldview is especially helpful for educational innovators: unpredictable, emergent factors invariably affect project outcomes, so it is necessary to assume that some users—students, teachers, administrators, institutions—will identify affordances the designers can or will not. In response, designers must build fail-safes capable of (a) inducing the adoption of specific, designer-aligned goals and (b) curbing behavior to conform to a particular model of thinking/action (i.e., giving users enough tethering to near the precipice of Epic Fail without falling over the ledge). That is the only way to adequately balance user desire for agency with developer need for consistency and ensure long-term implementation can be successful.

CASTLE UPON A HILL

Any game-based learning research aimed at supporting macroscopic educational reform requires researchers capable of ongoing school-level involvement, random fidelity checks, and two-way monitoring of the innovation through the creation of shared research–designer–teacher communities. The challenges outlined in this chapter are numerous and complex, but we believe project originators who are mindful about the maintenance of an active community role and leveraging educational changes at federal, state, and local levels can create instructional innovations that work and can be scaled for mass implementation. That is why we chose to focus on the particular cases featured throughout this chapter, to provide a foundation for understanding how and why repeated failure happens and to help guide the development of more engaging and long-lasting alternatives to current K–12 and higher education practices.

That said, we feel it appropriate to close with a (slightly modified) version of the offer we made at the start of this book: *"It's dangerous to go alone! Take this [situated cognition]."*

Ecopsychology is possibly the most powerful means of exploding the existing GBL castle and replacing it with a new, improved version. We hope our analyses and advice—in addition to those put forth by our coauthors—will point the field toward more sophisticated, thoughtful consideration of how and why games behave as complex learning ecologies. With your cooperation as our Player 2, we're confident that our collective educational endeavors will be stronger, more effective, and—above all—less susceptible to Epic Fail.

REFERENCES

Aronowsky, A., Sanzenbacher, B., Thompson, J., Villanosa, K., & Drew, J. (2012, June). *When simple is not best: Issues that arose using why reef in the conservation connection digital learning program.* Paper presented at GLS 8.0 Conference, Madison, WI.

Barab, S. A., Hay, K. E., Squire, K., Barnett, M., Schmidt, R., Karrigan, K., Yamagata-Lynch, L., & Johnson, J. (2000). Virtual solar system project: learning through a technology-rich, inquiry-based, participatory learning environment. *Journal of Science Education and Technology, 9*(1), 7–25.

Barron, B. (2003). When smart groups fail. *Journal of the Learning Sciences, 12*(3), 307–359.

Bergmann, J. & Sams, A. (2012). Flipping the classroom. *Tech & Learning, 32*(10), 42.

Clark, D. B., Tanner-Smith, E. E., & Killingsworth, S. S. (2016). Digital games, design, and learning: A systematic review and meta-analysis. *Review of Educational Research, 86*(1), 79–122. doi: 10.3102/0034654315582065

Cognition and Technology Group at Vanderbilt. (1992). Technology and the design of generative learning environments. In T. M. Duffy & D. Jonassen (Eds.), *Constructivism and the technology of instruction: A conversation.* Hillsdale NJ: Erlbaum.

Dusenbury, D., Brannigan, R., Falco, M., & Hansen, W. B. (2003). A review of research on fidelity of implementation: Implications for drug abuse prevention in school settings. *Health Education Research, 18*(2), 237–256.

Fretz, E. B., Wu, H., Zhang, B., Davis, E. A., Krajcik, J. S., & Soloway, E. (2002). An investigation of software scaffolds supporting modeling practices. *Research in Science Education, 32*(4), 567–589.

Hutchins, E. (1995). *Cognition in the wild.* Cambridge, MA: MIT Press.

Lave, J., & Wenger, E. (1991). *Situated learning: Legitimate peripheral participation.* Cambridge, England: Cambridge University Press.

National Research Council Committee on Science Learning: Computer Games, Simulations, and Education. (2011). Learning science through computer games and simulations. In M. A. Honey & M. Hilton (Eds.), Washington, DC: The National Academies Press.

Papert, S. (1980). *Mindstorms: Children, computers, and powerful ideas.* New York, NY: Basic Books.

Papert, S. (1993). *The children's machine.* New York, NY: Basic Books.

Papert, S. (1997). Why school reform is impossible. Review of Tyack and Cuban (1995). Retrieved from http://www.papert.org/articles/school_reform.html

Slota, S. T., Travis, R., & Ballestrini, K. (June, 2012). *Operation BIOME: The design of a situated, social constructivist ARG/RPG for biology education.* Paper presented at GLS 8.0 Conference, Madison, WI.

Sylvan, E., Larsen, J., Asbell-Clark, J., & Edwards T. (June, 2012). *The canary's not dead, it's just resting: The productive failure of a science-based augmented-reality game.* Paper presented at GLS 8.0 Conference, Madison, WI.

Tsurusaki, B., Amiel, T., & Hay, K. (2003). Using modeling-based inquiry in the virtual solar system. In D. Lassner & C. McNaught (Eds.), *Proceedings of EdMedia: World Conference on Educational Media and Technology 2003* (pp. 2237–2240). Association for the Advancement of Computing in Education (AACE).

Vogel, J. J., Vogel, D. S., Cannon-Bowers, J., Bowers, C. A., Muse, K., & Wright, M. (2006). Computer gaming and interactive simulations for learning: A meta-analysis. *Journal of Educational Computing Research, 34,* 229–243. doi:10.2190/FLHV-K4WA-WPVQH0YM

Wouters, P., van Nimwegen, C., van Oostendorp, H., & van der Spek, E. D. (2013). A metaanalysis of the cognitive and motivational effects of serious games. *Journal of Educational Psychology, 105,* 249–265. doi:10.1037/a0031311

Young, M., Slota, S., Cutter, A., Jalette, G., Lai, B., Mullin, G., . . . & Yukhymenko, M. (2012). Our princess is in another castle: A review of trends in video gaming for education. *Review of Educational Research, 82*(1), 61–89. doi:10.3102/0034654312436980

ABOUT THE EDITORS

Michael F. Young holds a PhD in cognitive psychology from Vanderbilt University and currently directs the University of Connecticut 2 Summers Learning Technology master's program. He has authored nine chapters on ecological psychology-driven instructional design and more than two dozen peer reviewed research papers on related topics. His work has appeared in a number of major journals, including the *Journal of Educational Computing Research, Journal of the Learning Sciences, Journal of Research on Science Teaching, Instructional Science,* and *Educational Technology Research and Development.*

Michael's research examines how individuals think and learn as well as the way technology can enhance thinking and learning. His NSF-funded project, GEEWIS (http://www.geewis.uconn.edu/), focuses on streaming real-time water quality pond data via the Internet and providing support for the integration of said data into secondary and higher education science classrooms. His approach to analytics and log files (which maintain time-stamped listing of navigation choices and lag time) has been applied to hypertext reading (Spencer Foundation grant), videodisc-based problem solving (Jasper project), and online navigation (Jason project).

Michael's most recent work concerns playful learning via video games and—as part of the UConn 2 Summers program—the creation and application of customized analog games (including a board game, a card game, and an online roleplaying game) to train K–12 technology coaches.

Stephen T. Slota, PhD (@steveslota) is an instructional design specialist and game design scientist at the University of Connecticut. He holds a PhD

Exploding the Castle, pages 285–286

in educational psychology: cognition, instruction, & learning technologies and has worked on a variety of game and instructional design projects with organizations including Arizona State University's Center for Games & Impact, UConn Health, Intel Corporation, Pfizer, and InSync Training, LLC. Separate from his other ventures, he co-owns and operates an educational game development and consultation company, the Pericles Group, LLC, which produces a variety of instructional language and science games for K–12, higher education, and recreation (www.practomime.com).

Stephen earned his bachelor of science in molecular & cellular biology and master's degree in curriculum and instruction from the University of Connecticut in 2007 and 2008, respectively. Prior to earning his doctoral degree, he taught a combination of biology, genetics, and human health at a public Connecticut high school. His research interests include technology, education, and instructional design; narrative and its effects on audience goal adoption and intentionality; player–game–context interactions in game-based learning instructional environments; prosocial learning through massive multiplayer online role-playing games (MMORPGs); and the relationship between imagination, dreams, and situated cognition.

CPSIA information can be obtained
at www.ICGtesting.com
Printed in the USA
BVHW04s2252200318
511126BV00002B/114/P

9 781681 239354